A Complete Price Guide to Coins of the United States

1981 Edition

A comprehensive illustrated valuation guide to coins struck by the United States Mints from the first issues in 1793 to date.

The history of United States Coins by Q. David Bowers.

The mintage quantity of each coin.

A Grading guide for each series.

A complete coin check list for all major United States coins.

A listing of U.S. Proof sets from 1936 to date.

H.E. Harris & Co., Inc. ®

BOSTON, MASS. 02117

COIN VALUES

Coin values listed in this book are intended as a guide only. Any radical fluctuation in the metallic values of gold and silver may cause most prices to depart considerably from those listed.

There are some coins listed without prices. This is caused by the lack of information on such coins because they have not, of late, been offered around or they are exceedingly rare.

MINTAGE QUANTITIES

The mintage figures in this book were concluded by the reports from the U. S. Mint. Quite often the Mint reports were inaccurate as to the actual coins minted during a given year. It should be pointed out that the mintage figure is for the number of coins struck and not for the number issued for circulation. Many coins were held by the Mint and later melted without ever passing into circulation.

Acknowledgments

A book as complex as this, in these years of inflation, could not have been accomplished without the help of others. We are indebted to Q. David Bowers for the outstanding introduction; to Richard A. Bagg of Bowers and Ruddy Galleries who was helpful in providing information on higher grade coins; to Rick and David Sundman of the Littleton Stamp and Coin Co. for their assistance in providing pricing information; also to still others too numerous to mention, our grateful thanks for your help.

SILVER AND GOLD COIN METALLIC VALUE CHART

	MULTIPLY TODAY'S BULLION VALUE* BY:
SILVER COINS	
1942-45 5¢ U.S. (.350 Fine) (War Time)	5.63%
U.S. 50¢ (.400 Fine) (1965-70)	14.79
U.S. $1.00 (.400 Fine) (1965-70)	31.67
1964 & Earlier 10¢ (.900 Fine)	7.23
1964 & Earlier 25¢ (.900 Fine)	18.09
1964 & Earlier 50¢ (.900 Fine)	36.17
1964 & Earlier U.S. $1.00 (.900 Fine)	77.36

GOLD COINS

U.S. $1.00 (.900 Fine)	4.84%
U.S. 2.50 (.900 Fine)	12.10
U.S. 3.00 (.900 Fine)	14.51
U.S. 5.00 (.900 Fine)	24.19
U.S. 10.00 (.900 Fine)	48.38
U.S. 20.00 (.900 Fine)	96.75

Generally gold coins will sell at a premium over their metallic value, depending on the coin and its condition.

The above percentages may normally be reduced by 15-20% when selling to dealers in order to cover their cost of handling.

*The bullion value may be found in most financial sections of daily and Sunday newspapers.

A History of American Coinage

by Q. David Bowers

Today there are just four denominations of United States coins which are seen in every day change: the cent, nickel, dime, and quarter. Half dollars, although minted in quantity, do not circulate readily. Eisenhower dollars and Susan B. Anthony dollars, although also made in large numbers, are not popular in every day transactions. It may come as a surprise to learn that at one time we had such curious denominations as the half cent, two-cent piece, two different varieties of three-cent pieces, nickels as well as half dimes (both being worth 5-cents), 20-cent pieces, three different types of metallic dollars (silver dollars, trade dollars, and gold dollars), and an array of gold coins extending up to the $20 denomination.

Coins have a rich history, one closely interwoven with political, economic, and other events. To study coins is to study the development of our nation.

The first official government mint was not established until 1792. Prior to that many different coins and other items served as media of exchange. In the early 17th century tobacco and ammunition traded at set rates in the colonies of Maryland and Virginia. On March 4, 1634, the Massachusetts General Court adopted legislation which provided: "It is likewise ordered that musket bullets of a full bore shall pass currently for a farthing apiece, providing that no man shall be compelled to take above XII (one shilling) at a time in them." In the same colony, grain, furs, and fish were also used in payment of debts.

In nearby New Hampshire, fish, lumber, and agricultural products saw service as currency. Citizens of the Carolinas often used tobacco, corn, peas, and even tar for the same purpose. In New York beaver skins were sometimes specified as payments in contracts.

In the early years many different foreign coins circulated throughout what is now the United States. Included were copper, silver, and gold issues from Spain, England, Portugal, Holland, France, Germany, and elsewhere. Most predominant were issues of Spain and England. It was not unusual for deeds, contracts, and other legal documents to be drawn in Spanish milled dollars or English pounds at the turn of the 19th century, well after the formation of the American government. Interestingly, the first paper money issues of the Continental Congress in the 1770s specified their values in Spanish dollars!

The first coins believed to have been specifically for use in America are those pieces made in England around 1616 for the Sommer Islands (Bermuda), which were once connected with the Virginia Company. Denominations comprised the twopence, threepence, sixpence, and shilling.

The first coins to be struck in what is now the United States were made in Massachusetts in 1652. From then until 1680 to, three decades later, many different varieties of silver coins were produced in the denominations of twopence, threepence, sixpence, and shilling. Early issues simply bore the notation NE (for New England) on one side and the denomination such as XII (for twelvepence or shilling) on the other. To discourage counterfeiting, designs became more complex, culminating in the famous Pine Tree shillings and other issues produced during the latter part of the period. Although coinage was effected until 1682, nearly all early Massachusetts silver coins bore the date of 1652.

In 1659 dies in England were prepared for use in Maryland, the colony established by Cecil Calvert, the second Lord of Baltimore. During the next several years silver pieces were produced of the denominations of groat (fourpence), sixpence and shilling.

In 1682 Mark Newby, who came to New Jersey from Ireland a year earlier, influenced the legislature of that state to pass an act which provided that halfpenny coins, imported from Ireland by Newby, would be legal tender within that colony, although they bore no specific legends or inscriptions pertaining to New Jersey.

William Wood, an English metallurgist, became interested in coinage as early as 1717, in which year he produced and prepared several patterns. In 1722 he obtained two patents or contracts from King George I which granted him the right to produce "tokens" for circulation in America and Ireland. Result was the Rosa Americana coinage which consisted of pieces of the halfpenny, penny, and twopence denomination bearing on the obverse a portrait of the King George I and on the reverse a rose. The pieces were light in weight, so despite intensive efforts they were not popular in America. Most merchants and citizens refused to use them. Related to these were Hibernia (Ireland) copper issues of 1722-1724, also produced by Wood. Some of these circulated in America to a limited extent.

Among the most curious of all early issues are the 1737-1739 copper threepence pieces produced by Dr. Samuel Higley of Granby, Connecticut. Higley owned his own copper mine and struck tokens from native metal which saw limited local circulation. Today these are extreme rarities and are valued at many thousands of dollars each.

In 1773 the British crown authorized a coinage of copper halfpennies for Virginia. These were struck in England and arrived two years later in the Virginia colony. By that time the seeds of independence had been sown and the British-made coins met with a limited reception.

Despite these and other issues made in or for America during the 1700s, the main coins in circulation were of Spanish origin. The Spanish milled dollar or 8-real piece was divided in eighths or "bits", each worth 12½ cents. From this term "two bits," for 25 cents passed into the modern idiom. Gold Spanish doubloons, valued at $16 each, were used for many large transactions.

Possibly the first coin specifically related to the United States government was the 1776 continental dollar which was struck in pewter and which bore the inscription similar to those found on certain continental paper money issues of the time. These dollars saw circulation throughout the period, possibly as a substitute for paper notes of the same denomination. Unfortunately, no specific legislation or authorization concerning the 1776 continental dollars survives today, so their history is largely unknown.

On March 13, 1776, the New Hampshire House of Representatives voted that a committee be established to consider the production of copper coinage. It was subsequently reported that it would be beneficial to issue such pieces. Apparently several patterns were made, and at least two varieties of these are known today.

On January 15, 1782, Robert Morris, Superintendent of Finance, proposed a national coinage in a report to Congress. On February 21st of the same year suggestions for a government mint were approved. In 1783 pattern silver pieces were made with Nova Constellatio designs. Despite intensive discussion, a mint did not materialize at the time. It was intended that the coinage be divided into a bit of 100 units, a quint of 500 units, and a mark of 1,000 units, as well as other divisions. The intent was to permit easy conversion of currency throughout the 13 colonies. At the time each colony had its own rate of exchange, and the traveler from one state to another was apt to encounter widely differing values.

Gouverneur Morris, Assistant Superintendent of Finance of the Continental Congress 1781-1785, ordered as a private venture a large quantity of copper coins bearing Nova Constellatio designs. Dated 1783 and 1785, these achieved wide circulation at the value of a half penny. In 1783 John Chalmers, an Annapolis, Maryland, goldsmith and silversmith, produced a series of silver coins of his own design. The values included threepence, sixpence, and shilling.

Following the formation of the United States government, states were given the right to produce their own coins. The first to take advantage of this was Vermont, an independent area which did not formally become a state until admitted to the Union in 1791. Ruben Harmon, Jr., of Rupert, Vermont, obtained the coinage privilege in 1785. From then through 1788 many different varieties of copper pieces were made. Later Vermont issues were produced at a private mint located in the neighboring state of New York. In the same year, 1785, the state of Connecticut granted four men the privilege to produce copper coins. Issues were made of several designs through the year 1788. From 1786 through 1788 New Jersey copper coins were struck. The design featured a horse head on the obverse and a shield on the reverse.

7

Although no official state authorization or legislation relating to the production of New York copper coins can be found, a number of pieces related to New York exist with dates from 1785 through 1788. Also associated with that date is the most famous of all American issues, the 1787 Brasher doubloon.

In 1787 Ephraim Brasher, a New York goldsmith and silversmith (who at one time produced articles for President George Washington, among other notables), produced gold doubloons and marked each with his "EB" counterstamp. These circulated at the value of $16 in the channels of commerce. Today only seven examples of the Brasher doubloon can be traced with certainty.

Although several varieties of pattern Massachusetts copper coins were produced in 1776, it was not until 1787-1788 that issues were made in quantity. Rather than contract coinage to a private individual, the Massachusetts General Court decided to establish a mint to be operated by the state. After severe difficulties, the mint was put into production and produced cents and half cents. In 1788 it was realized that each coin cost over twice its face value to produce so the venture was discontinued.

In 1787 Congress authorized a private contractor to produce copper coins, halfpenny size, bearing special legends. These became the first federally authorized pieces to circulate in large quantities. Known as the Fugio coppers, these featured a sundial on the obverse with the legend "Mind Your Business."

Many tokens and medals were issued to honor George Washington, our first president. These bear such dates at 1783, 1791, and 1792. Most were struck in England and distributed in America on speculation for profit. Certain varieties were struck as proposals for a regular United States coinage.

In addition to those mentioned, many other varieties of tokens and coins were made in England for circulation in America or were produced by various coiners within the United States. Standish Barry, a Baltimore silversmith, struck a distinctive silver threepence token dated July 4, 1790, particularly unusual in that it bore a day date in addition to the year. The First Presbyterian Church of Albany, New York, authorized the issue of 1,000 copper tokens during the same year. The 1796 Castorland jeton or "half dollar" pertained to a French settlement of that name made during the 1790s on the Black River in upstate New York. Talbot, Allum & Lee, New York City merchants in the India trade, distributed tokens bearing their advertisements.

On April 15, 1790, Congress instructed Secretary of the Treasury Alexander Hamilton to prepare a plan to establish a national mint. On March 3, 1791, President Washington approved a joint resolution of Congress to establish a coinage facility.

On April 2, 1792, an additional law, "establishing a mint and regulating the coins of the United States" was approved by Congress, which then proceeded to carry out the intention of the act.

Congress provided that United States coins be produced in the denominations of half cent, cent, half dime, dime, quarter dollar, half dollar, dollar, quarter eagle ($2.50 gold), half eagle ($5 gold), and eagle ($10).

The ratio of silver metal to alloy was 1,485 parts silver to 179 parts alloy, or about 892.5 fine. Gold coins were to be made to a standard of 11 parts gold to one part alloy, or 22 carats fine.

Land for the first mint was purchased in Philadelphia at Seventh Street between Market and Arch streets. David Ritenhouse, an astronomer, philosopher, and former Treasurer of Pennsylvania, was named by President Washington on July 1, 1792, to be the first Director of the Mint. The cornerstone for the structure was laid on July 31st. On September 11th, the first metal purchase, consisting of six pounds of old copper, was made. Coining presses ordered from England arrived on September 21st.

Toward the end of 1792 several different varieties of pattern coins were prepared. Important among these were the silver center cent and the Birch cents. Most famous were silver 5-cent pieces, called half dimes, which were made to the extent of about 2,000 pieces and which, it is believed, actually were put into circulation. As the mint facilities were not ready, it is believed that certain of these issues were produced nearby on the premises of John Harper.

In 1793 the first United States coinage for circulation appeared, cents and half cents. The cents bore on the obverse the head of Miss Liberty, and on the reverse a chain of links. It was stated that Miss Liberty "appeared in a fright" and that having a chain as part of the design was an "ill omen for Liberty." Because of this and similar sentiments the design was changed. From that time forward coinage motifs underwent constant evolution. During the first several decades of United States coinage there was a close relationship between the designs of different denominations. In modern times the trend has changed, and today different denominations have widely differing design subjects.

In 1794 the first American silver coins appeared, the half dime, half dollar, and dollar. The first shipment was made on October 15, 1774, and consisted of 1,758 silver dollars. On December 1st, 5,300 half dollars were shipped. The first gold coins, the half eagle and eagle, were made in the following year, 1795.

The Philadelphia Mint was beseiged by many problems during the early years. Yellow fever plagued Philadelphia on several occasions, and the institution closed its doors for periods during 1797, 1798, 1799, and 1803. Copper was in short supply, and it became a great struggle to locate adequate sources for the production of cents and half cents. Problems developed with the workmen, with production, and even with the acceptance of United States coins by certain banks. Congressional hearings were held, and on one occasion it was resolved to close the Mint forever. Fortunately for numismatists today, this never happened, and following several years of hardships, the Mint established proper procedures and was able to operate efficiently.

By 1804 the price of silver and gold bullion had risen in the market to the point at which it was profitable to export coins and melt them into their composite metals. For this reason coinage of the eagle and silver dollar was discontinued in 1804. In later years the Mint decided to "create" an 1804 silver dollar, a coin of which no original existed. Today only 15 of these pieces, struck at the Philadelphia Mint from about 1834 to the 1860s, are known to exist. The 1804 dollar has been called "the king of American coins."

In 1816 a fire at the Mint severely curtailed coinage. In 1817 new equipment was acquired, including presses which were suitable for the production of Proofs. Proof coins, struck from specially-prepared dies with mirror-like surfaces and using planchets (blank discs) prepared with exceptional care, were made for presentation purposes. Until 1858 these were mainly distributed to favored friends of the Mint, foreign dignitaries, politicians, and others. In the later year sales were made for the first time to the public. Since then Proof coins have been offered for sale at a premium above face value to collectors.

During the early years of Mint operation great emphasis was placed on the intrinsic value of silver and gold coins. It was felt that a $5 gold piece, for example, should contain very close to $5 worth of gold. Likewise, a silver dollar contained nearly $1 worth of silver. Problems arose when the metal market changed and bullion prices advanced. Each time this happened, vast quantities of United States coins went to the melting pot. In the 1830s this became particularly acute, when the price of gold rose sharply. Nearly all American gold issues produced during the 1820s and early 1830s were melted because of this. On August 1, 1834, a new law took effect which reduced the authorized weight of gold in coinage. After that date gold coins were again seen in circulation.

Of the different engravers associated with the Mint, none was more famous than Christian Gobrecht, who joined the staff in 1835. In 1836 he produced a design of Miss Liberty seated, a motif which was subsequently used on most silver issues through 1891 and which became a familiar part of Americana.

The financial panic of 1837 resulted in the hording of most coins in circulation. In their place appeared a large variety of cent-size copper pieces, known today as Hard Times tokens. Later the term was extended to cover privately-issued tokens during the years 1833-1834.

On January 1, 1837, substantial revisions were made in the coinage laws. Gold and silver coins were regulated to contain 90% valuable metal and 10% alloy. Silver dollar coinage, suspended since 1804, was resumed.

In 1838 branch mints were opened at New Orleans, Louisiana; Dahlonega, Georgia; and Charlotte, North Carolina. The expanding American frontier and increased needs of commerce made the New Orleans

Mint a logical supplier for western areas. Discoveries of gold in Georgia and the Carolinas necessitated the opening of mints in those areas to provide a repository for miners. To differentiate branch mint issues from those struck at Philadelphia, distinctive mintmarks were added to each coin produced. New Orleans pieces bore a distinctive "O," Dahlonega pieces a "D," and Charlotte a "C." Later additional mints were opened at San Francisco (1854, "S" mintmark), Carson City (1870, "CC" mintmark), and Denver (1906, "D," mintmark). Although both Dahlonega and Denver used D mintmarks, there was no confusion as the mints operated at different periods.

Just four coinage facilities operate today. The Philadelphia Mint, established in 1792, is in operation. With a few exceptions, Philadelphia Mint coins bear no mintmark. The Denver Mint, opened in 1906, is the second most important coinage facility. The San Francisco Mint, opened in 1854, produces only a limited amount of coins for circulation plus special Proof sets for collectors. In recent years a subsidiary coinage facility at West Point, New York, has been used to strike certain coins, although to prevent hording by collectors no mintmarks appear on such pieces, so they are indistinguishable from those made at Philadelphia.

The Charlotte and Dahlonega mints each operated from 1838 until 1851, when they were closed at the onset of the Civil War. The New Orleans Mint operated from 1838 to 1909. The Carson City facility operated from 1870 until 1893.

The discovery of gold in California in January 1848 led to the famed Gold Rush and sharply accelerated western expansion. Eventually this led to the establishment of the San Francisco Mint. During the 1849-1855 period many different varieties of gold coins were struck by merchants, bankers, and others in California in order to provide a convenient circulating medium for miners, in the absence of an official United States mint.

In 1849 two new gold denominations, the dollar and double eagle ($20), were introduced.

The Act of February 21, 1853, reduced the weight of all silver coins with the exception of the dollar. Prior to that it was profitable to melt silver coins for the bullion value. The denominations from the half dime through the half dollar had arrows added to the date to signify the weight change. These arrows were continued through 1855. Quarter dollars and half dollars of 1853 had in addition rays on the reverse.

In 1854 the $3 gold piece, a new denomination, was introduced. These coins proved unpopular, and issuance was discontinued in 1889.

In 1857 a sweeping coinage law abolished the old style large copper cent and half cent and provided for the new small-size cent made of copper-nickel alloy. Certain foreign coins, including Spanish and English pieces, which had been in active circulation and which were used in many commercial transactions, had their legal tender status revoked.

The Civil War resulted in the hording of coins of all kinds. The situation was particularly acute during the height of the war in 1862-1863, with the result that the government suspended payments of specie (gold and silver coins) through banks. In terms of United States paper money, coins rose to high premiums. On one occasion it took nearly $3 in United States paper money to buy a gold dollar. Specie payments were not resumed until 1876.

To fill the need for a circulating medium, encased postage stamps, Civil War tokens, and fractional currency paper notes were used. These latter pieces were called "stamps" by the general population.

The copper-nickel Indian head cent, which was introduced in 1859, was modified in 1864 to a smaller bronze format. In the same year the 2-cent piece was introduced, the first piece to bear the motto IN GOD WE TRUST. In the following year, 1865, the nickel-3-cent piece made its appearance, and the year after that, 1866, the nickel 5-cent piece was produced for the first time.

The Coinage Act of February 12, 1873, resulted in many changes. The standard silver dollar was suspended. The trade dollar, made of silver and of slightly heavier weight, was designed for use in the Orient. The 2-cent and silver-3-cent pieces were discontinued. The weights were adjusted slightly on certain silver coins, with the result that arrows again appeared in 1873 and 1874 on the denominations of 10 cents, 25 cents, and 50 cents.

On March 3, 1875, authorization was made for the coinage of a 20-cent piece which was intended to facilitate commerce in the West. Confusion with the quarter dollar soon resulted, and the denomination was discontinued in 1878.

The Bland-Allison Act of February 28, 1878, directed the Secretary of the Treasury to purchase between $2 and $4 million worth of silver each month to be made into silver dollars. In 1890 the Sherman Act supplanted the earlier legislation and provided that 4,500,000 ounces of silver per month would be acquired. Huge amounts of silver dollars, unwanted and unneeded by the public, accumulated in Treasury vaults. Of the over 500 million silver dollars produced through 1904, nearly 300 million went to the melting pot in 1918 under the Pittman Act. Silver dollars, minted in response to the political efforts of western mining interests, were controversial for many years.

In 1892 the first American commemorative coin made its appearance, the Columbian half dollar. From that time until 1954 many different commemorative issues were made, including 48 major designs of half dollars, one quarter, one silver dollar, and over a dozen gold coins, including two varieties of a special $50 denomination.

1892 saw the introduction of the Barber design for the dime, quarter, and half dollar, replacing the earlier Liberty seated design.

During the 20th century many new coinage designs appeared. In 1909 the old Lincoln cent motif was replaced by the new Lincoln design. The Indian head or Buffalo nickel appeared in 1913, to be replaced by the Jefferson nickel in 1938. The Mercury dime was first struck in 1916 and remained in use until 1946, when the Roosevelt design replaced it. The standing Liberty quarter, introduced in 1916, was used until 1930. It was replaced two years later, 1932, by the Washington design which has been with us since that time. The Liberty walking half dollar, introduced in 1916, was used until 1947. The Franklin half dollar appeared from 1948 through 1963. Kennedy half dollars have been made since that time. Morgan dollars, minted from 1878 to 1921, were replaced in the latter year by Peace dollars. These were produced until 1935. A lapse ensued and in 1971 the Eisenhower dollar, made of a special clad composition metal made its appearance. In 1979 the Susan B. Anthony dollar, which featured a smaller size and weight, was introduced.

On March 6, 1933, President Franklin D. Roosevelt declared that gold coins and paper gold certificates would not be paid out by banks and other institutions in the channels of commerce. Gold coinage in America effectively came to an end. Later, citizens were required to turn in their gold coins. Certain exceptions were made for numismatists. Possession of gold bullion without a permit became illegal. The permission to hold gold coins was not restored until December 31, 1974. The last United States gold coin was produced in 1933.

Today the numismatist can select from a wide variety of copper, nickel, silver and gold coins made as regular issues over the years in seven different United States mints. In addition, commemorative coins, tokens, and other special issues lend interest.

Grading of Coins

Grading is one of the essential parts of coin collecting today.
For most coins, there is a substantial value difference between each grade.
It is therefore important for the collector to familiarize himself with proper grading rules.

We give you here a brief grading guide. For those who indulge in rare coins or wish more details for grading United States coins, we suggest the publication "New Photograde," by James F. Ruddy.

About Good (abbreviated AG) worn almost smooth and can barely be identified. The date and mint must be distinguishable even though barely readable.

Good (G) heavily worn with all basic lettering and outlines visible but faint, date and mint clear.

Very Good (VG) Well worn. One letter in the word LIBERTY, on the headband or shield, is clearly legible with two or more letters faint but distinguishable. Details are clear but worn flat.

Fine (F) All major details are legible with definite wear on the high points only. The word LIBERTY is complete.

Very Fine (VF) Some of the very fine points of the design are clear but worn. The wear is even over the entire coin.

Extremely Fine (EF) all of the more intricate designs will be clear and show little signs of moderate wear.

Average Uncirculated (UNC) Has no trace of wear but may have small noticeable nicks and marks due to being bagged. Some may have lost part of their original luster.

There are a few other gradings of uncirculated coins, Brilliant Uncirculated, Choice Uncirculated and Perfect Gem Uncirculated, all of which command a higher price than the average uncirculated coin.

Proof Special struck coin, produced from a selected planchet. As a rule it has a mirror like finish without any traces of wear.

Regular Issues
of the United States

HALF CENTS
1793-1857

Authorized on April 2, 1792 and coined at the Philadelphia Mint. The authorized weight was to have been 132 grains, but by the Act of January 14, 1793, before any were coined, it was changed to 104 grains. On January 26, 1796 the weight was again changed to 84 grains. The half cent is the smallest denomination coin struck by the United States.

It was first thought the half cents would play an important part in American commerce but, after the first few years there was little demand for them. A little less than eight million were coined for circulation from 1793 until 1857 when the coinage Act of February 21, 1857 discontinued the half cents. By the beginning of the Civil War they were no longer seen in circulation and became scarce.

The composition of all half cents is copper.

Liberty Cap Type
1793
Designer Adam Eckfeldt

AG-Obverse: Clear outline of head. Date faint but legible.
    Reverse: About one half of design can be seen.

 G-Obverse: Most of Liberty can be seen.
    Reverse: Part of legend legible, outline of wreath complete.

VG-Obverse: Date and Liberty are strong. Hair outline clear.
    Reverse: Legend weak but complete.

 F-Obverse: Some of the hair details show.
    Reverse: Wreath leaves and berries worn but complete.

VF-Obverse: Hair ribbon sharp. Most of hair details show but weak around ear and forehead.
    Reverse: Some of the details in leaves show.

EF-Obverse: All hair details show but worn on high spots.
    Reverse: Most details of leaves show.

DATE	MINTAGE	AG-3	G-6	VG-10	F-15	VF-30	EF-45
1793	35,334	1500.00	2500.00	3000.00	3500.00	4500.00	8500.00

HALF CENTS

Design Change — Head Facing Right
1794
Designer Robert Scot

WITH POLE

DATE	MINTAGE	AG-3	G-6	VG-10	F-15	VF-30	EF-45
1794	81,600	210.00	350.00	575.00	695.00	1600.00	2500.00

1795-1797
Designer John Smith Gardner

NO POLE

1795 Lettered Edge with Pole	25,600	175.00	300.00	500.00	700.00	1195.00	2150.00
1795 Lettered Edge Punctuated Date ..		180.00	300.00	500.00	700.00	1200.00	2125.00
1795 Plain Edge No Pole	109,000	170.00	285.00	495.00	700.00	1175.00	2100.00
1795 Plain Edge Punctuated Date ..		170.00	285.00	495.00	700.00	1175.00	2100.00
1796 No Pole	1,390	— —	— —	RARE	— —	— —	— —
1796 With Pole ...	5090	1500.00	2500.00	3225.00	5250.00	— —	— —
1797 Plain Edge ...		195.00	325.00	500.00	695.00	1200.00	2150.00
1797 Lettered Edge	119,215	275.00	450.00	600.00	800.00	1700.00	3800.00
1797 1 above 1		180.00	300.00	495.00	700.00	1200.00	2150.00

HALF CENTS

Draped Bust Type
1800-1808
Designer Robert Scot

AG-Obverse: Clear outline of head with enough date to identify.
    Reverse: Part of wreath and legend shows.

G-Obverse: Lettering and date legible but weak.
    Reverse: Part of legend legible, outline of wreath complete.

VG-Obverse: Date and Liberty strong. Hair outline clear.
    Reverse: Legend weak but complete.

F-Obverse: Some hair details show. Drapery on bust worn but clear.
    Reverse: Some details in leaves visible.

VF-Obverse: Most hair details show. Details of Drapery on bust clear.
    Reverse: Legend strong. About half of leaves details show.

EF-Obverse: All hair details show but weak only around ear and forehead.
    Reverse: Most details of leaves show.

1802 NEW REVERSE   STEMLESS

DATE	MINTAGE	AG-3	G-6	VG-10	F-15	VF-30	EF-45	AU-50
1800	211,530	24.00	40.00	45.00	55.00	85.00	150.00	550.00
1802, 2 over 0 Reverse of 1800	14,366	1200.00	2000.00	2750.00	3725.00	6000.00	— —	— —
1802, 2 over 0 New Type Reverse . . .		120.00	200.00	275.00	465.00	1350.00	2500.00	— —
1803	97,900	27.50	45.00	50.00	60.00	85.00	150.00	575.00

SERF 4   1802 over 0   SPIKED CHIN

HALF CENTS

DATE	MINTAGE	AG-3	G-6	VG-10	F 15	VF-30	EF-45	AU-50
1804								
Regular w/ Stems		24.00	40.00	50.00	70.00	110.00	150.00	575.00
1804								
Regular w/o Stems		24.00	40.00	45.00	55.00	85.00	130.00	525.00
1804 Serf w/Stems	1,055,312	24.00	40.00	45.00	55.00	85.00	130.00	525.00
1804 Serf w/o Stems		24.00	40.00	45.00	55.00	85.00	130.00	525.00
1804 Spiked Chin		24.00	40.00	45.00	55.00	85.00	130.00	575.00
1805 Small								
w/o Stems		24.00	40.00	45.00	55.00	90.00	130.00	550.00
1805 Small								
5 w/Stems	814,464	60.00	100.00	175.00	400.00	700.00	1600.00	— —
1805 Large								
5 w/Stems		24.00	40.00	45.00	57.50	80.00	125.00	550.00
1806 Small 6								
w/o Stems		24.00	40.00	45.00	57.50	80.00	150.00	550.00
1806 Small								
6 w/Stems	356,000	40.00	65.00	100.00	170.00	280.00	650.00	— —
1806 Large								
6 w/Stems		24.00	40.00	45.00	57.50	80.00	150.00	550.00
1807	476,000	24.00	40.00	45.00	57.50	80.00	150.00	550.00
1808		24.00	40.00	45.00	57.50	80.00	150.00	550.00
1808, 8 over	400,000							
7		50.00	85.00	130.00	170.00	500.00	975.00	— —

Turban Head
1809-1836
Designer John Reich

AG-Obverse: Head visible, few stars but worn flat.
    Reverse: Half cent readable. Some letters of legend show.

G-Obverse: Complete head outlined. Liberty shows but weak letters.
              Date strong. All stars visible but very worn.
    Reverse: Legend readable but worn.

VG-Obverse: Full Liberty on hair band. Outline of ear shows.
    Reverse: Legend complete. Wreath strong but no details.

F-Obverse: Most hair details show Liberty strong.
    Reverse: Leaves show some details.

VF-Obverse: All hair details show but weak at ear and forehead.
    Reverse: Most of leaves show details.

EF-Obverse: Slight wear only on high points of hair details.
    Reverse: All leaves will show some details.

HALF CENTS

DATE	MINTAGE	AG-3	G-6	VG-10	F-15	VF-30	EF-45	AU-50
1809		22.50	37.50	42.50	50.00	75.00	90.00	165.00
1809, 9 over 6	1,154,572	22.50	37.50	42.50	50.00	75.00	90.00	165.00
1809 circle inside 0		22.50	37.50	42.50	50.00	75.00	90.00	165.00
1810	215,000	22.50	37.50	47.50	60.00	85.00	160.00	400.00
1811	63,140	57.50	95.00	115.00	225.00	475.00	950.00	— —
1825	63,000	24.00	40.00	50.00	55.00	70.00	110.00	250.00
1826	234,000	22.50	37.50	42.50	47.50	65.00	85.00	175.00
1828 13 Stars	606,000	22.50	37.50	42.50	47.50	65.00	95.00	175.00
1828 12 Stars		22.50	37.50	42.50	52.50	80.00	110.00	275.00
1829	487,000	22.50	37.50	42.50	50.00	60.00	85.00	175.00

LARGE BERRIES

SMALL BERRIES

MINTAGE		EF-45	UNC-65	PROOF-65
1831 Regular . . . 2,200		1200.00	2800.00	4500.00
1831 Restrike, Reverse of 1836, Large Berries				4000.00
1831 Restrike, Reverse of 1840-57, Small Berries				4700.00

DATE	MINTAGE	AG-3	G-6	VG-10	F-15	VF-30	EF-45	AU-50	UNC-65
1832	154,000	22.50	37.50	42.50	53.50	60.00	85.00	175.00	3150.00
1833	120,000	22.50	37.50	42.50	53.50	60.00	85.00	175.00	3150.00
1834	141,000	22.50	37.50	42.50	53.50	60.00	85.00	175.00	3150.00
1835	398,000	22.50	37.50	42.50	53.50	60.00	85.00	175.00	3150.00
1836 Original							PROOF ONLY		2800.00
1836 Reverse of 1840-57, Restrike							PROOF ONLY		3500.00

HALF CENTS

Braided Hair
1840-1857
Designer Christian Gobrecht

AG-Obverse: Well worn head, part of date showing.
    Reverse: Partial Legend, well worn but distinct chain.

G-Obverse: Part of Liberty shows. Some beads visible.
    Reverse: Complete legend and wreath but worn flat.

VG-Obverse: Liberty completely visible. Some hair details show.
    Reverse: Leaves strong but no details.

F-Obverse: Most hair details show. Beads complete and strong.
    Reverse: Leaves show some details.

VF-Obverse: All hair details show but weak at ear and forehead.
    Reverse: Most of leaves have some details.

EF-Obverse: Slight wear only on high points of hair details.
    Reverse: All leaves will show some details.

	PROOF-65
1840	3800.00
1840 Restrike	4000.00
1841	4000.00
1841 Restrike	4000.00
1842	4225.00
1842 Restrike	3800.00
1843	3900.00
1843 Restrike	3800.00
1844	4250.00
1844 Restrike	3900.00
1845	4800.00
1845 Restrike	3900.00
1846	3900.00
1846 Restrike	3800.00
1847	3875.00
1847 Restrike	3875.00
1848	3875.00
1848 Restrike	3800.00
1849 Small date	4950.00
1849 Restrike Small date	3900.00

HALF CENTS

SMALL DATE

DATE	MINTAGE	G-6	VG-10	F-15	VF-30	EF-45	AU-50	UNC-60	UNC-65	PROOF-65
1849 Large date	39,864	38.50	45.00	50.00	60.00	95.00	195.00	375.00	2500.00	7500.00
1850	39,812	38.50	45.00	50.00	60.00	95.00	195.00	375.00	2500.00	7500.00
1851	147,672	38.50	45.00	50.00	60.00	95.00	195.00	325.00	2500.00	7500.00
1852 Original								PROOF ONLY		7500.00
1852 Restrike								PROOF ONLY		7500.00
1853	129,694	38.50	45.00	50.00	60.00	95.00	250.00	350.00	3000.00	
1854	55,358	38.50	45.00	50.00	60.00	95.00	195.00	350.00	2500.00	7500.00
1855	56,500	38.50	45.00	50.00	60.00	95.00	195.00	350.00	2500.00	7500.00
1856	40,430	38.50	45.00	50.00	60.00	95.00	195.00	350.00	2500.00	7500.00
1857	35,180	38.50	45.00	50.00	60.00	95.00	195.00	350.00	2500.00	7500.00

LARGE CENTS
1793-1857

Authorized on April 2, 1792 and coined at the Philadelphia Mint. The law specified the Large Cent to weigh twice that of the Half Cent. Originally the weight was set at 264 grains but changed to 208 grains by the Act of January 14, 1793, in time for the first coins to be minted. Three years later it was changed again by a presidential order on January 26, 1796, to 164 grains. The mint had problems with the early coins and because of this numismatists today can assemble a very exciting collection of Large Cents. The first issue of 1793, engraved by Henry Volght, has an obverse of Liberty with flowing hair and a reverse of a linked chain. Objections were made to the linked chain not being a representative symbol of Liberty. A new design was made by Adam Eckfeild, showing a wreath on the reverse and a revised obverse of the flowing hair Liberty with a sharper profile. Objections continued to the untamed hair effect of Liberty. Another change was made by designer Joseph Wright to what is known as the Liberty Cap Cent, which seemed to satisfy most of the objections.

On the early coins, each die was cut by hand and frequently they cracked or broke. Replacing dies contained errors and variations creating a number of varieties which has made the Large Cents the most popular collectable series of United States coins.

The Large Cents were minted yearly from 1793 to 1857 with the exception of 1815 due to a shortage of copper. By 1857 the Large Cent became too costly to produce and was discontinued in favor of a smaller cent. The composition of all Large Cents is copper.

LARGE CENTS

Flowing Hair
1793
Chain Type
Designer Henry Voight

The head of the Chain Cent often comes with a weak strike. This should be considered when grading.

AG-Obverse: Well worn head, part of date showing.
    Reverse: Partial legend, well worn but distinct chain.

 G-Obverse: Head worn flat but clear, full date but weak.
    Reverse: Legend and One Cent weak but readable.

VG-Obverse: Head well outlined, distinct full date.
    Reverse: All letters of Legend and One Cent showing but worn.

 F-Obverse: Ends of hair will show balance of hair smooth.
    Reverse: All letters raised but high points worn.

VF-Obverse: Outline of ear faintly showing, half of hair showing.
    Reverse: One Cent and chain bold.

EF-Obverse: Details of hair will show but worn, ear showing.
    Reverse: Legend bold.

AMERI.
REVERSE

AMERICA
REVERSE

DATE	MINTAGE	AG-3	G-6	VG-10	F-15	VF-30	EF-45
1793		2100.00	3500.00	3875.00	4900.00	10250.00	22000.00
1793 Ameri. on reverse .	36,103	1950.00	3250.00	3600.00	4700.00	9500.00	21000.00
1973 Period after Date & Liberty		1950.00	3250.00	3600.00	4700.00	9500.00	21000.00

LARGE CENTS

Wreath Type
Designer Adam Eckfeldt

AG-Obverse: Well worn head, part of date showing.
    Reverse: Some letters showing, worn but distinct wreath.

 G-Obverse: Head worn flat but clear, full date but weak.
    Reverse: Wreath clear, all letters worn but readable.

VG-Obverse: Head well outlined, distinct full date and "Liberty."
    Reverse: All lettering clear but may be weak.

 F-Obverse: One half hair details visible, "Liberty" and date sharp.
    Reverse: Lettering sharp.

VF-Obverse: Most of hair details showing.
    Reverse: Beaded border sharp.

EF-Obverse: Hair details will show but worn on highest points and around ear.
    Reverse: Wreath will be worn only on high point.

DATE	MINTAGE	AG-3	G-6	VG-10	F-15	VF-30	EF-45
1793 Vine & Bar Edge ..	63,353	1000.00	1750.00	2000.00	2900.00	4900.00	10850.00
1793 Lettered Edge		1075.00	1800.00	2150.00	3000.00	5000.00	11000.00

There is an additional variety of this 1793 cent which is commonly called the Strawberry Leaf Variety. Instead of the normal three leaf sprig over the date there is a cluster of leaves and a blossom which resembles a strawberry plant. It is not known why this variety was made and is found only with considerable wear. Even in very worn condition it is extremely rare.

LARGE CENTS

Liberty Cap
1793-1796
Designers Joseph Wright 1793-95 Lettered Edge
John Smith Gardner 1795-96 Plain Edge

AG-Obverse: Head worn smooth but visible, date readable.
Reverse: About half of wreath and letters visible.

G-Obverse: Complete outline of head but no details showing.
Reverse: Wreath and all letters visible but weak.

VG-Obverse: Some hair details showing, "Liberty" and date clear.
Reverse: All letters clear.

F-Obverse: About half of hair details will show.
Reverse: Complete wreath, no details to leaves.

VF-Obverse: Most of hair details showing.
Reverse: Some details in leaves visible.

EF-Obverse: All hair details will show but worn on high spots and around ear.
Reverse: 1/100 sharp, Wreath worn only on high points.

DATE	MINTAGE	AG-3	G-6	VG-10	F-15	VF-30	EF-45
1793	11,056	600.00	1000.00	1400.00	2750.00	4700.00	9000.00

HEAD OF 1794		**HEAD OF 1795**			**STARRED REVERSE**		
1794		125.00	200.00	250.00	375.00	775.00	1400.00
1794 Head of 1793 .		195.00	325.00	450.00	950.00	2100.00	4500.00
1794 Head of 1795 .	918,521	125.00	200.00	250.00	375.00	775.00	1400.00
1794 Stars in Reverse rim		1200.00	2000.00	3250.00	6000.00	12500.00	23000.00
1795 Lettered Edge	37,000	135.00	225.00	375.00	450.00	675.00	1400.00
1795 Plain Edge . . .	501,500	125.00	215.00	360.00	425.00	675.00	1450.00
1796	109,825	135.00	225.00	375.00	450.00	650.00	1450.00

LARGE CENTS

Draped Bust
1796-1807
Designer Robert Scot

AG-Obverse: Head worn smooth but visible, date readable.
    Reverse: About half of wreath and letters visible.

G-Obverse: Complete outline of head but no details.
    Reverse: Wreath and all letters visible but weak.

VG-Obverse: Some hair details showing, "Liberty" and date clear.
    Reverse: All letters clear.

F-Obverse: Most of hair details showing but faint.
    Reverse: Complete wreath, no details to leaves.

VF-Obverse: All hair details showing but curls around ear are worn flat.
    Reverse: Some details in leaves visible.

EF-Obverse: High spots of hair and tops of curls around ear show wear.
    Reverse: Wreath worn only on high points of details.

REVERSE 1796

OBVERSE

REVERSE 1796

LIHERTY
ERROR

1797 STEMS

DATE	MINTAGE	AG-3	G-6	VG-10	F-15	VF-30	EF-45
1796		57.50	95.00	125.00	225.00	450.00	950.00
1796 Reverse of 1794 . . .	363,375	57.50	95.00	135.00	225.00	475.00	975.00
1796 Reverse of 1797 . . .		60.00	100.00	150.00	250.00	550.00	1000.00
1796 LIHERTY ERROR .		70.00	115.00	195.00	350.00	600.00	1500.00

LARGE CENTS

DATE	MINTAGE	AG 0	G-6	VG-10	F-15	VF-30	EF-45
1797 Plain edge reverse of 1796		40.00	65.00	100.00	175.00	375.00	800.00
1797 Milled edge reverse of 1796	897,500	35.00	60.00	100.00	160.00	350.00	795.00
1797 Reverse of 1797 with Stems		32.50	55.00	75.00	150.00	295.00	600.00
1797 Reverse of 1797 without Stems		45.00	75.00	125.00	225.00	500.00	975.00
1798, 8 over 7		32.50	55.00	100.00	195.00	525.00	1100.00
1798 Reverse of 1796	1,841,700	32.50	55.00	100.00	175.00	500.00	975.00
1798 Small date ...		20.00	35.00	50.00	95.00	200.00	485.00
1798 Large date ...		20.00	35.00	50.00	90.00	200.00	425.00
1799	42,500	350.00	600.00	1000.00	2000.00	4000.00	— —
1799, 9 over 8		400.00	675.00	1100.00	2100.00	4250.00	— —
1800		20.00	35.00	50.00	80.00	175.00	400.00
1800 over 1798	2,822,175	21.50	36.50	53.50	75.00	200.00	575.00
1800 over 79		24.00	40.00	55.00	80.00	175.00	400.00

FRACTION 1/000

SMALL FRACTION
1/100 over 1/000

1801		21.50	35.00	50.00	80.00	160.00	400.00
1801 Fraction 1/000		28.50	47.50	65.00	125.00	195.00	525.00
1801 1/100 over 1/000	1,362,837	24.00	40.00	60.00	130.00	250.00	575.00
1801 1/000, one Stem, "IINITED" ERROR		45.00	75.00	125.00	200.00	500.00	1100.00
1802		21.50	35.00	50.00	75.00	150.00	300.00
1802 1/000	3,435,100	22.50	37.50	45.00	80.00	200.00	400.00
1802 w/o Stems ..		21.50	35.00	45.00	65.00	175.00	350.00

LARGE CENTS

1803 SMALL DATE   LARGE FRACTION

DATE	MINTAGE	AG-3	G-6	VG-10	F-15	VF-30	EF-45
1803 Small Date							
Small Fract.		21.50	35.00	40.00	75.00	190.00	300.00
1803 Small Date							
Large Fract.		21.50	35.00	40.00	75.00	190.00	300.00
1803 Large Date ...	3,131,691						
Large Fract.		40.00	65.00	120.00	200.00	575.00	1100.00
1803 Large Date							
Small Fract.		225.00	375.00	650.00	1400.00	2750.00	— —
1803 1/100							
over 1/000		27.50	45.00	65.00	120.00	295.00	500.00
1803 w/o Stems ..		24.00	40.00	55.00	95.00	225.00	475.00

ORIGINAL 1804

1804	96,500	200.00	350.00	600.00	975.00	1875.00	3400.00
1804 Restrike Produced around 1860. Has an obverse of an 1803 and a reverse from a 1820 cent UNC 300.00							
1805 Blunt 1	941,116	21.50	35.00	45.00	67.50	175.00	325.00
1805 Pointed 1		21.50	35.00	45.00	67.50	175.00	325.00
1806	348,000	27.50	45.00	75.00	125.00	225.00	525.00
1807 Small Fract ..		21.50	35.00	45.00	82.50	150.00	550.00
1807 Large Fract ..	829,221	21.50	35.00	45.00	75.00	135.00	375.00
1807 Small 7 over 6		175.00	300.00	475.00	925.00	1850.00	4500.00
1807 Large 7 over 6		21.50	35.00	45.00	75.00	150.00	400.00

LARGE CENTS

Turban Head
1808-1814
Designer John Reich

AG-Obverse: Part of stars visible, date readable.
Reverse: About half of wreath and letters visible.

G-Obverse: All stars will show but well worn.
Reverse: All letters and wreath can be seen.

VG-Obverse: All letters of "Liberty" show, ear can be seen.
Reverse: Wreath well outlined but no details.

F-Obverse: Ear sharp, most of hair will show but weak.
Reverse: Slight details in some leaves.

VF-Obverse: All details of hair are visible but weak.
Reverse: All leaves and bow show some detail.

EF-Obverse: Hair sharp, worn only on high points of curls and hairlines.
Reverse: Sharp, wear on high points of leaves.

SERF 4

DATE	MINTAGE	AG-3	G-6	VG-10	F-15	VF-30	EF-45
1808	1,109,000	27.50	45.00	57.50	95.00	295.00	695.00
1809	222,867	57.50	95.00	150.00	280.00	500.00	975.00
1810		27.50	45.00	50.00	75.00	250.00	650.00
1810, 10 over 9	1,458,500	30.00	50.00	60.00	85.00	275.00	650.00
1811		50.00	85.00	125.00	225.00	425.00	850.00
1811, 1 over 0	218,025	55.00	90.00	135.00	230.00	425.00	875.00
1812	1,075,500	27.50	45.00	55.00	115.00	225.00	600.00
1813	418,000	31.50	52.50	75.00	115.00	250.00	675.00
1814		27.50	45.00	60.00	85.00	200.00	600.00
1814 with Serf 4 . . .	357,830	27.50	45.00	60.00	85.00	200.00	600.00

LARGE CENTS

Coronet Type
1816-1839
Designers: Obverse, Robert Scot
Reverse, John Reich

AG-Obverse: Part of stars visible, date readable.
    Reverse: About half of wreath and letters visible.

G-Obverse: All stars show, outline of head clear.
    Reverse: All letters and wreath can be seen.

VG-Obverse: All letters of "Liberty" and part of hair cords visible.
    Reverse: Wreath well outlined but no details.

F-Obverse: Hair cords show, most hair details visible.
    Reverse: Slight details in some leaves.

VF-Obverse: All details of hair show but weak.
    Reverse: All leaves and bow show some detail.

EF-Obverse: Hair cords sharp, Hair and stars worn only on high points.
    Reverse: Sharp, wear on high points of leaves.

13 STARS

15 STARS

DATE	MINTAGE	G-6	VG-10	F-15	VF-30	EF-45	AU-50	UNC-60	UNC-65
1816	2,820,982	20.00	27.50	33.50	42.50	110.00	245.00	500.00	3000.00
1817 13 Stars .		18.50	24.50	30.00	40.00	95.00	245.00	500.00	3000.00
1817 15 Stars ..	3,948,400	20.00	26.00	45.00	65.00	125.00	395.00	900.00	— —
1818	3,167,000	18.50	24.50	30.00	35.00	85.00	240.00	500.00	3000.00
1819		18.75	24.50	32.50	37.50	90.00	240.00	500.00	3000.00
1819, 9 over 8 .	2,671,000	19.50	24.50	35.00	40.00	90.00	240.00	500.00	3000.00
1820		18.50	24.50	29.50	35.00	90.00	240.00	500.00	3000.00
1820,20 over 19	4,407,550	18.75	24.75	30.00	37.50	95.00	250.00	500.00	3000.00
1821	389,000	35.00	45.00	65.00	110.00	285.00	550.00	975.00	— —
1822 Closed Date	2,072,339	18.75	24.50	32.00	37.50	95.00	275.00	525.00	3150.00
1822 Wide Date		18.75	24.50	32.00	37.50	95.00	275.00	525.00	3150.00

LARGE CENTS

DATE	MINTAGE	G-6	VG-10	F-15	VF-30	EF-45	AU-50	UNC-60	UNC-65
1823	855,730	50.00	65.00	125.00	200.00	700.00	— —	— —	— —
1823, 3 over 2 .		40.00	55.00	100.00	195.00	500.00	— —	— —	— —
1824 Closed Date		18.75	25.00	35.00	47.50	135.00	400.00	— —	— —
1824 Wide Date	1,262,000	18.75	25.00	37.50	50.00	135.00	400.00	— —	— —
1824, 4 over 2 .		35.00	45.00	67.50	110.00	275.00	525.00	— —	— —
1825 Small "A"		18.75	25.00	32.50	40.00	100.00	250.00	500.00	3000.00
1825 Large "A"	1,461,100	18.50	25.00	32.50	40.00	100.00	250.00	500.00	3000.00
1826 Closed Date		18.75	25.00	32.50	40.00	100.00	250.00	500.00	3000.00
1826 Wide Date	1,517,425	18.50	25.00	32.50	40.00	100.00	250.00	500.00	3000.00
1826, 6 over 5 .		35.00	45.00	75.00	120.00	250.00	500.00	750.00	4000.00
1827	2,357,732	18.50	22.50	30.00	37.50	100.00	250.00	500.00	3000.00
1828 Small Date	2,260,624	18.75	27.50	40.00	50.00	135.00	400.00	575.00	3250.00
1828 Large Date		18.75	22.50	32.50	37.50	100.00	250.00	500.00	3000.00
1829 Small Letters	1,414,500	25.00	35.00	60.00	85.00	225.00	450.00	625.00	3400.00
1829 Large Letters		18.50	27.50	37.50	45.00	140.00	400.00	575.00	3250.00
1830 Small Letters	1,711,500	19.50	35.00	60.00	135.00	300.00	700.00	— —	— —
1830 Large Letters		18.50	22.50	30.00	37.50	90.00	250.00	500.00	2900.00
1831 Small Letters	3,359,260	18.50	22.50	30.00	35.00	85.00	250.00	500.00	2900.00
1831 Large Letters		18.50	22.50	30.00	35.00	85.00	250.00	525.00	2900.00
1832 Small Letters	2,362,000	18.50	22.50	30.00	35.00	90.00	250.00	525.00	2950.00
1832 Large Letters		18.50	22.50	30.00	35.00	90.00	250.00	525.00	2950.00
1833	2,739,000	18.50	22.50	27.50	35.00	85.00	230.00	500.00	2900.00
1834 Sm. 8, Lg. Stars & Letters		18.50	22.50	27.50	35.00	85.00	230.00	500.00	2900.00
1834 Lg. 8, Stars & Letters	1,855,100	19.50	23.50	32.50	47.50	95.00	260.00	525.00	3100.00
1834 Lg. 8, Stars & Sm. Letters		21.50	27.50	42.50	75.00	165.00	450.00	600.00	3750.00
1834 Lg. 8, Sm. Stars & Letters		19.50	23.50	27.50	35.00	85.00	230.00	500.00	2900.00

LARGE CENTS

HEAD OF 1836

HEAD OF 1838

DATE	MINTAGE	G-6	VG-10	F-15	VF-30	EF-45	AU-50	UNC-60	UNC-65
1835 Lg. Date & Stars	3,878,400	19.50	25.00	32.50	45.00	125.00	650.00	575.00	3150.00
1835 Sm. Date & Stars		19.50	25.00	32.50	45.00	125.00	650.00	575.00	3150.00
1835 Head of 1836 . . .		18.50	20.00	27.50	32.50	100.00	230.00	500.00	2900.00
1836	2,111,000	18.50	20.00	27.50	32.50	85.00	230.00	500.00	2900.00
1837	5,558,300	18.75	23.75	32.50	45.00	115.00	500.00	600.00	3150.00
1837 Head of 1838 . . .		18.50	20.00	27.50	32.50	85.00	240.00	500.00	2900.00
1838	6,370,200	18.50	20.00	27.50	32.50	85.00	230.00	485.00	2900.00
1839	3,128,661	22.50	30.00	45.00	57.50	115.00	525.00	600.00	3150.00
1839 Head of 1838 . . .		19.75	27.50	42.50	47.50	115.00	525.00	700.00	3150.00
1839, 9 over 6		125.00	195.00	285.00	550.00	1750.00	2500.00	— —	— —

LARGE CENTS

Braided Hair
1840-1857
Designer Christian Gobrecht

AG-Obverse: Part of Stars visible, date readable.
   Reverse: About half of wreath and letters visible.

 G-Obverse: All stars show outline of head clear.
   Reverse: Wreath and all letters can be seen.

VG-Obverse: "Liberty" readable, outline of ear shows.
   Reverse: Wreath well outlined but no details.

 F-Obverse: Hair cords sharp, most hair details will show.
   Reverse: Slight details in some leaves.

VF-Obverse: All details of hair show but weak, ear sharp.
   Reverse: All leaves and bow show some detail.

 EF-Obverse: Details of hair strong but weak around ear.
   Reverse: Sharp, wear on high points of leaves.

DATE	MINTAGE	G-6	VG-10	F-15	VF-30	EF-45	AU-50	UNC-60	UNC-65
1840 Small Date	2,462,700	18.50	19.75	25.00	27.75	65.00	225.00	450.00	2500.00
1840 Large Date		18.75	20.00	25.00	27.75	65.00	225.00	450.00	2500.00
1841	1,597,367	19.50	22.50	25.00	27.75	65.00	235.00	450.00	2500.00
1842 Small Date		18.75	19.50	25.00	27.75	65.00	225.00	450.00	2500.00
1842 Large Date	2,383,390	18.50	19.50	25.00	27.75	65.00	225.00	450.00	2500.00
1843 Head of 1840 Sm. Letters		20.00	22.50	30.00	35.00	65.00	225.00	450.00	2500.00
1843 Head of 1840 Lg. Letters	2,428,320	30.00	45.00	85.00	110.00	185.00	400.00	675.00	3500.00
1843 Head of 1844 Lg. Letters		20.00	25.00	30.00	37.50	65.00	225.00	450.00	2500.00

LARGE CENTS

DATE	MINTAGE	G-6	VG-10	F-15	VF-30	EF-45	AU-50	UNC-60	UNC-65
1844		18.50	20.00	25.00	27.50	65.00	225.00	450.00	2500.00
1844 over 81 ..	2,398,752	22.50	27.50	35.00	45.00	85.00	275.00	500.00	2800.00
1845	3,894,804	18.50	19.50	22.00	25.00	65.00	210.00	450.00	2500.00
1846 Sm. Date		18.50	19.50	22.50	25.00	65.00	210.00	450.00	2500.00
1846 Med. Date .	4,120,800	18.50	19.50	22.50	25.00	65.00	210.00	450.00	2500.00
1846 Large Date .		18.50	20.00	25.00	27.50	65.00	210.00	450.00	2500.00
1847	6,183,669	18.50	19.50	21.50	25.00	65.00	210.00	450.00	2500.00
1847, 7 over sm. 7		20.00	27.50	35.00	45.00	95.00	250.00	500.00	3000.00
1848	6,415,799	18.50	19.50	21.50	25.00	65.00	210.00	450.00	2500.00
1849	4,178,500	18.50	19.50	21.50	25.00	65.00	210.00	450.00	2500.00
1850	4,426,844	18.50	19.50	21.50	25.00	65.00	210.00	450.00	2500.00
1851	9,889,707	18.50	19.50	21.50	25.00	65.00	210.00	450.00	2500.00
1851 over 81 ..		18.75	19.75	22.00	40.00	95.00	250.00	525.00	3150.00
1852	5,063,094	18.50	19.50	21.50	25.00	65.00	210.00	450.00	2500.00
1853	6,641,131	18.50	19.50	21.50	25.00	65.00	210.00	450.00	2500.00
1854	4,236,156	18.50	19.50	21.50	25.00	65.00	210.00	450.00	2500.00
1855 Knob on ear		18.50	19.50	27.50	35.00	75.00	220.00	465.00	2500.00
1855 Vertical 5's ...	1,574,829	18.50	19.50	21.50	27.50	60.00	210.00	450.00	2500.00
1855 Slanting 5's		18.50	19.50	21.50	27.50	60.00	200.00	450.00	2500.00
1856 Vertical 5	2,690,463	18.50	19.50	21.50	27.50	60.00	200.00	450.00	2500.00
1856 Slanting 5		18.50	19.50	21.50	27.50	60.00	200.00	450.00	2500.00
1857 Small Date .	333,456	40.00	50.00	60.00	75.00	100.00	280.00	550.00	3000.00
1857 Large Date .		40.00	50.00	60.00	75.00	100.00	280.00	550.00	3000.00

SMALL CENTS

Authorized on February 21, 1857 and coined at the Philadelphia Mint.
As early as 1849 the Mint was studying the idea of reducing the size of the one cent piece because the large copper cents were cumbersome and barely paid the cost of producing them. In 1856, Mint Director James Ross Snowden decided on the small size Flying Eagle design and had the engraver James B. Longacre produce the dies. From the new dies about 700 coins were struck in 1856, before the authorized date, and distributed to political dignitaries. In later years the 1856 cent was restruck as it became a popular collectors item.
In 1858, because of problems in striking the flying eagle design, it was discontinued.
The composition of the Flying Eagle cent is 88% copper and 12% nickel.

Flying Eagle
1856-1858
Designer, James B. Longacre

AG-Obverse: Eagle outline faint. Date readable.
    Reverse: About half of wreath and a few letters show.

G-Obverse: All letters legible. Eagle eye shows.
    Reverse: Wreath complete but worn. One cent clear.

VG-Obverse: Some feathers show. Letters sharp.
    Reverse: Little details in some leaves show.

F-Obverse: Eagle's head and some feathers sharp.
    Reverse: Ribbon shows little detail but well defined.

VF-Obverse: Tail feathers are complete. Most wing feathers sharp.
    Reverse: Some details in wreath and ribbon show.

EF-Obverse: Wear shows on breast and tip of wing only.
    Reverse: Most details will show with wear on high points.

DATE	MINTAGE	G-6	VG-10	F-15	VF-30	EF-45	AU-50	UNC-60	UNC-65	PROOF-65
1856	1000	1000.00	1175.00	1350.00	1650.00	1950.00	2650.00	3800.00	7000.00	8000.00
1857	17,450,000	22.50	25.00	26.50	45.00	97.50	250.00	550.00	2250.00	7000.00
1858 "AM" of America joined	24,600,000	20.00	22.50	27.50	47.50	100.00	300.00	575.00	2250.00	7000.00
1858 "AM" of America separated		20.00	22.50	27.50	47.50	100.00	300.00	575.00	2250.00	7000.00

SMALL CENTS

Indian Head
1859-1909
Designer, James B. Longacre

In 1859, a new design of small cent, engraved by James B. Longacre, with the head of an Indian girl, on the obverse and a laurel wreath on the reverse, was adopted. The following year, 1860, a shield, was added to the reverse to give it more national character, with an oak wreath in place of the laurel wreath. The composition of 88% copper and 12% nickel proved to be too hard causing frequent die breaks as well as being too costly. During 1864 a change in the alloy of the cent was made to 95% copper and 5% tin and zinc. Later in the same year the designers initial L, for Longacre was added on the ribbon just to the left of the lowest feather in the headdress.
In 1908 and 1909 the Indian head cents were struck at the San Francisco Mint as well as the Philadelphia Mint. This was the first production of a minor coin from a mint other than Philadelphia.
The Indian cent was discontinued in 1909 in favor of a new design.

AG-Obverse: Some letters show. Date legible enough to identify.
    Reverse: Most of wreath outline shows.

  G-Obverse: Outline of face and headdress clear.
    Reverse: Complete wreath outline shows.

VG-Obverse: Some letters of Liberty on headband will show.
    Reverse: Wreath is more than outline, some details show.

  F-Obverse: All letters of Liberty legible but worn.
    Reverse: All three arrowheads stand out from wreath.

VF-Obverse: Liberty sharp. Most details in feathers show.
    Reverse: Most details in wreath and ribbon show.

 EF-Obverse: Feather details complete and sharp.
    Reverse: Wear will show only on the high points.

**1859 TYPE WITHOUT
SHIELD ON REVERSE**

DATE	MINTAGE	G-6	VG-10	F-15	VF-30	EF-45	AU-50	UNC-60	UNC-65	PROOF-65
1859	36,400,000	11.00	12.50	17.50	35.00	95.00	210.00	500.00	1850.00	6500.00

SMALL CENTS

1860-1909 WITH
SHIELD ON REVERSE

DATE	MINTAGE	G-6	VG-10	F-15	VF-30	EF-45	AU-50	UNC-60	UNC-65	PROOF-65
1860	20,566,000	10.00	11.50	14.00	18.50	40.00	80.00	240.00	1275.00	3500.00
1861	10,100,000	15.50	18.50	25.00	40.00	70.00	110.00	350.00	1675.00	3750.00
1862	28,075,000	9.00	10.00	12.50	14.50	35.00	65.00	200.00	1275.00	3500.00
1863	49,840,000	8.75	9.75	12.75	18.00	33.50	60.00	175.00	1150.00	3500.00
1864	13,740,000	15.50	18.50	22.50	30.00	45.00	85.00	250.00	1650.00	3500.00

Bronze Type
1864-1909
Designer, James B. Longacre

A change of the alloy of the cent was made in 1864 to 95 percent copper and 5 percent tin and zinc. The design stayed the same except that later in the year the designer's initial "L" was added to the ribbon as it joins the hair at the back of the neck.

DATE	MINTAGE	G-6	VG-10	F-15	VF-30	EF-45	AU-50	UNC-60	UNC-65	PROOF-65
1864	39,233,714	7.25	9.00	16.50	25.00	40.00	60.00	100.00	900.00	3850.00
1864L		40.00	50.00	70.00	125.00	175.00	265.00	450.00	1550.00	10000.00
1865	35,429,286	7.50	10.00	16.50	22.50	40.00	55.00	90.00	875.00	1850.00
1866	9,826,500	32.00	40.00	50.00	70.00	100.00	150.00	245.00	1000.00	1450.00
1867	9,821,000	32.00	40.00	50.00	70.00	100.00	150.00	245.00	1000.00	1450.00
1868	10,266,500	32.00	40.00	50.00	70.00	100.00	150.00	245.00	1000.00	1450.00
1869	6,420,000	42.50	60.00	100.00	145.00	200.00	300.00	475.00	1550.00	1850.00
1869 over 8		110.00	130.00	265.00	425.00	625.00	950.00	1250.00	3500.00	— —
1870	5,275,000	36.50	45.00	75.00	100.00	150.00	225.00	325.00	1275.00	1500.00
1871	3,929,500	45.00	55.00	95.00	125.00	180.00	275.00	345.00	1650.00	1800.00
1872	4,042,000	60.00	75.00	120.00	155.00	210.00	325.00	515.00	1650.00	1800.00
1873	11,676,500	16.50	18.75	25.00	42.50	70.00	90.00	150.00	1100.00	1450.00
1874	14,187,500	16.50	18.75	25.00	40.00	65.00	85.00	140.00	1000.00	1450.00

SMALL CENTS

DATE	MINTAGE	G-6	VG-10	F-15	VF-30	EF-45	AU-50	UNC-60	UNC-65	PROOF-65
1875	13,528,000	16.50	18.75	25.00	40.00	65.00	85.00	140.00	1000.00	1450.00
1876	7,944,000	20.00	25.00	40.00	60.00	85.00	110.00	165.00	1000.00	1450.00
1877	852,500	395.00	485.00	600.00	795.00	950.00	1500.00	1975.00	6000.00	8750.00
1878	5,799,850	20.00	25.00	40.00	65.00	90.00	120.00	190.00	1000.00	1400.00
1879	16,231,200	6.75	8.50	12.50	18.50	35.00	45.00	85.00	1000.00	1400.00
1880	38,964,955	3.75	4.75	7.00	10.00	21.50	32.50	65.00	975.00	1400.00
1881	39,211,575	3.75	4.75	6.50	9.00	18.50	30.00	55.00	865.00	1175.00
1882	38,581,100	3.75	4.75	6.50	9.00	18.50	30.00	55.00	865.00	1175.00
1883	45,598,109	3.75	4.50	6.50	9.00	17.50	30.00	55.00	865.00	1175.00
1884	23,261,742	3.75	5.00	9.50	15.00	22.50	40.00	80.00	900.00	1175.00
1885	11,765,384	7.00	8.75	16.00	20.00	40.00	55.00	100.00	1000.00	1350.00
1886	17,654,290	4.00	6.50	12.50	17.00	25.00	45.00	90.00	900.00	1175.00
1887	45,226,483	3.50	4.75	6.50	8.50	18.50	28.00	52.50	725.00	1175.00
1888	37,494,414	3.50	4.25	5.50	7.00	17.50	27.50	52.50	725.00	1175.00
1889	48,869,361	3.25	4.00	5.50	7.00	17.50	27.50	52.50	725.00	1175.00
1890	57,182,854	3.25	4.00	5.00	7.00	17.50	27.50	52.50	725.00	1175.00
1891	47,072,350	3.50	4.25	5.50	7.50	17.50	28.00	52.50	725.00	1175.00
1892	37,649,832	3.25	4.25	5.50	7.50	17.50	27.50	52.50	725.00	1175.00
1893	46,642,195	3.50	4.00	5.50	7.50	17.50	27.50	52.50	725.00	1175.00
1894	16,752,132	4.25	6.00	10.00	15.50	22.50	35.00	55.00	650.00	1275.00
1895	38,343,636	2.50	3.00	5.00	7.00	17.50	26.50	50.00	650.00	1275.00
1896	39,057,293	2.25	3.00	5.50	7.50	17.50	26.50	50.00	650.00	1275.00
1897	50,466,330	2.15	3.25	4.75	7.00	16.75	25.50	50.00	650.00	1275.00
1898	49,823,079	2.15	3.00	4.00	7.00	16.50	25.50	50.00	650.00	1275.00
1899	53,600,031	2.15	3.00	4.00	7.00	16.50	25.50	50.00	650.00	1275.00
1900	66,833,764	1.80	2.25	3.75	6.50	15.00	25.50	50.00	600.00	1275.00
1901	79,611,143	1.80	2.25	3.75	6.50	15.00	22.00	50.00	600.00	1275.00
1902	87,376,722	1.80	2.25	3.75	6.50	15.00	22.00	50.00	600.00	1275.00
1903	85,094,493	1.80	2.25	3.75	6.50	15.00	22.00	50.00	600.00	1275.00
1904	61,328,015	1.75	2.00	3.50	6.50	15.00	22.00	50.00	600.00	1275.00
1905	80,719,163	1.80	2.25	3.50	6.50	15.00	22.00	50.00	600.00	1275.00
1906	96,022,255	1.80	2.00	3.50	6.50	15.00	22.00	50.00	600.00	1275.00
1907	108,138,618	1.75	2.00	3.50	6.50	15.00	22.00	50.00	600.00	1275.00

LOCATION
OF "S" MINT
MARK

1908	32,327,987	2.15	2.50	3.75	6.75	15.00	22.00	50.00	600.00	1275.00
1908S	1,115,000	32.00	37.50	42.00	45.00	60.00	125.00	250.00	1300.00	— —
1909	14,370,645	2.75	3.75	5.25	9.00	18.50	25.00	55.00	675.00	1350.00
1909S	309,000	155.00	175.00	225.00	250.00	320.00	400.00	550.00	2175.00	— —

SMALL CENTS

Lincoln Type
1909-1958
Designer, Victor D. Brenner

The Lincoln cent, designed by Victor D. Brenner, was issued to commemorate the 100th anniversary of Abraham Lincoln's birth. The original design had Brenner's initials on the bottom of the reverse. Later in 1909, after almost 28 million had been minted at Philadelphia and less than 500 thousand at the San Francisco mint, the V.D.B. initials were removed. It was not until 1918 that they were restored to the cent, on the obverse side under Lincoln's shoulder at the rim of the coin.

From 1909 through 1942 the cents continued to be made of 95 percent copper, 5 percent tin and zinc.

AG-Obverse: Date and mint marks legible enough to identify.
    Reverse: Wheat ears and letters worn into rim.

  G-Obverse: Letters complete but touching rim.
    Reverse: Wheat ears completely outlined.

VG-Obverse: Some hair details visible but faint.
    Reverse: Half of lines in wheat ears show.

  F-Obverse: Details show in bow tie. Legend sharp.
    Reverse: Lines in wheat ears show but worn.

VF-Obverse: Details of ear and hair complete but worn.
    Reverse: Lines in wheat ears strong and complete.

EF-Obverse: All details are sharp with wear on high points only.
    Reverse: Slight wear on wheat ears high points.

LOCATION OF
VDB

REVERSE FOR 1909-1958 ONLY.

LOCATION OF
MINT MARKS

DATE	MINTAGE	G-6	VG-10	F-15	VF-30	EF-45	AU-50	UNC-60	UNC-65	PROOF-65
1909										
V.D.B. ...	27,995,000	5.50	6.00	6.50	7.50	8.75	13.50	25.00	65.00	4500.00
1909S										
V.D.B. ...	484,000	395.00	450.00	500.00	550.00	650.00	750.00	900.00	1650.00	— —
1909	72,702,618	2.00	2.25	2.50	2.75	4.00	8.50	25.00	95.00	700.00
1909S	1,825,000	70.00	75.00	85.00	95.00	110.00	135.00	215.00	635.00	— —
1910	146,801,218	.70	1.00	1.25	1.50	2.75	6.50	25.00	75.00	800.00
1910S	6,045,000	13.50	16.50	17.50	20.00	30.00	50.00	100.00	415.00	— —

SMALL CENTS

DATE	MINTAGE	G-6	VG-10	F-15	VF-30	EF-45	AU-50	UNC-60	UNC-65	PROOF-65
1911	101,177,787	.85	1.00	1.25	2.00	6.50	10.00	30.00	100.00	775.00
1911D	12,672,000	9.25	11.00	12.75	18.50	32.50	65.00	120.00	485.00	— —
1911S	4,026,000	21.50	24.50	26.50	30.00	45.00	70.00	140.00	525.00	— —
1912	68,153,060	1.10	1.35	2.50	4.50	7.50	15.00	35.00	115.00	775.00
1912D	10,411,000	9.50	10.75	11.50	22.50	40.00	60.00	125.00	525.00	— —
1912S	4,431,000	21.50	22.50	24.00	25.00	40.00	60.00	110.00	550.00	— —
1913	76,532,352	1.00	1.25	1.75	3.50	7.50	10.00	40.00	115.00	775.00
1913D	15,804,000	5.50	6.50	7.75	12.50	26.50	52.00	90.00	400.00	— —
1913S	6,101,000	12.50	15.50	17.50	20.00	30.00	65.00	120.00	675.00	— —
1914	75,238,432	.90	1.50	2.75	4.75	6.75	18.50	85.00	225.00	875.00
1914D	1,193,000	125.00	140.00	160.00	225.00	425.00	675.00	1200.00	3350.00	— —
1914S	4,137,000	13.75	19.50	23.50	25.00	40.00	85.00	170.00	3000.00	— —
1915	29,092,120	2.50	3.00	6.00	12.50	38.00	75.00	125.00	450.00	900.00
1915D	22,050,000	1.85	2.25	3.50	6.75	13.00	30.00	50.00	425.00	— —
1915S	4,833,000	12.50	17.50	18.50	20.00	35.00	65.00	110.00	725.00	— —
1916	131,833,677	.70	1.00	1.25	1.75	3.75	8.75	17.50	100.00	900.00
1916D	35,956,000	.90	1.25	1.75	3.00	7.00	27.50	47.50	275.00	— —
1916S	22,510,000	2.75	3.00	3.75	5.25	12.75	25.00	55.00	350.00	— —
1917	196,429,705	.75	.95	1.00	1.25	1.75	6.50	25.00	100.00	— —
1917D	55,120,000	1.00	1.10	1.50	3.25	6.50	27.50	55.00	275.00	
1917S	32,620,000	1.10	1.25	1.50	3.25	6.50	30.00	65.00	350.00	
1918	288,104,634	.60	.85	1.00	1.50	2.75	8.75	25.00	95.00	
1918D	47,830,000	1.00	1.15	1.50	3.25	6.00	30.00	60.00	350.00	
1918S	34,680,000	1.00	1.25	1.50	3.00	6.00	27.50	65.00	300.00	— —
1919	392,021,000	.65	.85	1.00	1.25	2.00	7.50	18.00	95.00	— —
1919D	57,154,000	.65	.75	1.00	3.50	7.25	20.00	50.00	275.00	
1919S	139,760,000	.50	.75	1.00	2.00	3.50	18.50	45.00	300.00	
1920	310,165,000	.65	.85	1.25	1.50	2.25	7.50	25.00	75.00	
1920D	49,280,000	.85	1.00	1.25	2.25	6.25	26.50	85.00	295.00	
1920S	46,220,000	.65	.85	1.25	2.25	6.25	20.00	85.00	350.00	
1921	39,157,000	.75	1.00	1.25	2.25	6.50	18.75	85.00	200.00	
1921S	15,274,000	2.25	2.50	3.75	7.50	20.00	80.00	185.00	575.00	
1922*		250.00	300.00	415.00	525.00	775.00	1500.00	3750.00	8750.00	
1922D	7,160,000	9.50	12.50	13.00	18.50	30.00	60.00	95.00	325.00	

*Plain cent without mint mark caused by defective die.

DATE	MINTAGE	G-6	VG-10	F-15	VF-30	EF-45	AU-50	UNC-60	UNC-65	PROOF-65
1923	74,723,000	.75	1.00	1.25	1.50	2.75	6.50	25.00	45.00	
1923S	8,700,000	5.50	5.75	6.75	10.00	23.75	80.00	195.00	1075.00	
1924	75,178,000	.75	1.00	1.25	1.50	4.50	12.50	55.00	175.00	
1924D	2,520,000	23.50	24.50	25.50	35.00	60.00	130.00	290.00	1200.00	
1924S	11,696,000	2.00	2.25	2.50	4.50	8.25	45.00	165.00	575.00	
1925	139,949,000	.75	1.00	1.25	1.50	2.50	6.50	20.00	75.00	
1925D	22,580,000	1.00	1.25	1.50	2.25	4.75	18.75	55.00	225.00	
1925S	26,380,000	.75	1.00	1.25	1.75	3.50	17.50	75.00	350.00	
1926	157,088,000	.50	.75	1.00	1.25	2.50	6.50	20.00	100.00	
1926D	28,020,000	1.00	1.25	1.50	1.75	3.50	27.50	75.00	325.00	
1926S	4,550,000	8.25	8.75	9.75	11.00	18.75	55.00	165.00	450.00	
1927	144,440,000	.50	.75	1.00	1.25	2.50	6.50	20.00	55.00	
1927D	27,170,000	.65	.75	1.00	1.25	3.00	19.50	50.00	200.00	
1927S	14,276,000	2.00	2.25	2.50	2.75	4.50	30.00	90.00	300.00	
1928	134,116,000	.50	.75	1.00	1.25	2.00	6.00	20.00	50.00	
1928D	31,170,000	.65	.85	1.00	1.25	2.50	15.00	35.00	175.00	
1928S	17,266,000	1.35	1.50	1.75	1.95	2.75	21.50	85.00	325.00	

SMALL CENTS

DATE	MINTAGE	G-0	VG-10	F-15	VF-30	EF-45	AU-50	UNC-60	UNC-65	PROOF-65
1929	185,262,000	.45	.65	.75	.85	1.75	4.50	20.00	40.00	
1929D	41,730,000	.50	.75	.85	.95	1.75	7.50	25.00	65.00	
1929S	50,148,000	.50	.60	.75	.90	1.75	5.00	25.00	65.00	
1930	157,415,000	.45	.60	.75	.90	1.50	4.00	20.00	40.00	
1930D	40,100,000	.45	.60	.75	.90	1.50	6.50	20.00	45.00	
1930S	24,286,000	.75	1.00	1.25	1.50	1.75	4.00	25.00	65.00	
1931	19,396,000	1.95	2.25	2.50	2.75	3.50	8.25	25.00	85.00	
1931D	4,480,000	5.50	6.75	7.25	9.00	17.50	35.00	60.00	160.00	
1931S	866,000	55.00	57.50	60.00	65.00	70.00	75.00	80.00	175.00	
1932	9,062,000	5.00	5.50	6.00	6.50	7.00	9.00	25.00	65.00	
1932D	10,500,000		2.00	2.50	3.00	4.00	9.00	25.00	60.00	
1933	14,360,000		1.65	2.00	2.50	3.00	9.00	20.00	65.00	
1933D	6,200,000		5.25	6.00	6.75	7.50	9.00	25.00	75.00	
1934	219,080,000		.60	.70	.75	.85	1.00	4.50	20.00	
1934D	28,446,000		.60	.65	.70	.75	7.00	25.00	75.00	
1935	245,388,000		.60	.65	.70	.75	.85	2.50	10.50	
1935D	47,000,000		.65	.70	.75	.80	1.25	3.00	16.50	
1935S	38,702,000		.75	.80	.85	.90	2.50	7.50	32.50	
1936	309,637,569		.65	.70	.75	.80	.95	2.50	6.75	475.00
1936D	40,620,000		.65	.70	.75	.80	.90	2.75	12.00	
1936S	29,130,000		.85	.90	.95	1.00	1.25	2.75	11.50	
1937	309,179,320		.55	.60	.65	.70	.80	2.50	10.75	200.00
1937D	50,430,000		.55	.60	.65	.70	.75	2.75	8.50	
1937S	34,500,000		.65	.70	.75	.80	.85	2.50	8.00	
1938	156,696,734		.45	.50	.55	.60	.85	2.25	7.50	100.00
1938D	20,010,000		.85	.90	.95	1.00	1.25	2.25	13.50	
1938S	15,180,000		1.35	1.50	1.75	2.00	2.25	2.75	12.75	
1939	316,479,520		.45	.50	.55	.60	.75	1.50	4.50	75.00
1939D	15,160,000		1.35	1.50	2.00	2.25	2.50	4.50	17.00	
1939S	52,070,000		.50	.55	.60	.70	1.00	2.25	10.75	
1940	586,825,872			.40	.45	.50	.60	1.50	3.50	
1940D	81,390,000			.35	.40	.45	.55	1.75	7.75	
1940S	112,940,000			.35	.40	.45	.55	1.25	5.75	
1941	887,039,100			.35	.40	.45	.50	1.50	6.00	55.00
1941D	128,700,000			.40	.45	.50	1.00	2.75	11.75	
1941S	92,360,000			.45	.50	.60	1.25	5.00	20.00	
1942	657,828,600				.35	.40	.45	.60	2.25	55.00
1942D	206,698,000				.35	.40	.45	.70	3.00	
1942S	85,590,000				.40	.45	1.75	4.50	20.00	

During World War II the shortage of copper forced the Treasury Department to change the composition, in 1943, to steel coated with zinc.

DATE	MINTAGE	EF-45	AU-50	UNC-60	UNC-65	UNC-65
1943	684,628,670	.45	.50	.55	.90	3.25
1943D	217,660,000	1.10	1.15	1.25	1.50	6.25
1943S	191,550,000	1.10	1.15	1.25	2.25	12.50

The Steel cents proved to be unsatisfactory. In 1944 through 1946 the Treasury Department used salvaged shell cases to make the cents. In 1947 they returned to the original composition of 95 percent copper, 5 percent tin and zinc.

SMALL CENTS

DATE	MINTAGE	G-6	VG-10	F-15	VF-30	EF-45	AU-50	UNC-60	UNC-65	PROOF-65
1944	1,435,400,000				.25	.30	.35	.50	1.25	
1944D	430,578,000				.30	.35	.40	.65	2.75	
1944S	282,760,000				.30	.35	.40	.50	2.00	
1945	1,040,515,000				.30	.35	.40	.50	.80	
1945D	266,268,000				.30	.35	.40	.85	2.50	
1945S	181,770,000				.30	.35	.40	.70	1.60	
1946	991,655,000				.25	.30	.35	.45	.85	
1946D	315,690,000				.30	.35	.40	.50	1.00	
1946S	198,100,000				.35	.40	.45	.65	2.40	
1947	190,555,000				.25	.30	.35	.65	2.65	
1947D	194,750,000				.25	.30	.35	.45	2.00	
1947S	99,000,000				.35	.40	.45	.90	2.00	
1948	317,570,000				.25	.30	.35	.60	2.25	
1948D	172,637,500				.35	.40	.45	.60	2.35	
1948S	81,735,000				.40	.45	.50	1.00	3.25	
1949	217,490,000				.35	.40	.45	1.00	4.50	
1949D	154,370,500				.40	.45	.50	.75	3.00	
1949S	64,290,000				.40	.45	.50	2.00	7.00	
1950	272,686,386				.25	.30	.35	.60	3.50	45.00
1950D	334,950,000					.25	.30	.45	1.75	
1950S	118,505,000					.25	.30	.80	3.50	
1951	294,633,500					.25	.30	1.00	3.00	17.50
1951D	625,355,000					.25	.30	.45	1.35	
1951S	136,010,000					.25	.30	1.95	6.50	
1952	186,856,980					.35	.40	.85	1.60	15.00
1952D	746,130,000					.25	.30	.35	.85	
1952S	137,800,004					.25	.30	1.00	3.00	
1953	256,883,800					.25	.30	.35	.85	13.50
1953D	700,515,000					.25	.30	.35	.55	
1953S	181,835,000					.25	.30	.60	1.50	
1954	71,873,350					.35	.40	.75	2.25	7.50
1954D	251,552,500					.35	.40	.45	.70	
1954S	96,190,000					.30	.35	.40	.75	

**1955 DOUBLE
STRUCK ERROR**

DATE	MINTAGE	G-6	VG-10	F-15	VF-30	EF-45	AU-50	UNC-60	UNC-65	PROOF-65
1955	330,958,200					.30	.35	.40	.85	3.50
1955 Obverse with double impression						500.00	550.00	– –	3250.00	
1955D	563,257,500					.25	.30	.35	.70	
1955S	44,610,000					.85	1.00	1.25	1.50	
1956	421,414,384					.25	.30	.35	.55	2.85
1956D	1,098,201,100					.25	.30	.35	.45	
1957	283,787,952					.25	.30	.35	.45	2.75
1957D	1,051,342,000					.25	.30	.35	.40	
1958	253,400,652					.25	.30	.35	.40	3.50
1958D	800,953,300					.25	.30	.35	.30	

SMALL CENTS

Lincoln Memorial Type
1959 to Date
Designers: Obverse, Victor D. Brenner
Reverse, Frank Gasparro

The reverse of the cent was redesigned by Frank Gasparro, in 1959, to the Lincoln Memorial. This was the 150th anniversary of Lincoln's birth. In 1962 the metallic contents was changed to 95 percent copper 5 percent zinc.

LINCOLN MEMORIAL
REVERSE

DATE	MINTAGE	UNC-60	UNC-65	PROOF-65
1959	610,864,291		.20	1.50
1959D	1,279,760,000		.20	
1960 Large date	588,096,602		.20	1.50
1960 Small date		— —	8.00	25.00
1960D Large date	1,580,884,000		.20	
1960D Small date			.75	
1961	756,373,244		.20	
1961D	1,753,266,700		.20	
1962	609,263,019		.20	
1962D	1,793,148,400		.20	
1963	757,185,645		.20	
1963D	1,774,020,400		.20	
1964	2,652,525,762		.20	
1964D	3,799,071,500		.20	
1965	1,497,224,900		.20	
1966	2,188,147,783		.20	
1967	3,048,667,100		.30	
1968	1,707,880,970		.25	
1968D	2,886,269,600		.15	
1968S	261,311,510		.15	1.85
1969	1,136,910,000		.60	
1969D	4,002,832,200		.15	
1969S	547,309,631		.15	1.85
1970	1,898,315,000		.25	
1970D	2,891,438,900		.15	
1970S	693,192,814		.15	1.95
1971	1,919,490,000		.15	
1971D	2,911,045,600		.15	
1971S	528,354,192		.30	1.95

SMALL CENTS

DATE	MINTAGE		EF-45	UNC-65	PROOF-65
1972	2,933,255,000			.15	
1972 Double impression			250.00	450.00	
1972D	2,665,071,400			.15	
1972S	380,200,104			.15	1.95
1973	3,728,245,000			.15	
1973D	3,549,576,588			.15	
1973S . . . •	319,937,634			.15	1.95
1974	4,232,140,523			.15	
1974D	4,235,098,000			.15	
1974S	412,039,228			.20	2.25
1975	5,451,476,142			.15	
1975D	4,505,275,300			.15	
1975S	2,845,450	Proof only			20.00
1976	4,674,292,426			.15	
1976D	4,221,592,455			.15	
1976S	4,149,730	Proof only			9.00
1977	4,469,930,000			.15	
1977D	4,194,062,300			.15	
1977S	3,251,152	Proof only			9.00
1978	5,266,905,000			.15	
1978D	4,280,233,400			.15	
1978S	3,127,781	Proof only			10.75
1979	5,266,790,000			.15	
1979D	4,139,357,254			.10	
1979S	751,725,000			.15	10.50
1980	6,230,115,000			.10	
1980D	5,140,098,660			.10	
1980S	1,184,590,000			.15	12.00
1981				.10	
1981D				.10	
1981S				.15	12.00

Two Cent Coins
1864-1873
Designer, James B. Longacre

Authorized on April 22, 1864 and coined at the Philadelphia mint. There was a little more than 45 million two cent pieces made of which 33 million were minted in the first two years. This was the first coin to have the motto "In God We Trust" which was added due to increased religious sentiment during the Civil War. Two types exist, the 1864 small motto and 1864 large motto.
All two cent coins were made of 95 percent copper, 5 percent tin and zinc.

AG-Obverse: Little or no rim. Date just legible.
    Reverse: Some lettering visible.

  G-Obverse: The word GOD and first three letters of TRUST show.
    Reverse: All lettering shows but weak.

VG-Obverse: Part of the word WE is evident.
    Reverse: Wheat grains weak but visible.

  F-Obverse: Complete motto IN GOD WE TRUST shows.
    Reverse: Almost all wheat grains can be seen.

VF-Obverse: Leaves show some detail, Motto strong.
    Reverse: All wheat grains show strong.

EF-Obverse: Most details show in leaves.
    Reverse: Wreath and ribbon shows wear on high points.

DATE	MINTAGE	G-6	VG-10	F-15	VF-30	EF-45	AU-50	UNC-60	UNC-65	PROOF-65
1864 Small Motto	19,847,500	65.00	100.00	125.00	150.00	200.00	275.00	510.00	4200.00	— —
1864 Large Motto		12.50	14.50	16.50	20.00	40.00	85.00	310.00	1650.00	2750.00
1865	13,640,000	12.50	14.50	16.50	20.00	40.00	85.00	310.00	1650.00	2750.00
1866	3,177,000	15.50	17.50	20.00	23.50	40.00	85.00	325.00	1675.00	2750.00
1867	2,938,750	15.50	17.50	20.00	25.00	40.00	85.00	325.00	1675.00	2750.00
1868	2,803,750	15.50	17.50	20.00	25.00	40.00	85.00	325.00	1675.00	2750.00
1869	1,546,500	17.50	20.00	22.50	27.50	45.00	95.00	350.00	1750.00	2750.00
1870	861,250	20.00	22.50	25.00	30.00	55.00	115.00	415.00	1850.00	2750.00
1871	721,250	20.00	22.50	27.50	35.00	60.00	135.00	450.00	2150.00	2750.00
1872	65,000	85.00	110.00	150.00	275.00	325.00	425.00	850.00	2500.00	3000.00
1873	1,100	Proof Only								3500.00

THREE CENT—SILVER
1851-1873
Designer, James B. Longacre

Authorized on March 3, 1851 and coined at the Philadelphia mint, except the 1851 0 which was made at the New Orleans mint. It is the smallest of all the coins issued by the United States.
The three cent silver coins from 1851-1853 were made of 75 percent silver, 25 percent copper. A composition change was made in 1854-1873 to 90 percent silver 10 percent copper.

AG-Obverse: Some letters and outline of star shows.
    Reverse: About half of the design visible.

  G-Obverse: Complete legend and date but very weak.
    Reverse: All stars show but well worn.

VG-Obverse: Shield outline is weak. Legend and date strong.
    Reverse: Rim separated from stars.

  F-Obverse: Shield complete.
    Reverse: Design within "C" visible but weak.

VF-Obverse: Star sharp with wear on high points and tips.
    Reverse: Roman numeral III and stars sharp.

  EF-Obverse: Star and shield details clear. Star points show.
    Reverse: Design in "C" complete and bold.

LOCATION
OF
MINT MARK

TYPE 1851-1853   TYPE 1954

DATE	MINTAGE	G-6	VG-10	F-15	VF-30	EF-45	AU-50	UNC-60	UNC-65	PROOF-65
1851	5,447,400	16.50	18.50	27.50	40.00	75.00	160.00	575.00	3400.00	— —
1851 0	720,000	22.50	27.50	37.50	55.00	100.00	250.00	700.00	3500.00	— —
1852	18,663,500	15.00	17.50	22.50	37.50	70.00	160.00	550.00	3400.00	— —
1853	11,400,000	15.00	17.50	22.50	37.50	70.00	160.00	550.00	3400.00	— —
1854	671,000	20.00	23.50	27.50	50.00	110.00	310.00	950.00	5000.00	— —
1855	139,000	27.50	32.50	45.00	65.00	175.00	450.00	1100.00	5400.00	8100.00
1856	1,458,000	17.50	21.50	26.50	50.00	110.00	310.00	950.00	5000.00	8100.00
1857	1,042,000	18.50	22.50	27.50	50.00	110.00	310.00	950.00	5000.00	7900.00
1858	1,604,000	17.50	23.50	27.50	50.00	110.00	310.00	960.00	8000.00	6300 00
1859	365,000	20.00	27.50	32.50	55.00	110.00	180.00	550.00	3150.00	3750.00
1860	286,000	21.50	28.50	35.00	57.50	110.00	180.00	550.00	3150.00	4000.00
1861	497,000	20.00	27.50	32.50	55.00	110.00	180.00	550.00	3150.00	3750.00
1862	363,500	20.00	27.50	32.50	55.00	110.00	180.00	550.00	3150.00	3750.00

THREE CENT — SILVER

DATE	MINTAGE	G-6	VG-10	F-15	VF-30	EF-45	AU-50	UNC-60	UNC-65	PROOF 65
1863	21,460							650.00	6000.00	3750.00
1863 over 2								800.00	7500.00	4500.00
1864	12,470							700.00	6500.00	3750.00
1865	8,500							675.00	6250.00	3750.00
1866	22,725							735.00	5000.00	3750.00
1867	4,625							735.00	5250.00	3750.00
1868	4,100							735.00	5250.00	3750.00
1869	5,100							735.00	5250.00	3750.00
1870	4,000							735.00	4750.00	3750.00
1871	4,360							735.00	6800.00	3750.00
1872	1,950							800.00	4250.00	3750.00
1873	600	Proof only								4750.00

THREE CENT-NICKEL
1865-1889
Designer, James B. Longacre

Authorized on March 3, 1865 and coined at the Philadelphia Mint. It was designed to take the place of the silver-three cent pieces and saw a mintage of over eleven million the first year. However, the coin did not prove to be popular, so, much smaller quantities were struck in the following years, until it was discontinued in 1889.

All three cent nickels were made of 75 percent copper, 25 percent nickel.

AG-Obverse: Few letters and parts of letters show.
    Reverse: About two thirds of design can be seen.

G-Obverse: Legend complete but worn.
    Reverse: Wreath outline complete.

VG-Obverse: Rim complete. Head shows little or no details.
    Reverse: Wreath strong with evidence of details.

F-Obverse: Some hair details and curls.
    Reverse: Roman numeral III shows some weak lines.

VF-Obverse: Most hair details clear.
    Reverse: Wreath details can be seen.

EF-Obverse: Hair details sharp but worn about ear and forehead.
    Reverse: All lines in III visible, some may be faint due to weak strike.

THREE CENT-NICKEL

DATE	MINTAGE	G-6	VG-10	F-15	VF-30	EF-45	AU-50	UNC-60	UNC-65	PROOF-65
1865	11,382,000	12.50	13.50	15.00	18.50	25.00	52.00	280.00	1600.00	5000.00
1866	4,801,000	14.50	15.50	17.50	20.00	27.50	57.50	280.00	1600.00	2250.00
1867	3,915,000	14.50	15.50	17.50	20.00	27.50	57.50	280 00	1600.00	1850.00
1868	3,252,000	14.50	15.50	17.50	20.00	27.50	57.50	280.00	1600.00	1850.00
1869	1,604,000	15.50	16.50	18.50	20.00	27.50	57.50	280.00	1600.00	1850.00
1870	1,335,000	15.50	16.50	18.50	22.50	29.00	60.00	295.00	1750.00	1850.00
1871	604,000	17.50	18.50	20.00	23.50	30.00	60.00	325.00	1850.00	1850.00
1872	862,000	17.50	18.50	20.00	23.50	30.00	60.00	325.00	1850.00	1850.00
1873	1,173,000	15.50	16.50	18.50	22.50	30.00	60.00	285.00	1750.00	1850.00
1874	790,000	16.50	17.50	19.50	25.00	32.50	65.00	285.00	1650.00	1850.00
1875	228,000	18.50	21.50	23.50	27.50	35.00	90.00	350.00	2000.00	2000.00
1876	162,000	19.50	22.50	25.00	30.00	37.50	95.00	350.00	2000.00	1900.00
1877	510	Proof only								4500.00
1878	2,350	Proof only								2500.00
1879	41,200	45.00	50.00	55.00	65.00	80.00	190.00	500.00	1850.00	1850.00
1880	24,955	50.00	55.00	60.00	70.00	85.00	195.00	600.00	1850.00	1850.00
1881	1,080,575	15.50	16.50	18.50	20.00	25.00	60.00	285.00	1850.00	1850.00
1882	25,300	50.00	55.00	60.00	70.00	85.00	195.00	600.00	1850.00	1850.00
1883	10,609	75.00	90.00	110.00	130.00	170.00	275.00	600.00	1850.00	1850.00
1884	5,642	140.00	155.00	185.00	200.00	225.00	300.00	700.00	1850.00	1850.00
1885	4,790	200.00	225.00	250.00	275.00	325.00	400.00	725.00	2150.00	1850.00
1886	4,290	Proof only								1850.00
1887	7,961	160.00	175.00	200.00	225.00	250.00	300.00	700.00	2750.00	1950.00
1888	41,083	45.00	50.00	55.00	65.00	80.00	180.00	550.00	1850.00	1850.00
1889	21,561	50.00	55.00	60.00	70.00	95.00	190.00	575.00	1875.00	1850.00

FIVE CENT NICKELS

The first nickel, known as the shield type was authorized on May 16, 1866 and were all coined at the Philadelphia mint. The 1866 issue and a small amount of the 1867 issue were produced with rays between the stars on the reverse. These rays were eliminated during 1867 making two varieties that year. No further changes were made after that date. Made of 75 percent copper, 25 percent nickel.

Shield Type
1866-1883
Designer, James B. Longacre

AG-Obverse: Little or no rim. Date legible.
      Reverse: Some letters and a few stars show.

 G-Obverse: All letters in motto show but tops worn down.
      Reverse: All letters and stars show.

VG-Obverse: Some lines in shield visible.
      Reverse: Full rim separated from letters.

 F-Obverse: Some details showing in leaves.
      Reverse: Details on some of the stars show.

VF-Obverse: Most details of leaves and Shield are strong.
      Reverse: Details on most of the stars are complete.

EF-Obverse: Wear only on leave tips and high points of shield.
      Reverse: Stars full and sharp. On weak struck coins, only some of the stars will be full and sharp.

WITH RAYS ON REVERSE

DATE	MINTAGE	G-6	VG-10	F-15	VF-30	EF-45	AU-50	UNC-60	UNC-65	PROOF-65
1866	14,742,500	19.50	21.00	27.50	60.00	110.00	220.00	750.00	4800.00	7250.00
1867 Rays .	— —	20.00	22.50	30.00	60.00	120.00	225.00	850.00	4750.00	11500.00

FIVE CENT NICKELS

WITHOUT RAYS REVERSE

DATE	MINTAGE	G-6	VG-10	F-15	VF-30	EF-45	AU-50	UNC-60	UNC-65	PROOF-65
1867 without Rays	*30,909,500	14.50	17.50	20.00	25.00	35.00	63.50	350.00	1850.00	2350.00
1868	28,817,000	14.50	17.50	20.00	25.00	35.00	63.50	350.00	1850.00	2350.00
1869	16,395,000	14.50	17.50	20.00	25.00	36.50	65.00	360.00	1900.00	2500.00
1870	4,806,000	16.50	20.00	23.50	28.50	45.00	80.00	375.00	2000.00	2400.00
1871	561,000	45.00	55.00	80.00	110.00	150.00	250.00	550.00	2700.00	2700.00
1872	6,036,000	16.50	20.00	23.50	28.50	45.00	80.00	375.00	2200.00	2500.00
1873	4,550,000	16.50	20.00	23.50	28.50	45.00	80.00	385.00	2300.00	2400.00
1874	3,538,000	16.50	20.00	23.50	30.00	50.00	85.00	375.00	2200.00	2400.00
1875	2,097,000	20.00	23.50	30.00	45.00	60.00	110.00	425.00	2350.00	2400.00
1876	2,530,000	20.00	25.00	28.50	40.00	60.00	100.00	425.00	2300.00	2400.00
1877	500	Proof only								7500.00
1878	2,350	Proof only								2600.00
1879	29,100	275.00	340.00	400.00	475.00	600.00	650.00	800.00	2500.00	2000.00
1880	19,955	340.00	425.00	475.00	550.00	650.00	700.00	825.00	2500.00	2000.00
1881	72,375	260.00	325.00	375.00	425.00	550.00	600.00	800.00	2500.00	2000.00
1882	11,476,000	14.50	18.50	20.00	22.50	35.00	62.50	350.00	2250.00	2000.00
1883	1,456,919	14.50	18.50	20.00	22.50	35.00	62.50	350.00	2250.00	2000.00
1883 over 2	— —	60.00	80.00	115.00	160.00	290.00		575.00	3000.00	— —

*Mintage figure is the total of both kinds — with and without rays.

Liberty Head Type
1883-1912
Designer, Charles E. Barber

In 1883 the nickel design was changed from the shield type to the Liberty Head design. The first coin was produced without the word CENTS on the reverse and only the letter V resulting is some of the coins being gold plated and passed as gold pieces. Therefore the design was quickly changed to include the word CENTS.
Coined at the Philadelphia, Denver and San Francisco mints.
Made of 75 percent copper and 25 percent nickel.

AG-Obverse: Little or no rim. Few stars show. Date legible.
  Reverse: Almost all of the figure "V" and part of wreath will be visible.

  G-Obverse: Head of Liberty outline and all stars show.
  Reverse: All lettering around rim visible but weak.

VG-Obverse: A few letters of "LIBERTY" on headband will show.
  Reverse: "E. PLURIBUS UNUM" visible but very weak.

FIVE CENT NICKELS

F-Obverse: Complete legend "LIBERTY" readable
Reverse: "E. PLURIBUS UNUM" strong.

VF-Obverse: Most of hair detail shows.
Reverse: Part of wreath details show.

EF-Obverse: Complete details with little wear on forehead and around ear.
Reverse: Wear only on high points of wreath.

WITHOUT CENTS ON REVERSE

DATE	MINTAGE	G-6	VG-10	F-15	VF-30	EF-45	AU-50	UNC-60	UNC-65	PROOF-65
1883 w/o cents	5,479,519	8.95	9.75	10.50	12.00	13.00	21.50	82.50	975.00	2500.00

WITH CENTS ON REVERSE

DATE	MINTAGE	G-6	VG-10	F-15	VF-30	EF-45	AU-50	UNC-60	UNC-65	PROOF-65
1883	16,032,983	11.50	12.75	18.50	27.50	52.50	75.00	335.00	1750.00	1400.00
1884	11,273,942	12.50	14.00	20.00	35.00	57.50	80.00	345.00	1950.00	1500.00
1885	1,476,490	325.00	395.00	500.00	630.00	750.00	825.00	1350.00	4375.00	4375.00
1886	3,330,290	60.00	65.00	100.00	140.00	225.00	350.00	695.00	2950.00	3275.00
1887	15,263,652	11.50	12.75	17.00	25.00	45.00	75.00	340.00	1750.00	1350.00
1888	10,720,483	13.00	15.00	22.50	32.50	50.00	87.50	350.00	1850.00	1350.00
1889	15,881,361	8.25	9.75	16.50	25.00	40.00	75.00	330.00	1750.00	1350.00
1890	16,259,272	9.00	11.50	18.50	25.00	45.00	80.00	340.00	1800.00	1350.00
1891	16,834,350	7.50	9.00	15.50	24.00	40.00	75.00	325.00	1850.00	1350.00
1892	11,699,642	8.00	10.50	16.50	25.00	45.00	80.00	335.00	1850.00	1350.00
1893	13,370,195	7.75	9.50	15.50	24.50	40.00	75.00	325.00	1850.00	1350.00
1894	5,413,132	10.00	14.50	22.00	32.50	50.00	92.50	350.00	2150.00	1500.00

FIVE CENT NICKELS

DATE	MINTAGE	G-6	VG-10	F-15	VF-30	EF-45	AU-50	UNC-60	UNC-65	PROOF-65
1895	9,979,884	5.50	6.50	13.50	25.00	45.00	75.00	310.00	1750.00	1500.00
1896	8,842,920	5.50	7.50	15.00	25.00	45.00	85.00	320.00	1850.00	1500.00
1897	20,428,735	2.25	2.75	7.50	13.50	28.50	65.00	295.00	1725.00	1350.00
1898	12,532,087	2.25	2.75	7.50	15.00	30.00	70.00	300.00	1750.00	1350.00
1899	26,029,031	2.25	2.75	5.75	13.50	25.00	65.00	300.00	1700.00	1350.00
1900	27,255,995	2.00	2.50	4.00	11.75	23.50	60.00	300.00	1500.00	1350.00
1901	26,480,213	1.75	2.25	4.25	12.00	23.50	65.00	280.00	1500.00	1350.00
1902	31,480,579	1.75	2.25	4.00	11.75	23.50	60.00	280.00	1500.00	1350.00
1903	28,006,725	1.65	2.25	4.00	11.75	23.50	60.00	280.00	1500.00	1350.00
1904	21,404,984	1.75	2.25	4.25	12.00	23.50	60.00	280.00	1500.00	1350.00
1905	29,827,276	1.75	2.25	4.00	11.75	23.50	60.00	280.00	1500.00	1350.00
1906	38,613,725	1.65	2.25	4.00	11.75	23.50	60.00	280.00	1500.00	1350.00
1907	39,214,800	1.75	2.25	4.00	11.75	23.50	60.00	280.00	1500.00	1350.00
1908	22,686,177	1.65	2.25	4.00	11.75	23.50	60.00	280.00	1500.00	1350.00
1909	11,590,526	2.00	2.50	4.75	12.00	23.50	60.00	280.00	1500.00	1350.00
1910	30,169,353	1.65	2.25	3.75	11.75	23.50	60.00	280.00	1500.00	1350.00
1911	39,559,372	1.65	2.25	3.75	11.75	23.50	60.00	280.00	1500.00	1350.00
1912	26,236,714	1.75	2.25	3.75	11.50	23.50	60.00	280.00	1500.00	1350.00

Mint Marks are located on the reverse between the words United and Cents.

1912D	8,474,000	2.75	3.50	6.75	16.50	65.00	135.00	450.00	2250.00	— —
1912S	238,000	55.00	60.00	85.00	135.00	285.00	490.00	900.00	3200.00	— —

Buffalo Type
1913-1938
Designer, James Earle Fraser

The Buffalo type nickel first appeared in 1913 with an Indian Head on the obverse and a bison on the reverse.
Two varieties existed in 1913 one showing the bison on a mound the other on flat ground.
Coined at the Philadelphia, Denver and San Francisco Mints.
Made of 75 percent copper, 25 percent nickel.

AG-Obverse: Date very weak but legible.
    Reverse: Top of Buffalo head worn flat.

G-Obverse: "LIBERTY" readable but tops of letters worn into rim.
    Reverse: All letters visible.

VG-Obverse: Date full and clear.
    Reverse: Part of horn on Buffalo's head can be seen.

F-Obverse: Rim full, "LIBERTY" bold.
    Reverse: Most of horn visible.

VF-Obverse: Some details show in hair and cheek.
    Reverse: Full horn evident.

EF-Obverse: Only slight wear on Indian's hair braid.
    Reverse: Horn sharp. Slight wear on high point only.

FIVE CENT NICKELS

BUFFALO ON MOUND

DATE	MINTAGE	G-6	VG-10	F-15	VF-30	EF-45	AU-50	UNC-60	UNC-65	PROOF-65
1913 T1 . . .	30,993,520	8.00	8.75	10.50	12.50	23.50	45.00	82.50	625.00	4500.00
1913D	5,337,000	13.50	14.50	16.75	23.75	35.00	55.00	140.00	950.00	
1913S	2,105,000	18.00	21.50	26.50	40.00	52.50	85.00	240.00	1100.00	

BUFFALO ON FLAT GROUND

1937
3 LEGGED

DATE	MINTAGE	G-6	VG-10	F-15	VF-30	EF-45	AU-50	UNC-60	UNC-65	PROOF-65
1913 T2 . . .	29,853,700	8.00	9.00	10.00	12.50	18.00	35.00	82.50	600.00	5000.00
1913D	4,156,000	55.00	60.00	67.50	85.00	125.00	190.00	350.00	1100.00	
1913S	1,209,000	90.00	100.00	125.00	150.00	200.00	300.00	500.00	1500.00	
1914	20,665,738	9.50	12.00	12.50	14.00	18.50	42.50	110.00	525.00	4400.00
1914D	3,912,000	36.50	41.50	52.00	80.00	135.00	220.00	375.00	1500.00	
1914S	3,470,000	11.00	13.50	15.75	30.00	55.00	72.50	250.00	1150.00	
1915	20,987,270	5.00	6.75	9.75	12.50	21.50	36.50	100.00	550.00	4400.00
1915D	7,569,500	13.50	14.25	23.50	40.00	60.00	100.00	290.00	1125.00	
1915S	1,505,000	18.75	23.50	37.50	60.00	110.00	185.00	440.00	1675.00	
1916	63,498,066	1.75	2.25	3.95	6.50	11.00	38.50	70.00	400.00	4400.00
1916D	13,333,000	11.50	12.75	16.00	35.00	55.00	100.00	285.00	1250.00	
1916S	11,860,000	7.00	9.50	13.50	27.50	55.00	100.00	285.00	1125.00	
1917	51,424,029	2.00	2.50	3.95	7.00	16.00	38.00	82.50	500.00	
1917D	9,910,800	11.00	12.50	20.00	45.00	110.00	135.00	385.00	1500.00	
1917S	4,193,000	9.00	11.00	18.00	40.00	85.00	145.00	400.00	1750.00	
1918	32,086,314	2.00	2.75	5.25	12.00	26.50	55.00	175.00	775.00	
1918D	8,362,000	11.00	13.00	21.50	75.00	110.00	220.00	550.00	4200.00	
1918D over 7		750.00	825.00	950.00	1600.00	3250.00	6325.00	13500.00	38500.00	

FIVE CENT NICKELS

DATE	MINTAGE	G-6	VG-10	F-15	VF-30	EF-45	AU-50	UNC-60	UNC-65	PROOF-65
1918S	4,882,000	9.00	11.00	18.50	46.50	100.00	190.00	475.00	3600.00	
1919	60,868,000	1.50	1.85	2.80	6.25	13.50	35.00	75.00	475.00	
1919D	8,006,000	11.50	13.50	22.50	95.00	135.00	275.00	675.00	5500.00	
1919S	7,521,000	7.00	8.25	13.75	60.00	110.00	175.00	500.00	4400.00	
1920	63,093,000	1.75	1.85	2.80	6.25	14.00	36.50	80.00	500.00	
1920D	9,418,000	8.50	10.50	17.00	70.00	125.00	235.00	575.00	4400.00	
1920S	9,689,000	4.50	6.75	10.00	35.00	110.00	160.00	435.00	6300.00	
1921	10,663,000	2.00	2.75	4.50	12.75	30.00	57.50	175.00	750.00	
1921S	1,557,000	21.50	25.00	37.50	110.00	290.00	415.00	775.00	3850.00	
1923	35,715,000	1.25	1.50	2.25	5.25	12.00	30.00	82.50	500.00	
1923S	6,142,000	3.75	4.50	9.75	35.00	75.00	125.00	350.00	4400.00	
1924	21,620,000	1.50	1.75	2.25	6.75	15.50	42.50	110.00	675.00	
1924D	5,258,000	6.25	7.50	13.50	52.50	100.00	175.00	415.00	2550.00	
1924S	1,437,000	10.00	13.50	24.00	120.00	295.00	425.00	975.00	7150.00	
1925	35,565,100	1.20	1.50	2.00	5.25	12.50	35.00	75.00	125.00	
1925D	4,450,000	9.00	11.25	18.75	65.00	110.00	235.00	495.00	3700.00	
1925S	6,256,000	4.50	6.00	12.00	35.00	62.50	160.00	425.00	4100.00	
1926	44,693,000	1.00	1.20	1.50	3.75	10.00	37.50	70.00	365.00	
1926D	5,638,000	5.00	7.00	15.00	65.00	125.00	190.00	365.00	5175.00	
1926S	970,000	11.00	12.00	22.50	75.00	265.00	435.00	875.00	6600.00	
1927	37,981,000	1.25	1.20	1.50	3.75	10.00	40.00	65.00	365.00	
1927D	5,730,000	2.25	3.75	6.00	20.00	52.50	95.00	225.00	1100.00	
1927S	3,430,000	2.00	3.00	4.25	22.00	80.00	125.00	400.00	1675.00	
1928	23,411,000	1.25	1.50	2.00	3.75	10.00	40.00	70.00	380.00	
1928D	6,436,000	1.85	2.25	4.00	10.00	21.50	40.00	100.00	350.00	
1928S	6,936,000	1.20	1.50	3.00	5.50	18.75	45.00	160.00	465.00	
1929	36,446,000	1.00	1.20	1.50	3.00	7.50	37.00	65.00	330.00	
1929D	8,370,000	1.85	2.25	3.50	8.00	18.50	45.00	120.00	1000.00	
1929S	7,754,000	1.75	1.85	2.50	3.50	15.00	37.50	92.50	475.00	
1930	22,849,000	1.00	1.20	1.50	3.00	8.00	40.00	78.50	350.00	
1930S	5,435,000	1.50	1.75	1.85	3.85	12.50	37.50	125.00	650.00	
1931S	1,200,000	8.00	8.75	9.50	10.50	19.00	41.50	125.00	525.00	
1934	20,213,000	1.00	1.25	1.50	2.25	6.50	28.50	75.00	190.00	
1934D	7,480,000	1.30	1.75	2.25	3.00	7.50	38.75	145.00	375.00	
1935	58,264,000	1.00	1.10	1.25	1.75	2.75	26.00	45.00	100.00	
1935D	12,092,000	1.10	1.25	1.50	2.00	3.75	37.50	135.00	700.00	
1935S	10,300,000	1.65	2.00	2.25	2.50	3.50	28.00	65.00	170.00	
1936	119,001,420	1.00	1.15	1.25	1.50	2.75	25.00	42.50	90.00	3700.00
1936D	24,814,000	1.10	1.25	1.50	2.00	2.75	27.00	45.00	100.00	
1936S	14,930,000	1.25	1.50	1.75	2.00	2.75	27.00	55.00	140.00	
1937	79,485,769	1.00	1.25	1.50	1.75	3.00	26.00	38.50	100.00	3700.00
1937D	17,826,000	1.25	1.50	1.75	2.00	3.25	26.00	38.50	140.00	
1937D 3 Legged ..		250.00	300.00	350.00	425.00	500.00	650.00	900.00	4500.00	
1937S	5,635,000	1.50	1.75	2.00	2.50	3.50	26.00	38.50	65.00	
1938D	7,020,000	1.35	1.50	1.60	1.75	2.50	25.00	35.00	62.50	
1938D over S		— —	8.00	9.75	12.00	14.75	40.00	55.00	135.00	

FIVE CENT NICKELS

Jofferson Head
1938 To Date
Designer, Felix Schlag

A change in the design of the nickel took place in 1938 to the Jefferson Head Type. This was the first nickel to adopt a portrait in place of a symbolic motif.
Coined at the Philadelphia, Denver and San Francisco Mints.
From 1938 into 1942 and from 1946 to date, the composition was 75 percent copper, 25 percent nickel. During the World War II years, starting in October 1942 through 1945, the composition was changed to 56 percent copper, 35 percent silver and 9 percent manganese.

AG-Obverse: Letters worn down into rim. Only outline of head shows.
    Reverse: Outline of Monticello shows.

G-Obverse: All lettering worn but readable.
    Reverse: Monticello worn smooth with little evidence of detail.

VG-Obverse: Lettering clear and just touching rim.
    Reverse: Four middle pillars weak but visible.

F-Obverse: Some of the hair details show.
    Reverse: Pillars clear. Roof over pillars well worn.

VF-Obverse: Most hair details show.
    Reverse: Roof over pillars shows some details.

EF-Obverse: All hair details show. Wear on high points only.
    Reverse: Complete triangle of roof visible.

LOCATION
OF MINT MARKS
1938-1942D, 1946-1967

DATE	MINTAGE	G-6	VG-10	F-15	VF-30	EF-45	AU-50	UNC-60	UNC-65	PROOF-65
1938	19,515,365		.70	.80	.90	.95	1.00	1.15	5.75	80.00
1938D	5,376,000	2.50	2.60	2.65	2.70	2.75	9.00	18.50		
1938S	4,105,000	4.50	4.65	4.75	5.00	5.50	10.50	21.75		
1939	120,627,535	.65	.75	.85	.95	1.00	2.25	5.25	45.00
1939D	3,514,000	8.25	9.00	9.50	10.00	12.50	65.00	130.00		
1939S	6,630,000	1.60	1.75	1.85	2.00	3.00	40.00	95.00		
1940	176,499,158	.50	.60	.70	.80	1.00	1.50	3.00	45.00
1940D	43,540,000	.55	.60	.70	.80	1.00	3.50	7.00		
1940S	39,690,000	.55	.60	.70	.80	.85	2.25	5.25		
1941	203,283,720	.50	.60	.70	.80	.95	1.20	2.50	45.00
1941D	53,432,000	.55	.60	.70	.80	1.00	3.25	7.50		
1941S	43,445,000	.55	.60	.70	.80	1.20	5.00	10.75		
1942	49,818,600	.50	.60	.70	.80	.95	2.50	5.00	45.00
1942D	13,938,000	.75	.85	.90	.95	2.00	17.50	35.00		

FIVE CENT NICKELS

World War II Nickels
1942-1945

LOCATION OF MINT MARKS
CHANGED AND PLACED OVER
THE DOME OF MONTICELLO

DATE	MINTAGE	G-6	VG-10	F-15	VF-30	EF-45	AU-50	UNC-60	UNC-65	PROOF-65
1942P	57,900,600		1.25	1.30	2.50	3.50	4.00	4.75	60.00	500.00
1942S	32,900,000		1.25	1.30	2.50	3.75	4.25	5.00	32.50	
1943P	271,165,000		1.25	1.30	2.50	3.50	4.00	4.25	13.00	
1943D	15,294,000		1.25	1.30	2.50	3.75	4.25	4.50	13.00	
1943S	104,060,000		1.25	1.30	2.50	3.50	4.00	4.25	18.75	
1944P	119,150,000		1.25	1.30	2.50	3.50	4.00	4.25	14.75	
1944D	32,309,000		1.25	1.30	2.50	3.75	4.25	4.50	17.50	
1944S	21,640,000		1.25	1.30	2.50	3.75	4.25	4.50	18.75	
1945P	119,408,100		1.25	1.30	2.50	4.00	4.50	4.75	17.50	
1945D	37,158,000		1.25	1.30	2.50	3.50	4.00	4.25	13.00	
1945S	58,939,000		1.25	1.30	2.50	3.50	4.00	4.25	10.50	

Return to Prewar Composition
and Design.

LOCATION OF MINT MARK
CHANGED IN 1968 AND
PLACED UNDER THE DATE
ON THE OBVERSE

DATE	MINTAGE	G-6	VG-10	F-15	VF-30	EF-45	AU-50	UNC-60	UNC-65	PROOF-65
1946	161,116,000				.50	.55	.60	.75	1.60	
1946D	45,292,200				.55	.60	.65	.75	1.25	
1946S	13,560,000				.60	.65	.70	.75	2.00	
1947	95,000,000				.45	.50	.55	.65	1.00	
1947D	37,882,000				.50	.55	.60	.65	1.85	
1947S	24,720,000				.55	.60	.65	.75	2.00	

FIVE CENT NICKELS

DATE	MINTAGE	G-6	VG-10	F-15	VF-30	EF-40	AU-50	UNC-60	UNC-65	PROOF-65
1948	89,348,000				.50	.55	.60	.65	.75	
1948D	44,734,000				.55	.60	.65	.75	1.50	
1948S	11,300,000				.65	.65	.70	.75	1.00	
1949	60,652,000				.50	.55	.60	.65	1.25	
1949D	35,238,000				.55	.60	.65	.70	2.25	
1949S	9,716,000				.95	1.00	1.10	1.25	2.75	
1950	9,847,386				.90	.95	1.00	1.25	2.75	39.50
1950D	2,630,030	5.00	6.50	8.50	9.50	10.50	13.50	15.00	21.50	
1951	28,689,500				.50	.55	.60	.65	2.00	25.00
1951D	20,460,000				.65	.70	.75	.80	2.00	
1951S	7,776,000				.75	.80	.85	.95	7.00	
1952	64,069,980				.45	.50	.55	.60	2.00	14.75
1952D	30,638,000					.50	.55	.60	3.00	
1952S	20,572,000					.55	.60	.65	1.00	
1953	46,772,800							.45	.50	10.00
1953D	59,878,600							.20	.25	
1953S	19,210,900							.45	.50	
1954	47,917,350							.40	.50	7.00
1954D	117,183,060							.35	.50	
1954S	29,384,000							.45	.50	
1955	8,266,200							.75	1.50	4.00
1955D	74,464,100							.20	.25	
1956	35,885,384							.20	.25	2.00
1956D	67,222,940							.20	.25	
1957	39,655,952							.20	.25	1.75
1957D	136,828,900							.20	.25	
1958	17,963,652							.35	.55	1.50
1958D	168,249,120							.35	.40	
1959	28,397,291							.40	.45	
1959D	160,738,240							.30	.35	
1960	57,107,602							.35	.40	
1960D	192,582,180							.30	.35	
1961	76,668,244							.35	.40	
1961D	229,342,760							.30	.35	
1962	100,602,019							.35	.40	
1962D	280,195,720							.30	.35	
1963	178,851,645							.35	.40	
1963D	276,829,460							.25	.30	
1964	1,028,622,762							.25	.30	
1964D	1,787,297,160							.25	.30	
1965	136,131,380							.30	.35	
1966	156,208,283							.30	.35	
1967	107,325,800							.30	.35	
1968D	91,227,880							.25	.30	
1968S	103,437,510							.25	.30	1.10
1969D	202,807,500							.25	.35	
1969S	123,089,631							.20	.25	.95
1970D	515,485,380							.25	.30	
1970S	241,464,814							.25	.30	.95
1971	106,884,000							.30	.50	
1971D	316,144,800							.25	.35	
1971S	3,220,733	Proof only								2.00
1972	202,036,000							.15	.35	
1972D	351,694,600							.15	.35	
1972S	3,260,996	Proof only								1.75
1973	384,396,000							.15	.35	
1973D	261,405,400							.15	.35	
1973S	2,760,339	Proof only								2.75

FIVE CENT NICKELS

DATE	MINTAGE		UNC-60	UNC-65	PROOF-65
1974	601,752,000			.30	
1974D	277,373,000			.30	
1974S	2,612,568	Proof only			5.25
1975	181,772,000			.25	
1975D	401,875,300			.25	
1975S	2,845,450	Proof only			3.25
1976	367,124,000			.25	
1976D	563,964,147			.25	
1976S	4,125,000	Proof only			1.95
1977	585,376,000			.25	
1977D	297,313,422			.25	
1977S	3,251,000	Proof only			2.50
1978	391,308,000			.25	
1978D	313,092,780			.25	
1978S	3,127,781	Proof only			3.25
1979	463,188,000			.25	
1979D	325,867,672			.25	
1979S	3,677,175	Proof only			3.25
1980P	593,004,000			.15	
1980D	502,323,448			.15	
1980S	2,144,231	Proof only			2.75
1981P				.15	
1981D				.15	
1981S		Proof only			2.75

HALF DIMES
1794-1873

Authorized on April 2, 1792. The first issue was made in 1795 but dated 1794.
From 1794 through 1837 they were coined at the Philadelphia Mint. In 1838 the New Orleans Mint joined Philadelphia in making the half dimes and in 1863 the San Francisco Mint coined them with the Philadelphia Mint. Made of approximately 90 percent silver and 10 percent copper.

Flowing Hair
1794-1795
Designer, Robert Scot

DATE	MINTAGE	AG-3	G-6	VG-10	F-15	VF-30	EF-45	AU-50	UNC-60	UNC-65
1794	86,416	900.00	1500.00	1850.00	2500.00	4000.00	5500.00	7500.00	12000.00	— —
1795		875.00	1450.00	1650.00	2250.00	3200.00	5000.00	7500.00	12000.00	— —

Draped Bust, Small Eagle
1796-1797
Designer, Robert Scot

AG-Obverse: Outline of head and few stars show.
    Reverse: Worn smooth. Parts of eagle, wreath and some letters visible.

 G-Obverse: "LIBERTY" legible. Stars run into rim.
    Reverse: Complete outline of eagle and wreath.

VG-Obverse: All stars and lettering strong.
    Reverse: All lettering clear. Some feathers in deepest part of wing visible.

  F-Obverse: Some hair details show. Ear clear.
    Reverse: Both wings show some feathers.

VF-Obverse: Most details in hair and face show clearly.
    Reverse: Most feathers in wings show.

EF-Obverse: All details show clear. Slight wear on hairline at forehead.
    Reverse: All feathers visible but may be weak on breast because of weak striking.

HALF DIMES

DATE	MINTAGE	AG-3	G-6	VG-10	F-15	VF-30	EF-45	AU-50	UNC-60	UNC-65
1796	10,230	875.00	1450.00	1600.00	2400.00	3600.00	5150.00	7000.00	12000.00	— —
1796 over 5 ...		875.00	1450.00	1600.00	2500.00	3700.00	5300.00	7500.00	13000.00	— —
1797 13 stars ..		875.00	1450.00	1600.00	2400.00	3600.00	5150.00	7000.00	12000.00	— —
1797 15 stars ..	44,527	875.00	1450.00	1600.00	2400.00	3600.00	5150.00	7000.00	12000.00	— —
1797 16 stars ..		875.00	1450.00	1600.00	2400.00	3600.00	5150.00	7000.00	12000.00	— —

Draped Bust, Large Eagle
1800-1805
Designer, Robert Scot

DATE	MINTAGE	AG-3	G-6	VG-10	F-15	VF-30	EF-45	AU-50	UNC-60	UNC-65
1800	24,000	500.00	850.00	1400.00	2400.00	3650.00	5150.00	7000.00	— —	— —
1801	33,910	500.00	850.00	1400.00	2400.00	3600.00	5150.00	7000.00	— —	— —
1802	13,010	1450.00	2400.00	3000.00	7500.00	12000.00	45000.00	— —	— —	— —
1803	37,850	500.00	850.00	1400.00	2400.00	3600.00	5150.00	7000.00	— —	— —
1805	15,600	500.00	850.00	1400.00	2400.00	3600.00	5150.00	7000.00	— —	— —

Liberty Cap
1829-1837
Designer, William Kneass

AG-Obverse: Outline of head and most stars show.
    Reverse: Some letters show. Eagle visible.

G-Obverse: Part of "LIBERTY" readable.
    Reverse: "E. PLURIBUS UNUM" shows in part.

VG-Obverse: "LIBERTY" is complete. Some hair details.
    Reverse: "E. PLURIBUS UNUM" is complete.

F-Obverse: Most hair details and drapery folds show.
    Reverse: Some of the feathers show in the wings.

VF-Obverse: All of the hair details show except in the curls on the neck.
    Reverse: Most of the eagle's feathers show.

EF-Obverse: All hair details sharp. Wear evident on high points only.
    Reverse: Slight wear on edges of wings only.

HALF DIMES

DATE	MINTAGE	AG-3	G-6	VG-10	F-15	VF-30	EF-45	AU-50	UNC-60	UNC-65
1829	1,230,000	16.00	27.00	30.00	36.50	65.00	175.00	450.00	750.00	4800.00
1830	1,240,000	16.00	27.00	30.00	36.50	65.00	175.00	450.00	750.00	4800.00
1831	1,242,700	16.00	27.00	30.00	36.50	65.00	175.00	450.00	750.00	4800.00
1832	965,000	16.00	27.00	30.00	36.50	65.00	175.00	450.00	750.00	4800.00
1833	1,370,000	16.00	27.00	30.00	36.50	65.00	175.00	450.00	750.00	4800.00
1834	1,480,000	16.00	27.00	30.00	36.50	65.00	175.00	450.00	750.00	4800.00
1835 Lg. 5¢ & Date . . .			25.50	27.50	32.00	60.00	165.00	400.00	700.00	5000.00
1835 Sm. 5¢ Lg. Date . .			25.50	27.50	32.00	60.00	165.00	400.00	700.00	5000.00
1835 Lg. 5¢ Sm. Date .	2,7600,000		25.50	27.50	32.00	60.00	165.00	400.00	700.00	5000.00
1835 Sm. 5¢ Sm. Date .			25.50	27.50	32.00	60.00	165.00	400.00	700.00	5000.00
1836 Small 5¢	1,900,000		25.50	27.50	32.00	60.00	165.00	400.00	700.00	5000.00
1836 Large 5¢			25.50	27.50	32.00	60.00	165.00	400.00	700.00	5000.00
1837 Small 5¢	871,000		27.50	30.00	38.50	65.00	180.00	450.00	700.00	5000.00
1837 Large 5¢			25.50	27.50	32.00	60.00	165.00	400.00	700.00	5000.00

Seated Liberty
1837-1873
Designer, Christian Gobrecht

AG-Obverse: Rim worn smooth into the field.
    Reverse: At least one half of letters and wreath visible.

G-Obverse: Complete outline of Seated Liberty.
    Reverse: All letters worn but readable.

VG-Obverse: At least three letters of "LIBERTY" in shield visible.
    Reverse: Letters clear and separated from rim.

F-Obverse: "LIBERTY" in shield complete but some letters weak.
    Reverse: Wreath full with little details.

VF-Obverse: "LIBERTY" sharp. Some details in Seated Liberty's gown shows.
    Reverse: Leaves in wreath show some details.

EF-Obverse: Complete details with slight wear on knees and breast.
    Reverse: Wear only on high points of leaves.

HALF DIMES

WITHOUT STARS AND
NO DRAPERY AT ELBOW

WITH STARS AND
WITH DRAPERY AT ELBOW

THE MINT MARKS ARE LOCATED INSIDE THE WREATH ON REVERSE, THROUGH 1859.

DATE	MINTAGE	G-6	VG-10	F-15	VF-30	EF-45	AU-50	UNC-60	UNC-65
1837 Sm Date .	1,405,000	60.00	75.00	85.00	165.00	375.00	800.00	1700.00	— —
1837 Lg Date ..		55.00	70.00	80.00	150.00	350.00	800.00	1500.00	— —
1838 0 No									
Stars	70,000	75.00	115.00	230.00	400.00	800.00	1100.00	— —	— —
1838	2,255,000	17.50	22.50	25.00	45.00	87.50	300.00	950.00	— —
1839	1,069,150	19.50	25.00	28.00	45.00	87.50	300.00	950.00	— —
1839 0	981,550	20.00	27.50	35.00	55.00	100.00	350.00	1000.00	— —
1840 No									
Drapery	1,344,085	17.50	20.00	25.00	45.00	95.00	300.00	950.00	— —
1840 With									
Drapery		40.00	60.00	90.00	270.00	550.00	750.00	1800.00	
1840 0 No									
Drapery	935,000	20.00	27.50	35.00	55.00	100.00	600.00	1100.00	— —
1840 0 With									
Drapery		45.00	50.00	135.00	280.00	600.00	1100.00	— —	— —
1841	1,150,000	15.00	20.00	22.50	40.00	75.00	275.00	550.00	— —
1841 0	815,000	17.50	22.50	30.00	50.00	95.00	300.00	650.00	— —
1842	815,000	15.00	20.00	25.00	40.00	75.00	250.00	550.00	— —
1842 0	350,000	25.00	45.00	70.00	175.00	300.00	525.00	— —	— —
1843	1,165,000	15.00	20.00	25.00	40.00	87.50	300.00	550.00	— —
1844	430,000	15.00	20.00	25.00	40.00	87.50	300.00	550.00	— —
1844 0	220,000	70.00	85.00	225.00	375.00	900.00	— —	— —	— —
1845	1,564,000	15.00	20.00	25.00	40.00	87.50	300.00	575.00	— —
1846	27,000	135.00	165.00	300.00	425.00	900.00	— —	— —	— —
1847	1,274,000	15.00	20.00	25.00	40.00	87.50	300.00	550.00	— —
1848 Sm Date .		17.50	20.00	25.00	40.00	82.50	300.00	550.00	— —
1848 Lg Date ..	668,000	20.00	25.00	35.00	65.00	95.00	300.00	600.00	— —
1848 0	600,000	20.00	25.00	35.00	65.00	95.00	375.00	800.00	— —
1849		15.00	20.00	25.00	40.00	87.50	325.00	600.00	— —
1849 over 6 ...	1,309,000	17.50	22.50	30.00	45.00	87.50	350.00	700.00	3250.00
1849 over 8 ...		20.00	30.00	35.00	55.00	95.00	300.00	750.00	3750.00
1849 0	140,000	35.00	55.00	75.00	275.00	475.00	— —	— —	— —
1850	955,000	15.00	17.50	25.00	35.00	75.00	200.00	700.00	3500.00
1850 0	690,000	20.00	30.00	40.00	55.00	100.00	300.00	900.00	4500.00
1851	781,000	15.00	17.50	20.00	35.00	85.00	275.00	700.00	4250.00
1851 0	860,000	20.00	30.00	40.00	60.00	95.00	275.00	900.00	4250.00
1852	1,000,500	15.00	17.50	20.00	35.00	75.00	200.00	675.00	3500.00
1852 0	260,000	35.00	40.00	60.00	75.00	150.00	400.00	— —	— —

HALF DIMES

DATE	MINTAGE	G-6	VG-10	F-15	VF-30	EF-45	AU-50	UNC-60	UNC-65
1853 No Arrows	135,000	25.00	35.00	55.00	85.00	140.00	375.00	900.00	4500.00
1853 0 No Arrows		125.00	140.00	275.00	425.00	900.00	1700.00	— —	— —

IN 1853 A SLIGHT CHANGE IN THE WEIGHT OF THE COIN WAS MADE AND ARROWS WERE PLACED AT EACH SIDE OF THE DATE ON THE OBVERSE.

← 1853 →

DATE	MINTAGE	G-6	VG-10	F-15	VF-30	EF-45	AU-50	UNC-60	UNC-65	PROOF-65
1853	13,210,020	15.00	17.50	19.50	25.00	65.00	200.00	900.00	3750.00	6700.00
1853 0	2,200,000	15.00	17.50	19.50	25.00	65.00	250.00	925.00	3950.00	
1854	5,740,000	15.00	17.50	19.50	25.00	65.00	200.00	800.00	3500.00	6000.00
1854 0	1,560,000	17.50	19.50	25.00	50.00	100.00	275.00	1000.00	4000.00	
1855	1,750,000	15.00	17.50	19.50	30.00	75.00	200.00	800.00	3500.00	6000.00
1855 0	600,000	20.00	25.00	35.00	65.00	100.00	275.00	1200.00	4000.00	

IN 1856 THE ARROWS WERE REMOVED FROM BOTH SIDES OF THE DATE.

DATE	MINTAGE	G-6	VG-10	F-15	VF-30	EF-45	AU-50	UNC-60	UNC-65	PROOF-65
1856	4,880,000	15.00	17.50	20.00	35.00	75.00	200.00	550.00	3750.00	7000.00
1856 0	1,100,000	15.00	20.00	25.00	35.00	75.00	225.00	625.00	4750.00	
1857	7,280,000	15.00	17.50	20.00	35.00	75.00	200.00	550.00	3750.00	6500.00
1857 0	1,380,000	15.00	20.00	25.00	35.00	75.00	225.00	625.00	4750.00	
1858		15.00	17.50	20.00	35.00	75.00	200.00	550.00	3750.00	5500.00
1858 over date	3,500,000	50.00	65.00	85.00	225.00	325.00	500.00	1300.00	— —	
1858 0	1,660,000	15.00	20.00	25.00	35.00	75.00	250.00	700.00	4500.00	
1859	340,000	20.00	30.00	55.00	75.00	125.00	425.00	600.00	5000.00	5500.00
1859 0	560,000	20.00	25.00	35.00	45.00	75.00	250.00	800.00	4500.00	

HALF DIMES

Legend Added
1860-1873

LEGEND REPLACES STARS
ON OBVERSE AND REMOVED
FROM REVERSE

FROM 1860 THROUGH 1869 MINT MARKS ARE BELOW WREATH.

DATE	MINTAGE	G-6	VG-10	F-15	VF-30	EF-45	AU-50	UNC-60	UNC-65	PROOF-65
1860	799,000	12.50	15.50	25.00	30.00	55.00	125.00	450.00	2800.00	2800.00
1860 0	1,060,000	12.50	15.00	25.00	40.00	65.00	140.00	475.00	3000.00	
1861	3,360,000	12.50	15.00	25.00	30.00	60.00	110.00	425.00	2800.00	2800.00
1862	1,492,550	12.50	15.00	25.00	30.00	55.00	110.00	425.00	2800.00	
1863	18,460	65.00	75.00	110.00	170.00	225.00	500.00	850.00	4000.00	3000.00
1863S	100,000	20.00	25.00	35.00	50.00	125.00	375.00	900.00	3500.00	
1864	48,470	230.00	285.00	375.00	400.00	525.00	1000.00	1200.00	5000.00	4000.00
1864S	90,000	30.00	40.00	80.00	110.00	175.00	700.00	1200.00	3500.00	
1865	13,500	110.00	150.00	175.00	220.00	300.00	650.00	900.00	4500.00	3500.00
1865S	120,000	20.00	25.00	35.00	75.00	125.00	350.00	975.00	3500.00	
1866	10,725	115.00	160.00	200.00	235.00	300.00	750.00	1000.00	4000.00	3000.00
1866S	120,000	20.00	25.00	35.00	60.00	140.00	325.00	950.00	3500.00	
1867	8,625	150.00	225.00	275.00	325.00	425.00	750.00	1100.00	5000.00	2800.00
1867S	120,000	20.00	25.00	40.00	75.00	175.00	375.00	900.00	3000.00	
1868	89,200	25.00	35.00	45.00	85.00	175.00	300.00	600.00	3500.00	2800.00
1868S	280,000	20.00	22.50	25.00	35.00	65.00	125.00	500.00	3000.00	
1869	208,600	20.00	25.00	30.00	40.00	70.00	125.00	475.00	3000.00	2800.00
1869S	230,000	20.00	25.00	30.00	40.00	65.00	125.00	500.00	3000.00	
1870	536,000	17.50	20.00	25.00	35.00	65.00	125.00	450.00	2800.00	2800.00

IN 1871-1872 THE MINT MARKS WERE RETURNED TO INSIDE THE WREATH AND IN 1872-73 WERE PLACED AT THE BOTTOM OF THE WREATH.

DATE	MINTAGE	G-6	VG-10	F-15	VF-30	EF-45	AU-50	UNC-60	UNC-65	PROOF-65
1871	1,873,960	12.50	15.00	20.00	35.00	65.00	100.00	425.00	2800.00	2800.00
1871S	161,000	20.00	35.00	55.00	85.00	135.00	250.00	675.00	3250.00	
1872	2,947,950	12.50	15.00	20.00	35.00	65.00	100.00	425.00	2800.00	2800.00
1872S Mint Mark inside Wreath on Reverse . . .		15.00	17.50	25.00	35.00	55.00	100.00	425.00	2800.00	
1872S Mint Mark below Wreath . . .	837,000	12.50	15.00	25.00	35.00	65.00	100.00	475.00	2800.00	
1873	712,600	12.50	15.00	20.00	35.00	75.00	110.00	425.00	2800.00	2800.00
1873S	324,000	15.00	17.50	25.00	35.00	65.00	100.00	475.00	2800.00	

DIMES

Authorized on April 2, 1972. From 1796 through 1837 they were coined at the Philadelphia Mint. The Philadelphia Mint was assisted in 1838 by the New Orleans Mint, in 1856 by the San Francisco Mint, in 1871 by the Carson City Mint and in 1906 by the Denver Mint.
All dimes from 1796 through 1964 were made of approximately 90 percent silver and 10 percent copper. In 1965 the composition changed to a clad type coin of 75 percent copper, 25 percent nickel.

Draped Bust, Small Eagle
1796-1797
Designer, Robert Scot

DATE	MINTAGE	AG-3	G-6	VG-10	F-15	VF-30	EF-45	AU-50	UNC-60
1796	22,135	1200.00	2000.00	2400.00	3350.00	4700.00	6750.00	8700.00	15000.00
1797 13 Stars	25,261	1200.00	2000.00	2400.00	3350.00	4700.00	6750.00	8700.00	15000.00
1797 16 Stars		1200.00	2000.00	2400.00	3350.00	4700.00	6750.00	8700.00	15000.00

Draped Bust, Large Eagle
1798-1807
Designer, Robert Scot

AG-Obverse: Outline of head and some stars show.
    Reverse: More than half of eagle outline visible.

G-Obverse: "LIBERTY" legible. Stars run into rim.
    Reverse: Eagle will be completely outlined but no details.

VG-Obverse: All stars and lettering strong.
    Reverse: Part of "E PLURIBUS UNUM" show. Few feathers on wings evident.

F-Obverse: Some hair details show. Ear lobe visible.
    Reverse: "E PLURIBUS UNUM" complete but weak.

VF-Obverse: Most details in hair and face show clearly.
    Reverse: Most feathers show.

EF-Obverse: All details show clear. Slight wear on hairline at forehead.
    Reverse: All feathers visible some may be weak because of weak strike.

DIMES

DATE	MINTAGE	AG-3	G-6	VG-10	F-15	VF-30	EF-45	AU-50	UNC-60
1798		525.00	900.00	1100.00	1500.00	2200.00	3000.00	4500.00	7000.00
1798 over 97 13 Stars	27,550	— —	— —	— —	— —	— —	— —	— —	— —
1798 over 97 16 Stars		525.00	900.00	1100.00	1500.00	2200.00	3000.00	4500.00	6750.00
1800	21,760	525.00	900.00	1100.00	1450.00	1950.00	2900.00	4500.00	6500.00
1801	34,640	525.00	900.00	1100.00	1450.00	1950.00	2900.00	4500.00	6500.00
1802	10,975	525.00	900.00	1100.00	1450.00	1950.00	2900.00	4500.00	7000.00
1803	33,040	525.00	900.00	1100.00	1450.00	1950.00	2900.00	4500.00	7000.00
1804 13 Stars on rev.		775.00	1300.00	1700.00	2500.00	3500.00	4500.00	5000.00	— —
1804 14 Stars on rev.	8,265	825.00	1400.00	1700.00	2500.00	3500.00	4500.00	5000.00	— —
1805 4 Berries	120,780	525.00	900.00	1100.00	1450.00	1950.00	2900.00	4500.00	6500.00
1805 5 Berries		525.00	900.00	1100.00	1450.00	1950.00	2900.00	4500.00	6500.00
1807	165,000	525.00	900.00	1100.00	1450.00	1950.00	2900.00	4500.00	6500.00

Liberty Cap
1809-1837
Designer, John Reich

AG-Obverse: Outline of head and most stars show.
    Reverse: Some letters show. Eagle visible.

 G-Obverse: Some parts of letters in "LIBERTY" are evident. All stars can be seen but tops worn into rim.
    Reverse: All letters readable, some weak.

VG-Obverse: At least three letters of "LIBERTY" full.
    Reverse: Part of "E PLURIBUS UNUM" show.

 F-Obverse: "LIBERTY" complete. Ear visible.
    Reverse: "E PLURIBUS UNUM" complete.

VF-Obverse: Most of hair and cap details show.
    Reverse: Most of the eagle's feathers show sharply.

EF-Obverse: All hair details sharp, with wear evident on high points only.
    Reverse: Slight wear on high points of breast, wings and tail.

DIMES

DATE	MINTAGE	G-6	VG-10	F-15	VF-30	EF-45	AU-50	UNC-60	UNC-65
1809	51,065	95.00	140.00	200.00	300.00	500.00	2500.00	4200.00	18000.00
1811 over 9 ...	65,180	65.00	85.00	115.00	175.00	375.00	2000.00	4000.00	— —
1814 Sm Date .		32.50	50.00	70.00	110.00	275.00	1700.00	2500.00	12500.00
1814 Lg Date ..	421,500	30.00	40.00	60.00	95.00	275.00	1600.00	2500.00	11000.00
1814 StatesofAmerica		35.00	50.00	75.00	115.00	350.00	1800.00	2600.00	15000.00
1820 Small O ..		30.00	35.00	50.00	95.00	275.00	1100.00	2500.00	10000.00
1820 Large O	942,587	30.00	35.00	50.00	95.00	275.00	1100.00	2500.00	10000.00
1821 Sm Date .		30.00	35.00	50.00	95.00	275.00	1100.00	2500.00	10000.00
1821 Lg Date ..	1,186,512	30.00	35.00	50.00	95.00	275.00	1100.00	2500.00	10000.00
1822	100,000	70.00	90.00	145.00	285.00	575.00	2500.00	4000.00	— —
1823 3 over 2 ..	440,000	30.00	35.00	50.00	95.00	300.00	1000.00	2500.00	10000.00
1824 4 over 2 ..	100,000	40.00	50.00	70.00	95.00	300.00	1500.00	2500.00	12000.00
1825	410,000	30.00	35.00	50.00	100.00	300.00	1200.00	2500.00	11000.00
1827	1,215,000	30.00	35.00	50.00	95.00	300.00	1000.00	2500.00	10000.00
1828 Lg Date ..		45.00	60.00	75.00	125.00	275.00	1800.00	3000.00	14500.00
1828 Sm Date .	125,000	35.00	40.00	45.00	90.00	200.00	900.00	2350.00	10000.00
1829 Small 10¢		25.00	35.00	35.00	50.00	200.00	900.00	2350.00	7000.00
1829 Large 10¢	770,000	30.00	40.00	45.00	65.00	200.00	900.00	2350.00	8000.00
1830									
30 over 29		65.00	100.00	155.00	275.00	350.00	2000.00	— —	— —
1830 Small 10¢	510,000	25.00	30.00	35.00	57.50	200.00	900.00	2350.00	7000.00
1830 Large 10¢		25.00	30.00	35.00	57.50	200.00	900.00	2350.00	7000.00
1831	771,350	25.00	30.00	37.50	50.00	170.00	550.00	2100.00	6250.00
1832	522,500	25.00	30.00	37.50	67.50	175.00	550.00	2200.00	6250.00
1833									
1833 Last 3	485,000								
raised		25.00	30.00	37.50	67.50	175.00	550.00	2200.00	6250.00
1834 Small 4 ..		25.00	30.00	37.50	67.50	175.00	550.00	2200.00	6250.00
1834 Large 4 ..	635,000	25.00	30.00	37.50	67.50	175.00	550.00	2200.00	6250.00
1835	1,410,000	25.00	30.00	37.50	67.50	175.00	550.00	2100.00	6250.00
1836	1,190,000	25.00	30.00	37.50	67.50	175.00	550.00	2100.00	6250.00
1837	1,042,000	25.00	30.00	37.50	67.50	175.00	550.00	2100.00	6250.00

DIMES

Seated Liberty
1837-1891
Designer, Christian Gobrecht

AG-Obverse: Rim worn down into the field.
    Reverse: At least half of letters and wreath visible.

G-Obverse: Complete outline of Seated Liberty.
    Reverse: All letters worn but readable.

VG-Obverse: At least three complete letters of "LIBERTY" in shield visible.
    Reverse: Letters clear and separated from rim.

F-Obverse: "LIBERTY" in shield complete but some letters weak.
    Reverse: Wreath full with little details.

VF-Obverse: "LIBERTY" sharp. Some details in Seated Liberty's gown shows.
    Reverse: Leaves in wreath show some details.

EF-Obverse: Complete details with slight wear on knees and breast.
    Reverse: Wear only on high points of leaves.

WITHOUT STARS
NO DRAPERY FROM ELBOW

WITH STARS

MINT MARKS ARE LOCATED IN OR BELOW THE WREATH.

DATE	MINTAGE	G-6	VG-10	F-15	VF-30	EF-45	AU-50	UNC-60	UNC-65
1837 Sm Date	Included in	45.00	67.50	90.00	170.00	350.00	1000.00	2500.00	10000.00
1837 Lg Date	above	45.00	67.50	90.00	170.00	350.00	1000.00	2500.00	10000.00
1838 O	402,434	50.00	85.00	130.00	260.00	550.00	1700.00	4000.00	13500.00
1838 Small Stars	1,992,500	40.00	55.00	80.00	150.00	250.00	900.00	2000.00	9500.00
1838 Large Stars		15.00	20.00	25.00	47.50	75.00	400.00	900.00	7500.00
1838 Part Drapery		45.00	70.00	110.00	175.00	325.00	750.00	1500.00	9500.00
1839	1,053,115	15.00	20.00	25.00	40.00	70.00	400.00	900.00	7500.00
1839 O	1,243,272	20.00	25.00	30.00	60.00	100.00	400.00	975.00	7750.00
1840 No Drapery	1,358,580	15.00	20.00	25.00	40.00	70.00	750.00	1500.00	7500.00
1840 O	1,175,000	20.00	35.00	50.00	67.50	100.00	900.00	— —	— —
1840 with Drapery	Mintage included in 1840 above	30.00	45.00	70.00	80.00	400.00	1500.00	— —	— —

DIMES

DATE	MINTAGE	G-8	VG-10	F-15	VF-30	EF-45	AU-50	UNC-60	UNC-65
1841	1,622,500	15.50	17.50	20.00	40.00	60.00	300.00	700.00	4750.00
1841 O	2,007,500	20.00	25.00	35.00	50.00	80.00	700.00	1500.00	7000.00
1842	1,887,500	15.00	17.50	20.00	50.00	80.00	300.00	700.00	7000.00
1842 O	2,020,000	20.00	25.00	35.00	50.00	90.00	325.00	— —	— —
1843	1,370,000	15.00	17.50	20.00	40.00	70.00	300.00	700.00	4750.00
1843 O	150,000	55.00	70.00	130.00	275.00	850.00	1700.00	— —	— —
1844	72,500	40.00	60.00	90.00	250.00	550.00	1400.00	2000.00	— —
1845	1,755,000	15.00	16.50	20.00	35.00	60.00	150.00	700.00	4500.00
1845 O	230,000	20.00	50.00	75.00	160.00	800.00	1250.00	— —	— —
1846	31,300	75.00	85.00	140.00	250.00	525.00	1150.00	— —	— —
1847	245,000	20.00	30.00	50.00	75.00	200.00	375.00	1200.00	8500.00
1848	451,500	15.00	17.50	25.00	50.00	80.00	200.00	750.00	5500.00
1849	839,000	15.00	17.50	25.00	45.00	70.00	150.00	725.00	4500.00

DATE	MINTAGE	G-6	VG-10	F-15	VF-30	EF-45	AU-50	UNC-60	UNC-65	PROOF-65
1849 O	300,000	20.00	25.00	35.00	150.00	350.00	550.00	— —	— —	
1850	1,931,500	15.00	16.50	20.00	25.00	62.50	160.00	700.00	4500.00	
1850 O	510,000	17.50	20.00	30.00	80.00	125.00	325.00	1000.00	8500.00	
1851	1,026,500	15.00	16.50	20.00	30.00	65.00	160.00	700.00	4500.00	
1851 O	400,000	17.50	20.00	30.00	85.00	150.00	350.00	1500.00	8000.00	
1852	1,535,500	13.50	15.00	20.00	30.00	67.50	200.00	700.00	4500.00	
1852 O	430,000	20.00	25.00	40.00	85.00	175.00	600.00	1800.00	— —	
1853 No Arrows	95,000	35.00	40.00	60.00	100.00	225.00	600.00	1000.00	7500.00	

IN 1853 A SLIGHT CHANGE IN THE WEIGHT OF THE COIN WAS MADE AND ARROWS WERE PLACED AT EACH SIDE OF THE DATE ON THE OBVERSE.

← 1853 →

DATE	MINTAGE	G-6	VG-10	F-15	VF-30	EF-45	AU-50	UNC-60	UNC-65	PROOF-65
1853 with Arrows	12,078,010	13.50	15.00	18.50	30.00	67.50	300.00	950.00	5250.00	
1853 O	1,100,000	18.50	25.00	30.00	50.00	150.00	400.00	1000.00	8000.00	
1854	4,470,000	13.50	17.50	18.50	30.00	67.50	300.00	1000.00	5250.00	
1854 O	1,770,000	15.50	20.00	25.00	35.00	115.00	350.00	1000.00	6250.00	
1855	2,075,000	13.50	17.50	20.00	30.00	67.50	300.00	1100.00	5250.00	— —

IN 1856 THE ARROWS WERE REMOVED FROM BOTH SIDES OF THE DATE.

DATE	MINTAGE	G-6	VG-10	F-15	VF-30	EF-45	AU-50	UNC-60	UNC-65	PROOF-65
1856 Sm Date	5,780,000	13.50	15.50	17.50	20.00	55.00	210.00	700.00	4750.00	6500.00
1856 Lg Date		18.50	25.00	27.50	50.00	85.00	210.00	750.00	4500.00	
1856 O	1,180,000	15.50	17.50	18.50	25.00	65.00	210.00	750.00	4500.00	
1856 S	70,000	45.00	65.00	95.00	200.00	350.00	1200.00	— —	— —	
1857	5,580,000	13.50	17.50	19.50	25.00	55.00	210.00	700.00	4500.00	6500.00
1857 O	1,540,000	13.50	17.50	22.50	25.00	60.00	210.00	750.00	4500.00	
1858	1,540,000	13.50	15.50	20.00	25.00	55.00	210.00	700.00	4500.00	6750.00
1858 O	290,000	20.00	30.00	50.00	80.00	200.00	350.00	1200.00	8000.00	
1858 S	60,000	40.00	50.00	80.00	200.00	350.00	1150.00	— —	— —	
1859	430,000	13.50	15.50	20.00	30.00	65.00	225.00	1000.00	5000.00	5200.00
1859 O	480,000	13.50	17.50	20.00	45.00	85.00	500.00	1100.00	5500.00	
1859 S	60,000	35.00	55.00	85.00	200.00	375.00	1200.00	8000.00	16000.00	
1860 S	140,000	17.50	25.00	45.00	70.00	185.00	650.00	— —	— —	

DIMES

Legend Added
1860-1873

**LEGEND REPLACES STARS
ON OBVERSE AND REMOVED
FROM REVERSE**

DATE	MINTAGE	G-6	VG-10	F-15	VF-30	EF-45	AU-50	UNC-60	UNC-65	PROOF-65
1860	607,000	13.50	14.50	20.00	30.00	60.00	150.00	525.00	2750.00	2750.00
1860 O	40,000	400.00	725.00	900.00	1200.00	2300.00	— —	— —	— —	
1861	1,884,000	13.50	14.50	17.50	25.00	50.00	100.00	500.00	2750.00	2750.00
1861S	172,500	20.00	30.00	50.00	85.00	175.00	375.00	— —	— —	
1862	847,550	13.50	15.00	17.50	25.00	50.00	100.00	500.00	2750.00	2750.00
1862S	180,750	20.00	30.00	40.00	95.00	170.00	600.00	6750.00	— —	
1863	14,460	100.00	140.00	200.00	275.00	375.00	750.00	1300.00	7500.00	3000.00
1863S	157,500	20.00	35.00	45.00	75.00	180.00	600.00	1200.00	6750.00	
1864	11,470	90.00	130.00	200.00	250.00	350.00	700.00	1300.00	7500.00	3000.00
1864S	230,000	20.00	25.00	35.00	60.00	150.00	450.00	1200.00	6250.00	
1865	10,500	115.00	150.00	225.00	325.00	400.00	700.00	1100.00	7500.00	3000.00
1865S	175,000	20.00	30.00	35.00	70.00	150.00	800.00	3000.00	6000.00	
1866	8,725	125.00	175.00	300.00	400.00	450.00	850.00	1300.00	7500.00	3000.00
1866S	135,000	20.00	30.00	40.00	65.00	150.00	450.00	1500.00	6000.00	
1867	6,625	200.00	250.00	450.00	550.00	600.00	1175.00	1800.00	8500.00	3000.00
1867S	140,000	20.00	30.00	40.00	65.00	150.00	500.00	1200.00	6000.00	
1868	464,600	13.50	15.00	30.00	50.00	125.00	190.00	700.00	5000.00	2750.00
1868S	260,000	15.00	20.00	30.00	90.00	190.00	350.00	1000.00	5500.00	
1869	256,600	13.50	15.00	30.00	75.00	140.00	300.00	725.00	5500.00	2750.00
1869S	450,000	15.00	17.50	22.50	50.00	95.00	185.00	825.00	5000.00	
1870	471,500	13.50	15.00	22.50	50.00	100.00	190.00	450.00	5000.00	2750.00
1870S	50,000	70.00	110.00	165.00	250.00	400.00	1100.00	3200.00	— —	
1871	907,710	13.50	15.00	17.50	22.50	55.00	110.00	425.00	2750.00	2750.00
1871CC	20,100	300.00	400.00	850.00	1100.00	3000.00	— —	— —	— —	
1871S	320,000	15.00	25.00	40.00	75.00	140.00	375.00	1000.00	5250.00	
1872	2,396,450	13.50	15.00	17.50	20.00	50.00	125.00	425.00	2750.00	2750.00
1872CC	35,480	200.00	300.00	550.00	750.00	2100.00	— —	— —	— —	
1872S	190,000	25.00	40.00	80.00	125.00	200.00	500.00	1100.00	3250.00	
1873CC	12,400	Only one known, balance presumably melted.								
1873 Closed 3..	1,568,600	17.50	25.00	35.00	60.00	90.00	230.00	430.00	2750.00	
1873 Open 3		25.00	45.00	65.00	100.00	150.00	350.00	— —	— —	

FROM 1873 THROUGH 1874 THE ARROWS WERE PLACED ON EACH SIDE OF THE DATE.

DATE	MINTAGE	G-6	VG-10	F-15	VF-30	EF-45	AU-50	UNC-60	UNC-65	PROOF-65
1873	2,378,500	15.00	20.00	30.00	55.00	120.00	375.00	1250.00	5750.00	6500.00
1873CC	18,791	300.00	450.00	625.00	1000.00	2500.00	— —	13000.00	— —	
1873S	455,000	22.50	27.50	40.00	70.00	125.00	560.00	1500.00	6000.00	
1874	2,940,000	15.00	20.00	30.00	55.00	120.00	425.00	1200.00	5750.00	6500.00
1874CC	10,817	650.00	1200.00	2000.00	2500.00	4300.00	— —	— —	— —	
1874S	240,000	27.50	35.00	70.00	100.00	175.00	650.00	1500.00	6500.00	
1875	10,350,700	13.50	14.50	16.50	20.00	50.00	130.00	450.00	2750.00	2750.00

DIMES

DATE	MINTAGE	G-6	VG-10	F-15	VF-30	EF-45	AU-50	UNC-60	UNC-65	PROOF-65
1875CC Mint Mark under wreath ...	4,645,000	15.00	17.50	20.00	45.00	75.00	100.00	450.00	3250.00	
1875CC Mint Mark inside wreath ...		17.50	20.00	30.00	50.00	85.00	100.00	450.00	3250.00	
1875S M.M. under	9,070,000	13.50	14.50	16.50	25.00	60.00	125.00	450.00	2750.00	
1875S M.M. inside		20.00	40.00	85.00	150.00	215.00	235.00	465.00	2750.00	
1876	11,461,150	13.50	14.50	16.50	25.00	62.50	125.00	450.00	2750.00	2750.00
1876CC ...	8,270,000	13.50	14.50	16.50	30.00	62.50	125.00	450.00	2750.00	
1876S	10,420,000	13.50	14.50	16.50	25.00	62.50	125.00	450.00	2750.00	
1877	7,310,510	13.50	14.50	16.50	25.00	52.50	125.00	450.00	2750.00	2750.00
1877CC ...	7,700,000	13.50	14.50	16.50	20.00	52.50	125.00	450.00	2750.00	
1877S	2,340,000	13.50	14.50	16.50	25.00	57.50	125.00	450.00	2750.00	
1878	1,678,800	13.50	14.50	16.50	20.00	57.50	125.00	450.00	2750.00	2750.00
1878CC ...	200,000	30.00	35.00	60.00	100.00	200.00	450.00	900.00	5500.00	
1879	15,100	55.00	65.00	85.00	150.00	225.00	450.00	500.00	6000.00	3250.00
1880	37,355	45.00	55.00	75.00	125.00	160.00	325.00	475.00	5750.00	3250.00
1881	24,975	45.00	55.00	75.00	125.00	200.00	325.00	500.00	5750.00	3250.00
1882	3,911,100	13.25	14.50	16.50	20.00	50.00	75.00	450.00	2750.00	2750.00
1883	7,675,712	13.25	14.50	16.50	20.00	50.00	75.00	450.00	2750.00	2750.00
1884	3,366,380	13.25	14.50	16.50	20.00	50.00	75.00	450.00	2750.00	2750.00
1884S	564,969	17.50	20.00	30.00	50.00	95.00	160.00	475.00	4500.00	
1885	2,533,427	13.25	15.00	17.50	20.00	55.00	75.00	450.00	2750.00	2750.00
1885S	43,690	120.00	150.00	220.00	325.00	500.00	1500.00	3000.00	— —	
1886	6,377,570	13.50	15.00	17.50	20.00	50.00	75.00	450.00	2750.00	2750.00
1886S	206,524	20.00	30.00	40.00	55.00	90.00	175.00	525.00	4500.00	
1887	11,283,939	13.50	15.00	17.50	20.00	50.00	75.00	450.00	2750.00	2750.00
1887S	4,454,450	13.50	15.00	17.50	20.00	50.00	75.00	450.00	2750.00	
1888	5,496,487	13.50	15.00	17.50	20.00	50.00	75.00	450.00	2500.00	2750.00
1888S	1,720,000	13.25	14.50	17.50	20.00	55.00	75.00	450.00	2500.00	
1889	7,380,711	13.25	14.50	17.50	20.00	50.00	75.00	450.00	2500.00	2750.00
1889S	972,678	16.50	20.00	25.00	30.00	75.00	225.00	500.00	4000.00	
1890	9,911,541	13.50	15.00	17.50	20.00	50.00	75.00	450.00	2500.00	2750.00
1890S	1,423,076	15.00	20.00	25.00	40.00	70.00	125.00	500.00	3000.00	
1891	15,310,600	13.25	14.50	16.50	20.00	50.00	75.00	450.00	2500.00	2750.00
1891 0	4,540,000	13.25	14.50	16.50	20.00	50.00	75.00	500.00	2500.00	
1891S	3,196,116	13.25	14.50	16.50	25.00	55.00	85.00	525.00	2750.00	

DIMES

Barber Dimes
1892-1916
Designer, Charles E. Barber

THIS IS A LIBERTY HEAD DIME BUT HAS COMMONLY BEEN NAMED BARBER DIME AFTER ITS DESIGNER
CHARLES E. BARBER, THE CHIEF ENGRAVER OF THE MINT.

AG-Obverse: Outline of head visible. Letters evident but worn into rim.
  Reverse: About one half of wreath shows. "One Dime" legible.

 G-Obverse: All letters complete. Head worn smooth.
  Reverse: Complete outline of wreath.

VG-Obverse: At least the equivalent of three letters in "LIBERTY" will show.
  Reverse: All leaves outlined but little detail.

 F-Obverse: Full "LIBERTY" shows, but weak.
  Reverse: Some details show in wreath.

VF-Obverse: "LIBERTY" strong. Some details in wreath around head are clear.
  Reverse: Most details in wreath and ribbon show.

EF-Obverse: Wear is evident only on high points of cheek, tips of leaves and hair on forehead.
  Reverse: The tips of leaves show traces of wear.

DATE	MINTAGE	G-6	VG-10	F-15	VF-30	EF-45	AU-50	UNC-60	UNC-65	PROOF-65
1892	12,121,245	7.50	9.50	12.50	16.00	35.00	60.00	350.00	1575.00	2600.00
1892 0	3,841,700	11.50	13.50	15.75	22.00	36.50	35.00	450.00	2550.00	
1892S	990,710	45.00	50.00	60.00	75.00	110.00	190.00	575.00	3700.00	
1893/2	— —	— —	— —	— —	— —	215.00	325.00	750.00	7500.00	
1893	3,340,792	10.50	13.50	16.75	20.00	35.00	70.00	475.00	2300.00	2600.00
1893 0	1,760,000	24.50	28.50	38.50	42.50	60.00	135.00	650.00	4500.00	
1893S	2,491,401	12.50	15.00	21.50	30.00	38.50	80.00	450.00	2650.00	
1894	1,330,972	12.75	15.00	23.50	42.50	62.50	135.00	500.00	3150.00	2600.00
1894 0	720,000	50.00	65.00	90.00	135.00	300.00	675.00	3250.00	20000.00	
1894S	24	Proof only								— —
1895	690,880	90.00	100.00	115.00	135.00	215.00	400.00	1200.00	6300.00	3000.00
1895 0	440,000	210.00	240.00	275.00	375.00	425.00	650.00	2650.00	11000.00	
1895S	1,120,000	25.00	32.50	45.00	50.00	67.50	120.00	650.00	3400.00	
1896	2,000,762	10.75	13.50	22.50	28.50	43.50	82.50	450.00	2400.00	2600.00
1896 0	610,000	70.00	80.00	95.00	110.00	175.00	400.00	1350.00	7800.00	
1896S	575,056	55.00	70.00	90.00	95.00	140.00	325.00	800.00	4250.00	
1897	10,869,264	6.00	8.00	10.00	12.75	22.50	47.50	350.00	1350.00	2600.00
1897 0	666,000	55.00	75.00	100.00	110.00	240.00	475.00	2100.00	8200.00	
1897S	1,342,844	13.75	18.50	30.00	40.00	65.00	125.00	535.00	3250.00	
1898	16,320,735	5.75	7.50	9.75	12.75	22.50	47.50	350.00	1350.00	2600.00
1898 0	2,130,000	8.75	12.50	22.00	35.00	58.50	120.00	675.00	5400.00	
1898S	1,702,507	9.50	12.00	16.50	25.00	40.00	75.00	500.00	3200.00	

DIMES

DATE	MINTAGE	G 6	VG-10	F-16	VF-30	EF-45	AU-50	UNC-60	UNC-65	PROOF-65
1899	19,580,846	5.75	7.50	9.75	12.75	22.50	47.50	350.00	1350.00	2600.00
1899 O	2,650,000	7.75	11.00	20.00	35.00	58.50	110.00	675.00	5400.00	
1899S	1,867,493	8.00	10.50	16.50	26.00	37.50	75.00	475.00	3100.00	
1900	17,600,912	5.75	7.50	9.75	12.75	22.50	47.50	350.00	1350.00	2600.00
1900 O	2,010,000	10.50	13.50	22.50	35.00	65.00	150.00	700.00	6600.00	
1900S	5,168,270	5.75	7.75	11.00	16.50	32.50	68.50	450.00	3100.00	
1901	18,860,478	5.75	7.50	9.75	12.75	22.50	47.50	350.00	1350.00	2600.00
1901 O	5,620,000	5.75	7.75	11.00	20.00	55.00	150.00	675.00	6000.00	
1901S	593,022	55.00	70.00	110.00	150.00	250.00	475.00	1950.00	10000.00	
1902	21,380,777	5.50	7.25	9.75	12.75	22.50	47.50	350.00	1350.00	2600.00
1902 O	4,500,000	6.25	8.25	12.00	15.00	35.00	82.50	575.00	5200.00	
1902S	2,070,000	8.00	11.50	22.50	32.50	67.50	150.00	750.00	4850.00	
1903	19,500,755	5.50	7.25	9.75	12.75	22.50	47.50	350.00	1350.00	2600.00
1903 O	8,180,000	5.75	7.50	10.00	12.50	33.50	82.50	650.00	4500.00	
1903S	613,300	45.00	55.00	75.00	95.00	160.00	410.00	1600.00	9750.00	
1904	14,601,027	5.75	7.50	9.75	12.75	22.50	47.50	350.00	1350.00	2600.00
1904S	800,000	32.50	40.00	60.00	82.50	145.00	400.00	1600.00	9100.00	
1905	14,552,350	5.75	7.50	9.75	12.75	22.50	47.50	350.00	1350.00	2600.00
1905 O	3,400,000	7.00	9.00	12.50	17.50	33.50	75.00	525.00	3300.00	
1905S	6,855,199	6.00	8.50	11.50	16.25	32.50	80.00	525.00	3300.00	
1906	19,958,406	5.75	7.50	9.75	12.75	22.50	47.50	350.00	1350.00	2600.00
1906D	4,060,000	6.25	8.50	12.00	18.50	35.00	75.00	450.00	2400.00	
1906 O	2,610,000	8.50	10.75	18.00	25.00	35.00	80.00	525.00	3300.00	
1906S	3,136,640	6.50	8.50	13.50	18.50	36.00	75.00	525.00	3300.00	
1907	22,220,575	5.75	7.50	9.75	12.75	22.50	47.50	350.00	1350.00	2600.00
1907D	4,080,000	6.25	8.50	12.00	15.00	35.00	75.00	575.00	3400.00	
1907 O	5,058,000	5.75	8.00	12.50	16.50	35.00	62.50	450.00	1850.00	
1907S	3,178,470	6.50	8.50	13.00	15.50	36.00	80.00	575.00	3150.00	
1908	10,600,545	5.75	7.50	10.00	12.75	22.50	47.50	350.00	1350.00	2600.00
1908D	7,490,000	5.75	7.50	11.00	13.50	30.00	60.00	350.00	1700.00	
1908 O	1,789,000	8.75	12.00	18.50	26.50	45.00	100.00	575.00	3150.00	
1908S	3,220,000	7.00	9.00	11.50	17.50	33.50	75.00	550.00	2850.00	
1909	10,240,650	5.75	7.50	10.00	12.75	22.50	47.50	350.00	1350.00	2600.00
1909D	954,000	8.00	12.50	22.50	32.50	47.50	110.00	575.00	3150.00	
1909 O	2,287,000	7.00	9.50	13.50	20.00	35.00	75.00	475.00	2500.00	
1909S	1,000,000	8.00	11.50	23.50	34.00	50.00	110.00	550.00	3400.00	
1910	11,520,551	5.75	7.50	9.75	12.75	22.50	47.50	350.00	1350.00	2600.00
1910D	3,490,000	6.75	8.50	11.50	18.75	38.50	95.00	575.00	4100.00	
1910S	1,240,000	8.50	10.50	15.00	21.00	36.50	85.00	525.00	2850.00	
1911	18,870,543	5.75	7.50	9.75	12.75	22.50	47.50	350.00	1350.00	2600.00
1911D	11,209,000	5.75	7.75	10.00	13.50	26.00	48.50	375.00	1500.00	
1911S	3,520,000	6.75	8.50	11.50	14.00	32.50	70.00	475.00	2400.00	
1912	19,350,700	5.75	7.50	9.75	12.75	22.75	47.50	350.00	1350.00	2600.00
1912D	11,760,000	6.00	7.50	10.50	13.00	28.00	47.50	375.00	2300.00	
1912S	3,420,000	8.50	10.00	12.50	14.00	35.00	70.00	475.00	2400.00	
1913	19,760,622	5.75	7.50	9.75	12.75	22.75	47.50	350.00	1350.00	2600.00
1913S	510,000	13.75	27.50	40.00	57.50	120.00	235.00	700.00	3400.00	
1914	17,360,655	5.75	7.50	9.75	12.75	22.50	47.50	350.00	1350.00	2600.00
1914D	11,908,000	6.00	7.75	9.75	12.75	28.00	47.50	325.00	1600.00	
1914S	2,100,000	9.00	10.00	11.50	15.00	35.00	75.00	475.00	2850.00	
1915	5,620,450	6.00	8.50	12.00	14.00	23.50	48.00	350.00	1350.00	2650.00
1915S	960,000	12.00	13.00	14.50	18.75	36.50	95.00	550.00	3150.00	
1916	18,490,000	5.75	7.50	9.75	12.75	22.50	47.50	350.00	1575.00	
1916S	5,820,000	6.25	7.50	10.00	13.50	30.00	50.00	350.00	1575.00	

DIMES

Mercury Dime
1916-1945
Designer, Adolph A. Weinman

THIS COIN IS COMMONLY CALLED THE MERCURY DIME BUT IT IS LIBERTY WITH WINGS ON HER CAP.

AG-Obverse: Strong outline of head. Letters worn well into rim.
   Reverse: Fasces well outlined except top and bottom worn into rim.

G-Obverse: Letters legible but tops worn into rim.
   Reverse: Fasces outline complete. Tops of letters worn into rim.

VG-Obverse: Letters in "LIBERTY" complete. Strong outline of wing.
   Reverse: Some of the vertical lines in the Fasces show.

F-Obverse: Some of the wing feathers show. Rim sharp.
   Reverse: All of the vertical lines in the Fasces show, but weak.

VF-Obverse: Some hair details. Most of feathers show.
   Reverse: Top and bottom bands of the Fasces are complete.

EF-Obverse: Hair and wing are well detailed with wear only on high points.
   Reverse: Slight trace of wear only on the diagonal and horizontal bands.

DATE	MINTAGE	G-6	VG-10	F-15	VF-30	EF-45	AU-50	UNC-60	UNC-65	PROOF-65
1916	22,180,080	6.75	7.50	9.50	10.00	14.00	22.50	40.00	90.00	
1916D	264,000	525.00	700.00	900.00	1350.00	1800.00	2300.00	3000.00	5250.00	
1916S	10,450,000	8.00	8.75	9.25	13.00	19.25	30.00	57.50	250.00	
1917	55,230,000	5.00	5.50	7.25	8.75	10.00	17.50	35.00	85.00	
1917D	9,402,000	8.00	8.75	11.00	18.50	42.50	85.00	185.00	500.00	
1917S	27,330,000	5.50	5.75	7.50	9.50	13.00	26.50	67.50	290.00	
1918	26,680,000	5.50	5.75	8.75	14.00	28.50	52.50	95.00	310.00	
1918D	22,674,800	6.50	7.00	8.25	12.50	26.50	55.00	115.00	425.00	
1918S	19,300,000	6.00	6.50	7.75	10.00	17.50	36.50	85.00	330.00	
1919	35,740,000	4.75	5.00	7.25	8.50	10.00	19.00	42.50	150.00	
1919D	9,939,000	7.50	8.25	9.25	17.50	37.50	87.50	240.00	550.00	
1919S	8,850,000	6.75	7.25	8.25	17.00	35.00	87.50	270.00	700.00	
1920	59,030,000	4.50	4.75	5.25	8.75	10.00	17.50	36.50	100.00	
1920D	19,171,000	6.25	6.75	8.00	10.00	17.50	42.50	110.00	425.00	
1920S	13,820,000	6.25	6.75	7.75	9.50	18.00	35.00	100.00	375.00	
1921	1,230,000	35.00	47.50	95.00	190.00	360.00	850.00	1300.00	2550.00	
1921D	1,080,000	52.00	67.50	125.00	250.00	375.00	850.00	1300.00	2550.00	
1923	50,130,000	4.25	4.50	5.25	7.75	9.50	16.50	35.00	95.00	
1923S	6,440,000	6.25	6.75	8.00	10.50	25.00	50.00	150.00	550.00	

73

DIMES

DATE	MINTAGE	G-8	VG-10	F-15	VF-30	EF-45	AU-50	UNC-60	UNC-65	PROOF-65
1924	24,010,000	5.00	5.25	5.50	8.75	11.00	22.50	52.00	165.00	
1924D	6,810,000	5.75	6.50	8.25	11.00	22.00	52.50	175.00	525.00	
1924S	7,120,000	5.75	6.50	7.75	9.50	19.00	47.50	175.00	585.00	
1925	25,610,000	4.50	4.75	5.25	8.00	9.50	17.50	58.50	165.00	
1925D	5,117,000	8.75	9.00	12.50	28.00	80.00	165.00	410.00	975.00	
1925S	5,850,000	5.50	6.25	7.75	10.50	22.00	60.00	200.00	685.00	
1926	32,160,000	4.25	4.50	5.50	7.50	8.50	13.75	32.50	90.00	
1926D	6,828,000	5.50	6.25	8.00	10.00	19.00	35.00	120.00	450.00	
1926S	1,520,000	13.50	16.00	20.00	37.50	100.00	325.00	625.00	2200.00	
1927	28,080,000	4.25	4.50	5.50	7.50	8.25	13.50	31.50	90.00	
1927D	4,812,000	6.75	7.50	8.25	16.00	38.50	100.00	350.00	850.00	
1927S	4,770,000	5.25	5.75	7.50	8.75	18.50	47.50	150.00	575.00	
1928	19,480,000	4.25	4.50	5.50	7.50	8.50	13.50	31.50	95.00	
1928D	4,161,000	7.50	8.25	10.00	17.50	37.50	95.00	230.00	— —	
1928S	7,400,000	5.50	5.75	6.75	8.50	16.00	36.50	90.00	395.00	
1929	25,970,000	4.25	4.50	5.50	7.25	8.00	11.50	25.00	78.50	
1929D	5,034,000	6.75	7.50	8.75	9.50	13.50	25.00	50.00	210.00	
1929S	4,730,000	4.75	5.25	5.50	7.75	9.00	17.50	57.50	250.00	
1930	6,770,000	4.75	5.25	5.25	7.75	9.50	18.00	36.50	135.00	
1930S	1,843,000	8.50	8.75	9.00	9.25	17.00	47.00	140.00	— —	
1931	3,150,000	5.25	5.75	6.75	8.75	13.50	26.50	60.00	185.00	
1931D	1,260,000	13.50	14.50	16.50	22.75	42.50	82.50	175.00	— —	
1931S	1,800,000	8.25	8.50	8.75	9.50	16.50	45.00	135.00	— —	
1934	24,080,000	4.50	4.75	5.00	5.25	5.50	— —	26.50	90.00	
1934D	6,772,000	7.25	7.50	7.75	8.00	8.25	— —	100.00	300.00	
1935	58,830,000	4.00	4.25	4.50	4.75	5.00	— —	22.50	75.00	
1935D	10,477,000	6.25	6.50	6.75	7.00	7.25	— —	175.00	— —	
1935S	15,840,000	5.75	6.00	6.25	6.50	6.75	— —	60.00	215.00	
1936	87,504,130	4.00	4.25	4.50	4.75	5.00	— —	22.50	75.00	2000.00
1936D	16,132,000	5.25	5.50	5.75	6.00	6.50	— —	90.00	280.00	
1936S	9,210,000	5.75	6.00	6.25	6.50	6.75	— —	48.50	150.00	
1937	56,865,756	4.25	4.50	4.75	5.00	5.25	— —	20.00	70.00	1100.00
1937D	14,146,000	5.75	6.00	6.25	6.50	6.75	— —	72.50	230.00	
1937S	9,740,000	6.95	7.25	7.50	7.75	8.00	— —	62.50	180.00	
1938	22,198,728	4.75	5.00	5.25	5.50	5.75	— —	26.50	110.00	1000.00
1938D	5,537,000	7.00	7.25	7.50	7.75	8.00	— —	82.50	255.00	
1938S	8,090,000	5.75	6.00	6.25	6.50	6.75	— —	35.00	90.00	
1939	67,749,321	4.25	4.50	4.75	5.00	5.25	— —	18.50	57.50	800.00
1939D	24,394,000	5.00	5.25	5.50	5.75	6.00	— —	20.00	57.50	
1939S	10,540,000	5.50	5.75	6.00	6.25	6.50	— —	50.00	150.00	
1940	65,361,827		4.00	4.25	4.50	4.75	— —	16.50	36.50	650.00
1940D	21,198,000		4.75	5.00	5.25	5.50	— —	38.00	125.00	
1940S	21,560,000		4.75	5.00	5.25	5.50	— —	17.50	50.00	
1941	175,106,557		3.95	4.10	4.25	4.50	— —	9.00	30.00	600.00
1941D	45,634,000		4.25	4.50	4.75	5.00	— —	32.50	65.00	
1941S	43,090,000		4.25	4.50	4.75	5.00	— —	12.00	39.00	
1942	205,432,329		3.95	4.10	4.25	4.50	— —	9.50	28.50	575.00
1942 over 1			450.00	475.00	500.00	550.00	— —	2250.00	4500.00	
1942D	60,740,000		4.00	4.25	4.50	4.75	— —	15.00	45.00	
1942D over 1			450.00	475.00	500.00	550.00	— —	2500.00	4750.00	

DIMES

DATE	MINTAGE	G-6	VG-10	F-15	VF-30	EF-45	UNC-60	UNC-65	PROOF-65
1942S	49,300,000		4.25	4.50	4.75	5.00	25.00	95.00	
1943	191,710,000		3.95	4.10	4.25	4.50	10.00	28.50	
1943D	71,949,000		4.00	4.25	4.50	4.75	11.00	36.50	
1943S	60,400,000		4.00	4.25	4.50	4.75	22.50	60.00	
1944	231,410,000		3.95	4.10	4.25	4.50	10.00	28.50	
1944D	62,224,000		4.25	4.50	4.75	5.00	10.00	36.50	
1944S	49,490,000		4.50	4.75	5.00	5.25	10.00	38.00	
1945	159,130,000		3.95	4.10	4.25	4.50	10.00	29.00	
1945D	40,245,000		4.00	4.25	4.50	4.75	10.00	36.50	
1945S	41,920,000		4.00	4.25	4.50	4.75	11.00	37.50	
1945 Micro S			5.75	6.00	6.50	7.00	20.00	77.50	

Roosevelt Dimes
1946 to Date
Designer, John R. Sinnock

G-Obverse: Rim and letters very clear. Hair worn smooth.
   Reverse: Letters worn into rim. Torch outline complete.

VG-Obverse: Few hair lines show.
   Reverse: Letters free from rim. The vertical lines on each side of torch show.

F-Obverse: Ear sharp. Part of hair details distinct.
   Reverse: Most vertical lines in torch show.

VF-Obverse: Most hair details visible.
   Reverse: All of the vertical lines are evident but some weak.

EF-Obverse: All hair details show but weak from ear to forehead.
   Reverse: All vertical lines in torch are strong.

DIMES

DATE	MINTAGE	G-6	VG-10	F-15	VF-30	EF-45	UNC-65	PROOF-65
1040	225,250,000	3.50	3.75	4.00	4.25	4.50	5.50	
1946D	61,043,500	3.50	3.75	4.00	4.25	4.50	8.50	
1946S	27,900,000	3.50	3.75	4.00	4.25	4.50	9.00	
1947	121,520,000	3.50	3.75	4.00	4.25	4.50	9.25	
1947D	46,835,000	3.50	3.75	4.00	4.25	4.50	20.00	
1947S	34,840,000	3.50	3.75	4.00	4.25	4.50	9.00	
1948	74,950,000	3.50	3.75	4.00	4.25	4.50	9.50	
1948D	52,841,000	3.50	3.75	4.00	4.25	4.50	26.50	
1948S	35,520,000	3.50	3.75	4.00	4.25	4.50	14.50	
1949	30,940,000	4.00	4.50	5.25	6.00	10.00	40.00	
1949D	26,034,000	3.50	3.75	4.00	4.50	5.25	19.00	
1949S	13,510,000	3.75	4.00	4.75	5.25	11.00	75.00	
1950	50,181,500	3.50	3.75	4.00	4.25	4.50	9.00	80.00
1950D	46,803,000	3.50	3.75	4.00	4.25	4.50	9.50	
1950S	20,440,000	3.50	3.75	4.00	4.50	5.00	40.00	
1951	130,937,602	3.50	3.75	4.00	4.25	4.50	7.25	80.00
1951D	56,529,000	3.50	3.75	4.00	4.25	4.50	8.25	
1951S	31,630,000	3.50	3.75	4.25	4.50	5.00	32.50	
1952	99,122,073	3.50	3.75	4.00	4.25	4.50	7.50	50.00
1952D	122,100,000	3.50	3.75	4.00	4.25	4.50	9.00	
1952S	44,419,500	3.50	3.75	4.00	4.25	4.75	11.50	
1953	53,618,920	3.50	3.75	4.00	4.25	4.50	8.25	35.00
1953D	136,433,000	3.50	4.00	4.50	5.50	6.00	7.75	
1953S	39,180,000	3.50	4.00	4.50	5.00	5.50	6.50	
1954	114,243,503	3.50	3.75	4.00	4.25	4.50	5.00	15.00
1954D	106,397,000	3.50	3.75	4.00	4.25	4.50	4.75	
1954S	22,860,000	3.50	3.75	4.00	4.25	5.00	6.00	
1955	12,828,381	3.50	3.75	4.00	4.25	5.75	7.25	15.00
1955D	13,959,000	3.50	3.75	4.00	4.25	4.75	5.50	
1955S	18,510,000	3.50	3.75	4.00	4.25	4.75	5.50	
1956	109,309,384	3.50	3.75	4.00	4.25	4.50	5.00	8.00
1956D	108,015,100	3.50	4.25	4.50	4.75	5.00	5.50	
1957	161,407,952	2.75	2.85	3.00	3.25	3.50	4.00	5.50
1957D	113,354,330	3.50	3.75	4.00	4.25	4.50	5.50	
1958	32,785,652	3.50	3.75	4.00	4.25	4.50	5.00	5.50
1958D	136,564,600	3.50	3.75	4.00	4.25	4.50	5.00	
1959	86,929,291	2.25	2.50	2.75	3.00	3.25	3.50	
1959D	164,919,790	2.25	2.50	2.75	3.00	3.25	3.50	
1960	72,081,602	2.10	2.25	2.50	2.75	3.00	3.25	
1960D	200,160,400	2.10	2.25	2.50	2.75	3.00	3.25	
1961	96,758,244	2.10	2.25	2.50	2.75	3.00	3.25	
1961D	209,146,550	2.10	2.25	2.50	2.75	3.00	3.25	
1962	75,668,019	2.10	2.25	2.50	2.75	3.00	3.25	
1962D	334,948,380	2.10	2.25	2.50	2.75	3.00	3.25	
1963	126,725,645	2.10	2.25	2.50	2.75	3.00	3.25	
1963D	421,476,530	2.10	2.25	2.50	2.75	3.00	3.25	
1964	933,310,762	2.10	2.25	2.50	2.75	3.00	3.25	
1964D	1,357,517,180	2.10	2.25	2.50	2.75	3.00	3.25	

DIMES

MINTAGE   UNC-65 PROOF-65

Clad Dimes

DATE	MINTAGE		UNC-65	PROOF-65
1965	1,652,140,570		.60	
1966	1,382,734,540		.60	
1967	2,244,007,320		.60	
1968	424,470,400		.60	
1968D	480,748,280		.55	
1968S	3,041,506	Proof only		1.65
1969	145,790,000		.55	
1969D	563,323,870		.55	
1969S	2,934,631	Proof only		1.50
1970	345,570,000		.55	
1970D	754,942,100		.55	
1970S	2,632,810	Proof only		2.75
1971	162,690,000		.55	
1971D	377,914,240		.55	
1971S	3,220,733	Proof only		1.50
1972	431,540,000		.55	
1972D	330,290,000		.50	
1972S	3,260,996	Proof only		1.50
1973	315,670,000		.50	
1973D	455,032,426		.45	
1973S	2,760,339	Proof only		2.50
1974	470,248,000		.45	
1974D	571,083,000		.45	
1974S	2,612,568	Proof only		2.85
1975	585,673,900		.45	
1975D	313,705,300		.45	
1975S	2,845,450	Proof only		3.50
1976	568,760,000		.45	
1976D	695,222,774		.45	
1976S	4,149,730	Proof only		1.95
1977	796,930,000		.35	
1977D	376,607,228		.35	
1977S	3,251,152	Proof only		1.95
1978	663,980,000		.35	
1978D	282,847,540		.35	
1978S	3,127,781	Proof only		2.40
1979	315,440,000		.35	
1979D	390,921,184		.35	
1979S	3,677,175	Proof only		3.00
1980P	735,170,000		.35	
1980D	719,354,321		.35	
1980S	2,144,231	Proof only		3.00
1981P			.35	
1981D			.35	
1981S		Proof only		3.00

TWENTY CENTS
1875-1878
Designer: William Barber

Authorized on March 3, 1875 and coined at the Philadelphia, Carson City and San Francisco Mints. Made of 90 percent silver, 10 percent copper.

AG-Obverse: Rim and stars worn flat into each other.
    Reverse: Rim flat. Most of eagle outline shows.

 G-Obverse: All stars worn but visible.
    Reverse: All letters readable but tops worn into rim.

VG-Obverse: Some of the letters in "LIBERTY" are complete.
    Reverse: Some of the eagle's wing feathers show.

 F-Obverse: The "LIBERTY" is almost complete but quite weak.
    Reverse: Most of eagle's feathers show. Breast worn flat.

VF-Obverse: "LIBERTY" complete. Some details of gown clear.
    Reverse: All feathers visible but very weak on high points.

EF-Obverse: Only slight wear on knees and breast.
    Reverse: Wing edges and breast show trace of wear.

**MINT MARKS ARE LOCATED
BELOW THE EAGLE ON THE REVERSE**

DATE	MINTAGE	G-6	VG-10	F-15	VF-30	EF-45	AU-50	UNC-60	UNC-65	PROOF-65
1875	39,700	65.00	80.00	100.00	150.00	275.00	525.00	2100.00	8800.00	7000.00
1875CC . . .	133,290	55.00	70.00	85.00	135.00	250.00	500.00	1400.00	8800.00	
1875S	1,155,000	55.00	70.00	85.00	135.00	250.00	500.00	1700.00	12000.00	
1876	15,900	125.00	150.00	175.00	200.00	350.00	675.00	2100.00	12000.00	7550.00
1876CC . . .	10,000	Most melted at the mint						— —		
1877	510	Proof only								8750.00
1878	600	Proof only								8500.00

QUARTER DOLLARS
1796 to Date

Authorized on April 2, 1972. From 1796 through 1839 they were coined at the Philadelphia Mint. The Philadelphia Mint was assisted in 1840 by the New Orleans Mint, in 1855 by the San Francisco Mint, in 1870 by the Carson City Mint and in 1906 by the Denver Mint.
All quarter dollars from 1796 through 1964 were made of approximately 90 percent silver, 10 percent copper. In 1965 the composition changed to a clad type coin of 75 percent copper, 25 percent nickel.

Draped Bust Small Eagle
1796
Designer, Robert Scot

AG-Obverse: Outline of head and few stars show.
    Reverse: Worn smooth. Parts of eagle, and some letters visible.

 G-Obverse: "LIBERTY" legible. Tops of stars run into rim.
    Reverse: Eagle outline complete, but no details.

VG-Obverse: All stars and lettering strong.
    Reverse: Part of "E PLURIBUS UNUM" shows. Few feathers on wings evident.

 F-Obverse: Some hair details show. Ear lobe visible.
    Reverse: "E PLURIBUS UNUM" complete but weak.

VF-Obverse: Most details in hair and face show clearly.
    Reverse: "E PLURIBUS UNUM" clear and sharp. Most feathers show.

EF-Obverse: All details show clearly. Slight wear on hairline at forehead.
    Reverse: All feathers visible, some may be faint because of poor strike.

DATE	MINTAGE	AG-3	G-6	VG-10	F-15	VF-30	EF-45	AU-50	UNC-60	UNC-65
1796	6,146	2250.00	3750.00	4500.00	6500.00	8750.00	18000.00	29000.00	35000.00	— —

QUARTER DOLLARS

Draped Bust Large Eagle
1804-1807
Designer, Robert Scot

DATE	MINTAGE	AG-3	G-6	VG-10	F-15	VF-30	EF-45	AU-50	UNC-60	UNC-65
1804	6,738	425.00	700.00	1000.00	1800.00	4000.00	7500.00	15000.00	22000.00	45000.00
1805	121,394	210.00	350.00	525.00	750.00	1300.00	2625.00	4500.00	— —	8200.00
1806	206,124	180.00	300.00	350.00	650.00	1300.00	2425.00	4200.00	— —	8200.00
1806 over 5		180.00	300.00	350.00	650.00	1600.00	2750.00	5000.00	— —	— —
1807	220,643	180.00	300.00	350.00	650.00	1300.00	2400.00	4250.00	— —	8200.00

Liberty Cap
1815-1838
Designer, John Reich

AG-Obverse: Outline of head and few stars show.
    Reverse: Some letters show. Eagle outline visible.

G-Obverse: Some parts of letters in "LIBERTY" are evident. All stars can be seen but tops worn into rim.
    Reverse: All letters around rim readable but weak.

VG-Obverse: At least three letters of "LIBERTY" can be seen.
    Reverse: Part of "E PLURIBUS UNUM" shows.

F-Obverse: "LIBERTY" complete. Ear visible. Some hair details show.
    Reverse: "E PLURIBUS UNUM" complete.

VF-Obverse: Most of details show in hair, cap and drapery.
    Reverse: Most of the eagle's feathers show sharply.

EF-Obverse: All hair details sharp, with wear evident on high points only.
    Reverse: Only slight wear on high points of wings and tail.

QUARTER DOLLARS

DATE	MINTAGE	AG-3	G-6	VG-10	F-15	VF-30	EF-45	AU-50	UNC-60	UNC-65
1815	89,235	38.50	65.00	80.00	100.00	300.00	700.00	2000.00	3850.00	12000.00
1818		38.50	65.00	80.00	100.00	300.00	700.00	1900.00	3800.00	12000.00
1818 over 15 . .	361,174	38.50	65.00	80.00	100.00	300.00	700.00	2000.00	3850.00	12000.00
1819 Small 9 . .		38.50	65.00	80.00	90.00	250.00	650.00	1900.00	3750.00	12000.00
1819 Large 9 . .	144,000	38.50	65.00	80.00	90.00	250.00	650.00	1900.00	3750.00	12000.00
1820 Small O . .		38.50	65.00	80.00	100.00	235.00	650.00	1275.00	3800.00	12000.00
1820 Large O . .	127,444	42.50	70.00	85.00	100.00	250.00	650.00	1275.00	3800.00	12000.00
1821	216,851	38.50	65.00	80.00	100.00	240.00	650.00	1250.00	3800.00	13000.00
1822		38.50	65.00	80.00	100.00	250.00	650.00	1250.00	3800.00	13000.00
1822 25 over 50¢	64,080	150.00	250.00	350.00	450.00	1250.00	2000.00	3750.00	4200.00	14000.00
1823 over 22 . .	17,800	900.00	1500.00	6000.00	7500.00	15000.00	25000.00	— —	— —	— —
1824	24,000	38.50	65.00	80.00	100.00	275.00	700.00	1400.00	3750.00	13000.00
1825 over 22 . .		38.50	65.00	80.00	100.00	250.00	650.00	1500.00	3800.00	12000.00
1825 over 23 . .	148,000	38.50	65.00	80.00	100.00	250.00	650.00	1500.00	3800.00	12000.00
1825 over 24 . .		38.50	65.00	80.00	100.00	250.00	650.00	1500.00	3800.00	12000.00
1827 Original . .	4,000									75000.00
1827 Restrike .										50000.00
1828		38.50	65.00	80.00	100.00	400.00	650.00	1500.00	3800.00	12000.00
1828 25 over 50¢	102,000	57.50	95.00	150.00	200.00	450.00	900.00	2000.00	3900.00	— —

IN 1831 THE COIN WAS REDUCED IN SIZE AND THE MOTTO OVER THE EAGLE WAS REMOVED.

DATE	MINTAGE	AG-3	G-6	VG-10	F-15	VF-30	EF-45	AU-50	UNC-60	UNC-65
1831 Sm Letters		32.50	55.00	60.00	65.00	135.00	250.00	650.00	2200.00	9450.00
1831 Lg Letters	398,000	32.50	55.00	60.00	65.00	135.00	250.00	650.00	2200.00	9450.00
1832	320,000	32.50	55.00	60.00	65.00	135.00	250.00	650.00	2200.00	9450.00
1833	156,000	32.50	55.00	80.00	100.00	175.00	275.00	750.00	2300.00	10000.00
1834	286,000	32.50	55.00	60.00	65.00	135.00	250.00	650.00	2200.00	9450.00
1835	1,952,000	32.50	55.00	60.00	65.00	135.00	250.00	650.00	2200.00	9450.00
1836	472,000	32.50	55.00	60.00	65.00	135.00	250.00	650.00	2200.00	9450.00
1837	252,400	32.50	55.00	60.00	65.00	135.00	250.00	650.00	2200.00	9450.00
1838	366,000	32.50	55.00	60.00	65.00	135.00	250.00	650.00	2200.00	9450.00

QUARTER DOLLARS

Seated Liberty
1838-1891
Designer, Christian Gobrecht

AG-Obverse: Rim worn down into stars.
   Reverse: At least half of letters and eagle visible.

G-Obverse: All stars show but tops touching rim.
  Reverse: All letters will show, some touching rim.

VG-Obverse: At least three complete letters of "LIBERTY" in shield visible.
   Reverse: Letters clear and separated from rim.

F-Obverse: "LIBERTY" in shield complete but some letters weak.
  Reverse: Some of eagle's feathers show.

VF-Obverse: "LIBERTY" sharp. Some details in gown show.
  Reverse: Most of the eagle's feathers show.

EF-Obverse: Most details show. Slight wear on knees and breast.
  Reverse: All details show with wear on the high points only.

WITHOUT DRAPERY
FROM ELBOW

DATE	MINTAGE	G-6	VG-10	F-15	VF-30	EF-45	AU-50	UNC-60	UNC-65
1838	466,000	20.00	22.50	30.00	58.50	180.00	550.00	3150.00	23500.00
1839	491,146	20.00	22.50	30.00	58.50	170.00	550.00	3150.00	23500.00
1840 0 No Drapery	425,200	22.50	29.50	37.50	65.00	175.00	600.00	3350.00	26000.00
1840 0 Drapery		24.50	30.00	55.00	80.00	175.00	525.00	1600.00	8000.00
1840	188,127	22.50	30.00	45.00	85.00	180.00	525.00	2500.00	8000.00
1841	120,000	52.50	75.00	100.00	150.00	275.00	475.00	1000.00	7500.00
1841 0	452,000	32.50	50.00	75.00	100.00	200.00	525.00	1000.00	8000.00
1842 Lg Date ..	88,000	75.00	90.00	150.00	300.00	400.00	1200.00	2700.00	10000.00
1842 0 Sm Date	769,000	400.00	500.00	700.00	1000.00	2000.00	3000.00	--	--
1842 0 Lg Date		30.00	37.50	50.00	65.00	125.00	250.00	--	--

QUARTER DOLLARS

DATE	MINTAGE	G-6	VG-10	F-15	VF-30	EF-45	AU-50	UNC-60	UNC-65
1843	645,600	20.00	22.50	28.00	45.00	85.00	275.00	850.00	— —
1843 0	968,000	22.50	30.00	75.00	100.00	275.00	550.00	— —	— —
1844	421,200	20.00	25.00	30.00	45.00	90.00	275.00	875.00	6000.00
1844 0	740,000	20.00	25.00	30.00	55.00	100.00	300.00	1200.00	— —
1845	922,000	20.00	22.50	28.00	45.00	85.00	225.00	850.00	5500.00
1846	510,000	20.00	25.00	30.00	45.00	87.50	250.00	850.00	5500.00
1847	734,000	20.00	22.50	28.00	45.00	87.50	250.00	850.00	5500.00
1847 0	368,000	30.00	50.00	75.00	125.00	250.00	500.00	850.00	— —
1848	146,000	25.00	30.00	37.50	85.00	175.00	425.00	850.00	7500.00
1849	340,000	25.00	30.00	37.50	50.00	125.00	300.00	850.00	6000.00
1849 0	16,000	425.00	600.00	900.00	2000.00	3200.00	6500.00	— —	— —
1850	190,800	25.00	33.50	50.00	75.00	140.00	400.00	1000.00	7500.00
1850 0	396,000	32.50	55.00	75.00	100.00	175.00	425.00	1000.00	7500.00
1851	160,000	28.00	32.50	65.00	85.00	150.00	425.00	1000.00	— —
1851 0	88,000	175.00	225.00	350.00	500.00	1300.00	3500.00	— —	— —
1852	177,060	32.50	45.00	65.00	85.00	150.00	425.00	900.00	— —
1852 0	96,000	250.00	400.00	500.00	800.00	1500.00	3850.00	— —	— —
1853	44,200	200.00	250.00	300.00	475.00	650.00	1750.00	4500.00	— —

**WITH ARROWS ADDED TO EACH SIDE
OF THE DATE AND RAYS AROUND EAGLE**

DATE	MINTAGE	G-6	VG-10	F-15	VF-30	EF-45	AU-50	UNC-60	UNC-65	PROOF-65
1853	15,210,020	18.50	20.00	25.00	55.00	150.00	375.00	2250.00	12500.00	
1853 0	1,332,000	20.00	25.00	30.00	60.00	175.00	425.00	3000.00	13500.00	

**IN 1854 THE RAYS AROUND THE EAGLE WERE REMOVED BUT THE ARROW ON EACH SIDE OF THE DATE
STAYED, UNTIL 1856 WHEN THEY WERE REMOVED.**

DATE	MINTAGE	G-6	VG-10	F-15	VF-30	EF-45	AU-50	UNC-60	UNC-65
1854	12,380,000	18.50	20.00	22.50	37.50	75.00	200.00	1575.00	6000.00
1854 0 small O	1,484,000	18.50	20.00	25.00	40.00	85.00	225.00	2500.00	6500.00
1854 0 Large O		150.00	250.00	350.00	700.00	1200.00	— —	— —	— —

QUARTER DOLLARS

DATE	MINTAGE	G-6	VG-10	F-15	VF-30	EF-45	AU-50	UNC-60	UNC-65	PROOF-65
1855	2,857,000	18.50	20.00	25.00	37.50	75.00	200.00	1575.00	6000.00	10000.00
1855 0	176,000	50.00	80.00	100.00	175.00	350.00	1000.00	1850.00	— —	
1855S	396,400	50.00	75.00	95.00	150.00	300.00	950.00	1750.00	— —	
1856	7,264,000	18.50	20.00	22.50	45.00	85.00	175.00	850.00	5500.00	5300.00
1856 0	968,000	25.00	32.50	45.00	65.00	145.00	225.00	875.00	6000.00	
1856S	286,000	37.50	55.00	75.00	160.00	225.00	900.00	— —	— —	
1857	9,644,000	18.50	20.00	22.50	45.00	85.00	175.00	850.00	5500.00	6600.00
1857 0	1,180,000	22.50	27.50	35.00	55.00	110.00	200.00	900.00	5750.00	
1857S	82,000	50.00	75.00	175.00	260.00	450.00	1200.00	— —	— —	
1858	7,368,000	18.50	20.00	22.50	45.00	85.00	175.00	850.00	5500.00	6600.00
1858 0	520,000	25.00	30.00	45.00	65.00	145.00	275.00	900.00	6500.00	
1858S	121,000	40.00	45.00	150.00	225.00	300.00	900.00	— —	— —	
1859	1,344,000	20.00	25.00	30.00	50.00	85.00	175.00	900.00	5500.00	6600.00
1859 0	260,000	35.00	55.00	80.00	115.00	225.00	400.00	900.00	6000.00	
1859S	80,000	60.00	100.00	150.00	250.00	450.00	1500.00	— —	— —	
1860	805,400	20.00	22.50	28.00	45.00	85.00	185.00	900.00	6500.00	6600.00
1860 0	388,000	27.50	35.00	50.00	75.00	160.00	275.00	925.00	6500.00	
1860S	56,000	95.00	150.00	250.00	450.00	650.00	2500.00	— —	— —	
1861	4,854,600	18.50	20.00	25.00	45.00	85.00	175.00	875.00	6500.00	6600.00
1861S	96,000	40.00	50.00	75.00	100.00	300.00	1500.00	2600.00	10000.00	
1862	932,550	20.00	22.50	28.00	65.00	125.00	175.00	850.00	6500.00	6600.00
1862S	67,000	45.00	55.00	85.00	150.00	300.00	1500.00	— —	— —	
1863	192,000	22.50	28.00	45.00	60.00	100.00	325.00	1200.00	7500.00	6600.00
1864	94,070	45.00	50.00	75.00	100.00	185.00	550.00	1200.00	— —	6600.00
1864S	20,000	150.00	200.00	350.00	500.00	1200.00	4000.00	— —	— —	
1865	59,300	50.00	60.00	75.00	125.00	175.00	600.00	1250.00	8500.00	
1865S	41,000	47.50	50.00	90.00	175.00	300.00	1250.00	2000.00	— —	6900.00

In 1866 THE MOTTO "IN GOD WE TRUST" WAS ADDED TO THE REVERSE ABOVE THE EAGLE.

DATE	MINTAGE	G-6	VG-10	F-15	VF-30	EF-45	AU-50	UNC-60	UNC-65	PROOF-65
1866	17,525	175.00	225.00	300.00	400.00	525.00	1500.00	1750.00	13000.00	5000.00
1866S	28,000	75.00	100.00	150.00	250.00	425.00	1275.00	— —	— —	
1867	20,625	100.00	125.00	175.00	275.00	400.00	1350.00	1500.00	12500.00	5000.00
1867S	48,000	50.00	75.00	100.00	175.00	275.00	700.00	3000.00	— —	
1868	30,000	75.00	100.00	130.00	185.00	290.00	800.00	1200.00	9500.00	5000.00
1868S	96,000	40.00	65.00	90.00	140.00	200.00	650.00	2500.00	9000.00	
1869	16,600	175.00	225.00	300.00	400.00	525.00	1600.00	1800.00	13000.00	5000.00
1869S	76,000	45.00	70.00	100.00	150.00	225.00	700.00	— —	— —	
1870	87,400	30.00	40.00	60.00	125.00	200.00	650.00	1200.00	9000.00	4900.00
1870CC . . .	8,340	700.00	1300.00	2000.00	2500.00	3000.00	7500.00	— —	— —	

QUARTER DOLLARS

DATE	MINTAGE	G-6	VG-10	F-15	VF-30	EF-45	AU-50	UNC-60	UNC-65	PROOF-65
1871	119,160	20.00	21.50	35.00	65.00	100.00	350.00	1000.00	7500.00	4900.00
1871CC	10,890	450.00	575.00	900.00	1200.00	2000.00	5000.00	— —	— —	
1871S	30,900	150.00	375.00	450.00	550.00	900.00	2200.00	3000.00	— —	
1872	182,950	18.50	22.50	30.00	55.00	100.00	350.00	1000.00	7900.00	4900.00
1872CC	22,850	225.00	350.00	500.00	750.00	2000.00	3500.00	— —	— —	
1872S	83,000	150.00	300.00	400.00	500.00	850.00	3000.00	4900.00	— —	
1873 Closed 3 .	212,600	65.00	85.00	175.00	220.00	350.00	700.00	— —	— —	4900.00
1873 Open 3 ..		30.00	40.00	60.00	115.00	200.00	675.00	1000.00	9000.00	
1873CC	4,000	Only a few known				Rare				

IN 1873 ARROWS WERE PLACED ON EACH SIDE OF THE DATE. THEY WERE REMOVED IN 1875.

1873	1,271,000	25.00	30.00	50.00	70.00	190.00	550.00	2000.00	7000.00	8100.00
1873CC	12,462	450.00	575.00	800.00	1500.00	2500.00	5500.00	— —	— —	
1873S	156,000	25.00	35.00	50.00	80.00	225.00	700.00	2000.00	7500.00	
1874	471,900	25.00	30.00	50.00	75.00	200.00	600.00	2000.00	6750.00	8100.00
1874S	392,000	25.00	35.00	50.00	80.00	225.00	700.00	2000.00	7500.00	
1875	4,293,500	17.50	20.00	22.50	40.00	75.00	250.00	900.00	5000.00	8100.00
1875CC	140,000	40.00	50.00	100.00	150.00	300.00	1000.00	1500.00	12000.00	
1875S	680,000	20.00	27.50	40.00	65.00	100.00	375.00	900.00	8000.00	
1876	17,817,150	17.50	20.00	25.00	40.00	75.00	275.00	900.00	4900.00	5000.00
1876CC	4,944,000	17.50	20.00	30.00	50.00	100.00	375.00	900.00	8000.00	
1876S	8,596,000	17.50	20.00	22.50	40.00	75.00	200.00	800.00	4500.00	
1877	10,911,710	17.50	20.00	22.50	40.00	75.00	200.00	800.00	4900.00	4900.00
1877CC	4,192,000	17.50	20.00	28.50	50.00	100.00	350.00	900.00	7500.00	
1877S		17.50	20.00	27.50	45.00	80.00	175.00	800.00	5000.00	
1877S over S ..	8,996,000	50.00	100.00	125.00	150.00	250.00	800.00	1400.00	10000.00	
1878	2,260,800	17.50	20.00	25.00	40.00	75.00	190.00	800.00	4900.00	4900.00
1878CC	996,000	20.00	25.00	30.00	50.00	95.00	275.00	800.00	6750.00	
1878S	140,000	50.00	75.00	100.00	150.00	250.00	800.00	1500.00	7700.00	
1879	14,700	85.00	100.00	125.00	190.00	275.00	800.00	1000.00	7500.00	5500.00
1880	14,955	85.00	100.00	125.00	190.00	275.00	800.00	1000.00	7500.00	5500.00
1881	12,975	100.00	125.00	150.00	200.00	300.00	775.00	1000.00	7500.00	5500.00
1882	16,300	100.00	125.00	150.00	200.00	300.00	775.00	1000.00	7500.00	5500.00
1883	15,439	100.00	125.00	150.00	200.00	300.00	775.00	1000.00	7500.00	5500.00
1884	8,875	125.00	175.00	200.00	275.00	350.00	775.00	1000.00	8000.00	5500.00
1885	14,530	100.00	135.00	150.00	200.00	300.00	800.00	1000.00	7500.00	5500.00
1886	5,886	200.00	250.00	300.00	350.00	525.00	875.00	1100.00	8500.00	5750.00
1887	10,710	100.00	125.00	175.00	225.00	300.00	775.00	1000.00	7500.00	5500.00
1888	10,833	100.00	125.00	175.00	225.00	300.00	775.00	1000.00	7500.00	5500.00
1888S	1,216,000	17.50	20.00	25.00	40.00	75.00	250.00	1000.00	4900.00	
1889	12,711	100.00	125.00	150.00	200.00	300.00	700.00	1000.00	7500.00	5500.00
1890	80,590	45.00	55.00	75.00	100.00	150.00	650.00	1000.00	7500.00	5500.00
1891	3,920,600	17.50	20.00	25.00	40.00	75.00	200.00	1000.00	4900.00	5250.00
1891 0	68,000	150.00	175.00	250.00	450.00	775.00	2000.00	— —	— —	
1891S	2,216,000	19.50	25.00	28.00	45.00	75.00	200.00	1000.00	4900.00	

QUARTER DOLLARS

Barber Quarters
1892-1916
Designer, Charles E. Barber

AG-Obverse: Outline of head visible. Letters evident but worn partly into rim.
Reverse: Most of eagle outline visible.

G-Obverse: Stars complete but worn. Motto readable.
Reverse: Tops of some letters run into rim.

VG-Obverse: At least the equivalent of three letters in "LIBERTY" show.
Reverse: Some letters in "E PLURIBUS UNUM" can be seen.

F-Obverse: "LIBERTY" is complete but weak.
Reverse: Some of the wing feathers show.

VF-Obverse: Complete wreath outline with considerable details in top part.
Reverse: "E PLURIBUS UNUM" is complete. Most of the feathers show.

EF-Obverse: Wear only on high points of forehead and leaves.
Reverse: All details show, with slight wear on wing edges.

THIS IS A LIBERTY HEAD QUARTER BUT HAS
COMMONLY BEEN NAMED BARBER QUARTER
AFTER ITS DESIGNER CHARLES E. BARBER,
CHIEF ENGRAVER OF THE MINT.

DATE	MINTAGE	G-6	VG-10	F-15	VF-30	EF-45	AU-50	UNC-60	UNC-65	PROOF-65
1892	8,237,245	13.00	18.50	21.50	28.00	75.00	135.00	600.00	2500.00	4350.00
1892 0	2,640,000	15.00	20.00	25.00	35.00	90.00	175.00	725.00	4100.00	
1892S	964,079	27.50	35.00	45.00	70.00	125.00	275.00	975.00	6000.00	
1893	5,444,815	13.00	17.50	21.50	28.00	75.00	135.00	650.00	2750.00	4350.00
1893 0	3,396,000	13.50	18.50	25.00	35.00	90.00	190.00	800.00	4100.00	
1893S	1,454,535	15.00	20.00	27.50	45.00	100.00	200.00	850.00	4100.00	
1894	3,432,972	13.50	17.50	21.50	28.00	75.00	140.00	675.00	3500.00	4350.00
1894 0	2,852,000	13.50	18.50	22.50	32.50	85.00	200.00	875.00	4500.00	
1894S	2,648,821	13.75	18.50	22.50	32.50	85.00	200.00	875.00	4500.00	
1895	4,440,880	13.00	19.50	21.50	28.00	75.00	140.00	675.00	3600.00	4350.00
1895 0	2,816,000	13.75	25.00	25.00	35.00	95.00	225.00	900.00	6250.00	
1895S	1,764,681	14.75	22.50	27.50	45.00	90.00	200.00	800.00	4250.00	
1896	3,874,762	13.00	17.50	20.00	30.00	75.00	160.00	675.00	3000.00	4350.00
1896 0	1,484,000	14.75	25.00	55.00	130.00	575.00	2750.00	14000.00		
1896S	188,039	300.00	475.00	750.00	950.00	1575.00	3375.00	6750.00	24000.00	
1897	8,140,731	12.50	13.50	18.75	25.00	55.00	125.00	550.00	2500.00	4350.00
1897 0	1,414,800	11.50	19.50	25.00	65.00	135.00	535.00	2950.00	10000.00	
1897S	542,229	20.00	30.00	40.00	70.00	120.00	350.00	1075.00	5500.00	

QUARTER DOLLARS

DATE	MINTAGE	G-6	VG-10	F-15	VF-30	EF-45	AU-50	UNC-60	UNC-65	PROOF-65
1898	11,100,735	11.50	13.50	18.75	25.00	55.00	125.00	550.00	2500.00	4350.00
1898 0	1,868,000	13.00	17.50	20.00	40.00	90.00	290.00	1275.00	8750.00	
1898S	1,020,592	13.00	18.50	21.50	35.00	85.00	225.00	1075.00	5700.00	
1899	12,624,846	11.75	13.50	18.75	25.00	55.00	125.00	550.00	2500.00	4350.00
1899 0	2,644,000	14.75	19.50	22.50	45.00	100.00	275.00	1125.00	7800.00	
1899S	708,000	18.50	25.00	30.00	60.00	110.00	275.00	975.00	5000.00	
1900	10,016,912	11.75	13.50	18.75	25.00	55.00	125.00	550.00	2500.00	4350.00
1900 0	3,416,000	14.50	18.50	22.50	50.00	110.00	300.00	1300.00	10000.00	
1900S	1,858,585	14.00	17.50	21.50	40.00	80.00	185.00	800.00	4500.00	
1901	8,892,813	11.50	13.50	18.75	25.00	55.00	125.00	550.00	2500.00	4350.00
1901 0	1,612,000	22.50	35.00	50.00	95.00	175.00	480.00	2450.00	16000.00	
1901S	72,644	1100.00	1450.00	1950.00	2375.00	3950.00	6000.00	22000.00	55000.00	
1902	12,197,744	11.50	13.50	18.75	25.00	55.00	125.00	550.00	2500.00	4350.00
1902 0	4,748,000	13.00	18.00	21.50	35.00	85.00	215.00	1200.00	7500.00	
1902S	1,524,612	19.00	22.50	25.00	50.00	85.00	275.00	1000.00	6400.00	
1903	9,670,064	11.50	13.50	18.75	25.00	55.00	125.00	550.00	2500.00	4350.00
1903 0	3,500,000	18.00	25.00	27.50	47.00	75.00	200.00	875.00	5700.00	
1903S	1,036,000	18.00	20.00	25.00	55.00	85.00	325.00	1100.00	6750.00	
1904	9,588,813	11.50	13.50	18.75	25.00	55.00	125.00	550.00	2500.00	4350.00
1904 0	2,456,000	13.50	18.50	25.00	55.00	90.00	500.00	2900.00	12150.00	
1905	4,968,250	11.50	13.50	18.75	25.00	55.00	125.00	550.00	2500.00	4350.00
1905 0	1,230,000	13.50	19.50	22.50	45.00	75.00	200.00	925.00	4500.00	– –
1905S	1,884,000	14.50	20.00	22.50	40.00	70.00	175.00	850.00	4450.00	
1906	3,656,435	11.50	13.50	18.75	25.00	55.00	125.00	550.00	2500.00	4350.00
1906D	3,280,000	12.00	18.75	20.00	30.00	70.00	165.00	750.00	3375.00	
1906 0	2,056,000	12.00	18.75	20.00	35.00	65.00	175.00	850.00	3875.00	
1907	7,192,575	11.50	13.50	18.75	25.00	55.00	125.00	550.00	2500.00	4350.00
1907D	2,484,000	12.00	18.75	20.00	30.00	70.00	185.00	875.00	4125.00	
1907 0	4,560,000	12.00	18.75	20.00	30.00	70.00	165.00	800.00	3875.00	
1907S	1,360,000	12.00	15.50	20.00	35.00	75.00	210.00	1000.00	5625.00	
1908	4,232,545	11.50	13.50	18.75	25.00	55.00	125.00	550.00	2500.00	4350.00
1908D	5,788,000	12.00	15.50	18.75	30.00	75.00	165.00	750.00	3500.00	
1908 0	6,244,000	12.00	15.50	18.75	30.00	70.00	165.00	750.00	3500.00	
1908S	784,000	16.50	20.00	30.00	55.00	85.00	285.00	1200.00	6200.00	
1909	9,268,650	11.50	13.50	18.75	25.00	55.00	125.00	550.00	2500.00	4350.00
1909D	5,114,000	12.00	15.50	18.75	30.00	70.00	165.00	750.00	3750.00	
1909 0	712,000	20.00	30.00	50.00	85.00	180.00	450.00	2000.00	8625.00	
1909S	1,348,000	12.00	15.00	18.50	30.00	75.00	180.00	950.00	5625.00	
1910	2,244,551	11.50	13.50	18.75	25.00	55.00	125.00	550.00	2500.00	4350.00
1910D	1,500,000	12.00	15.50	19.00	30.00	70.00	180.00	950.00	5625.00	
1911	3,720,543	11.50	13.50	18.50	25.00	55.00	125.00	550.00	2500.00	4350.00
1911D	933,600	12.00	15.50	18.75	30.00	70.00	165.00	725.00	3250.00	
1911S	988,000	12.50	15.50	18.75	30.00	75.00	175.00	875.00	4200.00	
1912	4,400,700	11.50	13.50	18.50	25.00	55.00	125.00	550.00	2500.00	4350.00
1912S	708,000	12.00	18.75	20.00	30.00	80.00	190.00	900.00	4500.00	
1913	484,613	20.00	25.00	65.00	140.00	475.00	950.00	4100.00	12500.00	
1913D	1,450,800	12.50	14.50	20.00	35.00	80.00	165.00	675.00	3500.00	
1913S	40,000	400.00	600.00	875.00	1200.00	1750.00	2975.00	6875.00	21250.00	
1914	6,244,610	11.50	13.50	18.75	25.00	55.00	125.00	550.00	2500.00	4350.00
1914D	3,046,000	12.00	14.50	20.00	27.50	65.00	140.00	625.00	3000.00	
1914S	264,000	26.50	35.00	60.00	125.00	300.00	600.00	2100.00	8000.00	
1915	3,480,450	11.50	13.50	18.75	25.00	55.00	125.00	550.00	2500.00	4350.00
1915D	3,694,000	12.00	14.50	20.00	27.50	65.00	170.00	575.00	2850.00	
1915S	704,000	13.50	16.00	25.00	35.00	80.00	175.00	675.00	3500.00	
1916	1,788,000	11.50	13.50	18.75	25.00	55.00	125.00	550.00	2500.00	
1916D	6,540,800	12.00	18.75	20.00	27.50	65.00	170.00	575.00	2800.00	

QUARTER DOLLARS

Standing Liberty
1916-1930
Designer, Hermon A. MacNeil

AG-Obverse: Date must be legible. Complete outline of Liberty shows.
  Reverse: Eagle outline near complete. Stars and lettering worn down into rim.

G-Obverse: Letters in "LIBERTY" and date easily readable.
  Reverse: All letters and stars show.

VG-Obverse: All numerals of date are complete but still show considerable wear.
  Reverse: Letters are free from rim.

F-Obverse: Date is sharp. Some details show in shield and drapery on sides of right leg.
  Reverse: Some of the feathers show in both wings.

VF-Obverse: Leg and thighs are rounded with heavy wear at knees.
  Reverse: Most of the eagle's feathers show in detail.

EF-Obverse: Slight wear on breast and knees only.
  Reverse: All feathers visible with wear on high points only.

NO STARS UNDER EAGLE

DATE	MINTAGE	G-6	VG-10	F-15	VF-30	EF-45	AU-50	UNC-60	UNC-65	PROOF-65
1916	52,000	1450.00	1650.00	2400.00	3150.00	3900.00	4500.00	5250.00	9600.00	17500.00
1917	8,792,000	22.50	23.50	25.00	45.00	80.00	160.00	300.00	1125.00	3000.00
1917D	1,509,200	26.50	27.50	47.50	77.50	170.00	300.00	400.00	1275.00	3750.00
1917S	1,952,000	24.50	26.50	34.00	65.00	150.00	275.00	390.00	1275.00	3750.00

STARS UNDER EAGLE AND OTHER MINOR CHANGES.

QUARTER DOLLARS

DATE	MINTAGE	G-6	VG-10	F-15	VF-30	EF-45	AU-50	UNC-60	UNC-65	PROOF-65
1917	13,880,000	22.00	25.00	28.50	36.00	55.00	100.00	260.00	1500.00	4275.00
1917D	6,224,400	34.00	40.00	65.00	75.00	140.00	190.00	325.00	2000.00	5700.00
1917S	5,552,000	32.00	36.00	40.00	65.00	110.00	165.00	290.00	2000.00	5700.00
1918	14,240,000	26.50	30.00	34.00	45.00	65.00	115.00	275.00	1500.00	4950.00
1918D	7,380,000	37.50	40.00	55.00	70.00	120.00	190.00	375.00	2400.00	8000.00
1918S		26.50	29.50	35.00	40.00	75.00	120.00	265.00	1600.00	7500.00
1918S over 17	11,072,000	1450.00	1600.00	2350.00	3100.00	4750.00	7500.00	12000.00	26950.00	60000.00
1919	11,324,000	42.00	50.00	65.00	80.00	90.00	135.00	290.00	1750.00	4250.00
1919D	1,944,000	70.00	100.00	135.00	190.00	320.00	425.00	800.00	3500.00	16800.00
1919S	1,836,000	67.50	80.00	130.00	165.00	300.00	400.00	750.00	3200.00	14000.00
1920	27,860,000	24.50	27.50	30.00	35.00	55.00	95.00	250.00	1350.00	4250.00
1920D	3,586,400	40.00	47.50	70.00	100.00	150.00	265.00	400.00	2400.00	7000.00
1920S	6,380,000	27.50	30.00	37.50	43.50	70.00	120.00	260.00	1600.00	8500.00
1921	1,916,000	90.00	110.00	180.00	215.00	300.00	450.00	675.00	2450.00	5000.00
1923	9,716,000	26.50	30.00	32.50	37.50	65.00	100.00	300.00	1350.00	5400.00
1923S	1,360,000	115.00	165.00	220.00	275.00	450.00	565.00	850.00	2850.00	5750.00
1924	10,920,000	26.50	30.00	32.50	37.50	65.00	100.00	300.00	1350.00	5175.00
1924D	3,112,000	40.00	47.50	60.00	80.00	125.00	170.00	300.00	1275.00	5400.00
1924S	2,860,000	30.00	32.50	35.00	40.00	65.00	110.00	300.00	1650.00	7475.00
1925	12,280,000	12.75	14.75	20.00	24.50	40.00	80.00	260.00	1075.00	3275.00
1926	11,316,000	13.00	15.00	20.00	24.50	40.00	80.00	260.00	1075.00	3275.00
1926D	1,716,000	18.50	22.50	26.50	30.00	60.00	115.00	300.00	1175.00	7750.00
1926S	2,700,000	17.50	18.50	25.00	30.00	72.50	160.00	365.00	2400.00	13850.00
1927	11,912,000	12.75	14.75	21.50	24.50	40.00	80.00	260.00	1075.00	3175.00
1927D	976,400	18.50	25.00	30.00	45.00	82.50	135.00	300.00	1950.00	4200.00
1927S	396,000	33.00	47.50	140.00	300.00	975.00	1500.00	3250.00	8500.00	19250.00
1928	6,336,000	15.00	16.50	18.75	24.50	42.50	80.00	260.00	1050.00	4125.00
1928D	1,627,600	17.50	18.50	22.50	30.00	62.50	110.00	280.00	1150.00	6250.00
1928S	2,644,000	17.50	19.00	21.50	25.00	45.00	90.00	265.00	1125.00	3750.00
1929	11,140,000	12.75	14.50	18.75	24.50	42.50	80.00	260.00	1050.00	3375.00
1929D	1,358,000	17.50	20.00	24.00	27.50	55.00	100.00	280.00	1150.00	6000.00
1929S	1,764,000	14.75	18.75	21.50	25.00	45.00	85.00	260.00	1050.00	3375.00
1930	5,632,000	14.75	15.75	18.75	24.50	42.50	80.00	260.00	1050.00	3375.00
1930S	1,556,000	14.75	18.75	21.50	25.00	45.00	85.00	260.00	1050.00	3750.00

QUARTER DOLLARS

Washington Head
1932 To Date
Designer, John Flanagan

AG-Obverse: Complete outline of head. Letters run deep into rim.
    Reverse: Almost all eagle and wreath outlines shows. Letters are deep into the rim.

  G-Obverse: All letters are clear, with the tops worn into the rim.
    Reverse: Tops of the letters are worn into the rim.

VG-Obverse: Letters are full and just touching the rim.
    Reverse: Wing tips visible. Letters are full and just touching the rim.

  F-Obverse: The rim will be full. Some hairlines show about the ear.
    Reverse: Feathers will be evident but weak, on both sides of the eagle's breast.

VF-Obverse: Most hair details show. Curls still show considerable wear.
    Reverse: Feathers are distinct on both sides of eagle's breast.

EF-Obverse: All details in curls show but wear on high points.
    Reverse: Wear only on legs and center of breast.

DATE	MINTAGE	G-6	VG-10	F-15	VF-30	EF-45	AU-50	UNC-60	UNC-65	PROOF-65
1932	5,404,000	14.50	15.50	16.50	17.50	22.50	26.50	60.00	285.00	
1932D	436,800	90.00	95.00	115.00	150.00	250.00	450.00	1150.00	4175.00	
1932S	408,000	85.00	90.00	95.00	115.00	150.00	260.00	675.00	2850.00	
1934	31,912,052	9.75	10.50	11.00	11.75	12.50	16.00	25.00	125.00	
1934D	3,527,200	16.50	17.50	18.50	22.00	35.00	62.75	260.00	975.00	
1935	32,484,000	9.50	10.00	10.75	11.75	12.50	15.75	20.00	90.00	
1935D	5,780,000	13.50	16.50	18.50	22.50	30.00	55.00	250.00	975.00	
1935S	5,660,000	13.50	15.50	16.50	17.50	19.75	37.50	200.00	700.00	
1936	41,303,837	9.50	10.00	10.75	11.75	12.50	15.75	20.00	90.00	600.00
1936D	5,374,000	13.50	14.50	18.00	23.50	40.00	135.00	550.00	1650.00	
1936S	3,828,000	16.50	18.75	20.00	21.50	23.50	35.00	135.00	325.00	
1937	19,701,542	10.50	11.50	12.00	12.50	13.50	16.50	20.00	90.00	175.00
1937D	7,189,600	12.75	14.50	16.50	18.50	21.50	320.00	80.00	275.00	
1937S	1,652,000	17.50	18.50	19.75	22.50	30.00	61.50	275.00	750.00	
1938	9,480,045	12.75	13.50	16.50	19.75	24.50	35.00	130.00	350.00	150.00
1938S	2,832,000	17.50	18.50	18.50	19.50	21.50	32.00	115.00	265.00	
1939	33,548,795	9.50	10.00	10.50	11.00	11.50	12.00	12.50	58.50	100.00
1939D	7,092,000	12.75	13.50	14.50	17.50	20.00	28.50	70.00	265.00	
1939S	2,628,000	17.50	18.50	19.50	21.50	22.50	32.50	100.00	300.00	

QUARTER DOLLARS

DATE	MINTAGE	G-6	VG-10	F-15	VF-30	EF-45	AU-50	UNC-60	UNC-65	PROOF-65
1940	35,715,246	9.50	10.00	10.50	11.00	11.50	12.00	12.50	53.50	90.00
1940D	2,797,600	17.00	18.50	19.50	21.50	22.50	36.50	125.00	335.00	
1940S	8,244,000	12.75	13.50	14.50	15.50	16.50	17.50	20.00	90.00	
1941	79,047,287	8.95	9.25	10.00	10.50	11.00	11.50	12.50	20.00	85.00
1941D	16,714,800	11.50	12.50	13.50	14.00	14.75	16.50	18.50	57.50	
1941S	16,080,000	11.75	12.75	13.50	14.00	14.50	16.50	22.50	62.50	
1942	102,117,123	8.75	9.25	10.00	10.50	11.00	12.00	12.75	20.00	85.00
1942D	17,487,200	11.50	12.50	13.00	13.50	14.00	15.00	16.50	35.00	
1942S	19,384,000	10.50	11.50	12.00	12.50	15.50	17.50	25.00	175.00	
1943	99,700,000	8.95	9.25	9.75	10.50	11.00	11.50	12.50	20.00	
1943D	16,095,600	11.50	12.50	12.50	13.00	13.50	14.00	14.75	42.50	
1943S	21,700,000	11.00	11.50	12.00	12.50	15.50	20.00	27.50	150.00	
1944	104,956,000		8.75	9.25	10.00	10.50	11.00	11.50	17.50	
1944D	14,600,000		11.75	12.50	13.00	13.50	14.50	16.50	40.00	
1944S	12,560,000		12.00	13.00	14.00	15.00	16.50	20.00	47.50	
1945	74,372,000		9.25	10.50	11.00	11.50	12.00	12.50	28.50	
1945D	12,341,600		12.00	13.00	14.00	14.50	15.00	16.00	27.50	
1945S	17,004,001		11.50	12.00	13.50	14.50	15.50	16.50	30.00	
1946	53,436,000			9.50	10.00	10.50	11.00	11.50	18.50	
1946D	9,072,800			12.75	13.25	14.00	14.50	15.00	18.50	
1946S	4,204,000			14.50	15.00	15.50	16.00	16.50	19.00	
1947	22,556,000			11.00	12.00	12.50	13.00	13.50	20.00	
1947D	15,338,400			11.50	12.00	12.50	13.00	14.50	25.00	
1947S	5,532,000			13.50	14.00	14.50	15.00	15.50	19.00	
1948	35,196,000			9.50	10.00	10.50	11.00	11.50	18.50	
1948D	16,766,800			11.50	12.00	12.50	13.00	13.50	18.50	
1948S	15,960,000			11.50	12.50	13.00	13.75	14.50	25.00	
1949	9,312,000			12.00	13.00	14.00	15.00	17.50	77.50	
1949D	10,068,400			12.00	13.00	14.00	14.50	15.00	31.50	
1950	24,971,512			11.00	11.50	12.00	12.50	13.00	17.50	80.00
1950D	21,075,600			11.00	11.50	12.00	12.50	13.50	18.50	
1950S	10,284,004			11.50	12.50	13.50	15.00	16.50	35.00	
1951	43,505,602			9.50	10.00	10.50	11.00	11.50	17.50	80.00
1951D	35,354,800			9.75	10.50	11.00	11.50	12.00	18.00	
1951S	9,048,000				12.50	13.50	14.50	15.00	28.50	
1952	38,862,073				9.75	10.50	11.00	11.50	17.50	50.00
1952D	49,795,200				9.50	10.00	10.50	11.00	18.00	
1952S	13,707,800				12.00	12.50	13.00	13.50	22.50	
1953	18,664,920				11.50	12.00	12.50	13.00	16.00	35.00
1953D	56,112,400				9.50	10.00	10.50	11.00	14.50	
1953S	14,016,000				11.75	12.50	13.00	13.50	17.50	
1954	54,645,503				9.50	10.00	10.50	11.00	13.00	20.00
1954D	46,305,500					9.75	10.00	10.25	13.50	
1954S	11,834,722					11.00	11.25	11.50	12.75	
1955	18,558,381					10.75	11.00	11.25	12.50	17.00
1955D	3,182,400					16.50	16.75	17.00	18.00	
1956	44,813,384					9.50	9.75	10.00	12.50	15.00
1956D	32,334,500					9.75	10.00	10.25	12.50	
1957	47,779,952					9.50	9.75	10.00	11.75	12.00
1957D	77,924,160					9.00	9.25	9.50	11.75	
1958	7,235,652							12.75	13.50	13.50
1958D	78,124,900							9.00	11.50	
1959	25,533,291							11.00	12.50	12.50
1959D	62,054,232							9.00	11.50	

QUARTER DOLLARS

DATE	MINTAGE	G-6	VG-10	F-15	VF-30	EF-45	AU-50	UNC-60	UNC-65	PROOF-65
1960	30,855,602							9.50	11.00	12.50
1960D	63,000,324							9.00	11.00	
1961	40,064,244							9.25	11.00	12.50
1961D	83,656,928							8.75	11.00	
1962	39,374,019							9.50	11.00	12.50
1962D	127,554,756							8.75	11.00	
1963	77,391,645							8.95	11.00	12.50
1963D	135,288,184							8.75	11.00	
1964	564,341,347							8.75	11.00	12.50
1964D	704,135,528							8.75	11.00	

IN 1965 THE COMPOSITION OF THE QUARTER CHANGED TO A CLAD SANDWICH TYPE COIN. THE OUTER LAYERS ARE COPPER NICKEL WITH A CORE OF PURE COPPER.

MINT MARK
HAS BEEN PLACED
ON THE OBVERSE

1965	1,819,717,540							1.25		
1966	821,101,500							1.25		
1967	1,524,031,848							1.25		
1968	220,731,500							1.15		
1968D	101,534,000							1.35		
1968S	3,041,506	Proof only								2.25
1969	176,212,000							1.25		
1969D	114,372,000							1.80		
1969S	2,934,631	Proof only								2.00
1970	136,420,000							1.10		
1970D	417,341,364							1.15		
1970S	2,632,810	Proof only								2.50
1971	109,284,000							1.10		
1971D	258,634,428							.95		
1971S	3,220,733	Proof only								1.85
1972	215,048,000							1.10		
1972D	311,067,732							1.10		
1972S	3,260,996	Proof only								1.85
1973	346,924,000							1.10		
1973D	232,977,400							1.10		
1973S	2,760,399	Proof only								2.65
1974	801,456,000							.95		
1974D	353,160,300							.95		
1974S	2,612,568	Proof only								2.95

QUARTER DOLLARS

**BICENTENNIAL QUARTERS DATED
1776-1976. COINED IN 1975 AND 1976.**

DATE	MINTAGE		UNC-65	PROOF-65
1976	809,784,016		.95	
1976D	860,118,839		.95	
1976S	7,059,099	Proof only		2.25

**1976 SILVER CLAD COINS. OUTER LAYERS 80 PERCENT SILVER 20 PERCENT COPPER. INNER CORE 21 PER-
CENT SILVER 79 PERCENT COPPER.**

DATE	MINTAGE		UNC-65	PROOF-65
1976S	Silver Clad	MINTAGE FIGURES NOT RELEASED	3.25	7.00

Return to Regular Washington Issue

DATE	MINTAGE		UNC-65	PROOF-65
1977	468,556,000		.75	
1977D	256,524,978		.75	
1977S	3,251,152	Proof only		2.25
1978	521,452,000		.75	
1978D	287,373,152		.75	
1978S	3,127,781	Proof only		2.75
1979	515,708,000		.50	
1979D	489,789,780		.50	
1979S	3,677,175	Proof only		2.95
1980P	635,832,000		.50	
1980D	518,327,487		.50	
1980S	2,144,231	Proof only		3.25
1981P			.50	
1981D			.50	
1981S		Proof only		3.25

Commemorative Quarter Dollar

Isabella
1893
Designer, Charles E. Barber

Authorized April 2, 1893 for the Columbian Exposition. Weight 96.45 grains, .900 fine.

**QUEEN ISABELLA
OF SPAIN**

**WOMEN'S
INDUSTRY**

DATE	ISSUED QUANTITY		EF-45	AU-50	UNC-60	UNC-65
1893	24,214		275.00	550.00	775.00	2000.00

HALF DOLLARS
1794 to Date

Authorized on April 2, 1792. From 1794 through 1837 they were coined at the Philadelphia Mint. The Philadelphia Mint was assisted in 1838 by the New Orleans Mint, in 1855 by the San Francisco Mint, in 1870 by the Carson City Mint, and in 1906 by the Denver Mint.

All Half Dollars from 1794 through 1964 were made of approximately 90 percent silver, 10 percent copper. In 1965 the composition changed to a clad type coin of nickel and copper.

Flowing Hair
1794-1795
Designer, Robert Scot

AG-Obverse: Head outline is faint. Few stars visible.
    Reverse: Some letters visible. Eagle outline faint.

 G-Obverse: Head well outlined. All stars show but well worn.
    Reverse: Complete eagle outline but worn smooth.

VG-Obverse: Some hair details show at the back of the neck.
    Reverse: Some feathers visible on tail and left wing.

 F-Obverse: Some details show on face and hair.
    Reverse: Some feathers visible on both wings.

VF-Obverse: Most of hair details show.
    Reverse: Leaves in wreath are distinct.

EF-Obverse: All the hair details show with little wear on top of the head.
    Reverse: Most of the feathers show. Wreath is well defined.

DATE	MINTAGE	AG-3	G-6	VG-10	F-15	VF-30	EF-45	AU-50	UNC-60
1794	23,464	825.00	1375.00	1525.00	2400.00	3800.00	6500.00	9250.00	— —
1795		750.00	1275.00	1450.00	2300.00	3500.00	6350.00	9000.00	24000.00
1795 3 leaves	299,680								
under wings		875.00	1450.00	1650.00	2500.00	4000.00	5800.00	10250.00	— —

HALF DOLLARS

Draped Bust, Small Eagle
1796-1839
Designer, Robert Scot

AG-Obverse: Outline of head and few stars show.
    Reverse: Parts of eagle and some letters visible.

 G-Obverse: "LIBERTY" clear. Tops of stars run into rim.
    Reverse: Eagle outline complete, but no details.

VG-Obverse: All stars and lettering clear and separated from rim.
    Reverse: Part of "E PLURIBUS UNUM" shows.

 F-Obverse: Some hair details show. Ear lobe clear.
    Reverse: Most of "E PLURIBUS UNUM" shows. Some feathers show.

VF-Obverse: Most details in hair and face show clearly.
    Reverse: "E PLURIBUS UNUM" is complete. Most feathers show.

 EF-Obverse: All details show clearly. Slight wear on high hairlines at forehead.
    Reverse: All feathers visible. Edges of wings show slight wear.

DATE	MINTAGE	AG-3	G-6	VG-10	F-15	VF-30	EF-45	AU-50	UNC-60
1796									
15 Stars ..	934	8250.00	13750.00	16500.00	23500.00	40000.00	48500.00	68000.00	— —
1796									
16 Stars ..		8250.00	13800.00	16500.00	23500.00	40000.00	48500.00	66000.00	— —
1797	2,984	8250.00	13800.00	16500.00	23500.00	40000.00	48500.00	66000.00	— —

HALF DOLLARS

Draped Bust, Large Eagle
1801-1807
Designer, Robert Scot

DATE	MINTAGE	AG-3	G-6	VG-10	F-15	VF-30	EF-45	AU-50	UNC-60
1801	30,289	180.00	300.00	475.00	800.00	1075.00	1850.00	3100.00	11000.00
1802	29,820	150.00	250.00	375.00	800.00	1075.00	1350.00	2600.00	10500.00
1803 Small 3 . .	188,234	130.00	225.00	325.00	400.00	550.00	1175.00	2300.00	10000.00
1803 Large 3 . .		100.00	165.00	230.00	275.00	500.00	1050.00	1775.00	10000.00
1805	211,722	65.00	135.00	185.00	450.00	900.00	1400.00	10000.00	
1805 over 4		110.00	180.00	235.00	285.00	525.00	1200.00	2100.00	10000.00
1806	839,576	65.00	135.00	185.00	450.00	900.00	1400.00	10000.00	
1806 over 5 . . .		80.00	135.00	165.00	265.00	475.00	1025.00	1775.00	10000.00
1806 over inverted 6		95.00	160.00	225.00	275.00	500.00	1175.00	1875.00	9750.00
1807	301,076	65.00	110.00	135.00	185.00	450.00	900.00	1425.00	9750.00

HALF DOLLARS

Liberty Cap
1807-1839
Designer, John Reich

AG-Obverse: Outline of head and few stars show.
Reverse: Some letters show. Outline of eagle visible.

G-Obverse: Some of the letters in "LIBERTY" are complete.
Reverse: All letters around rim are readable but weak.

VG-Obverse: "LIBERTY" is complete. Some of the hair details show.
Reverse: Feathers evident in eagle's left wing.

F-Obverse: Most of hair details show.
Reverse: Some feathers show in both wings.

VF-Obverse: All hair, cap and drapery details show, with wear on the hair waves and curls and the top of the cap.
Reverse: Most of the feathers will show.

EF-Obverse: Curls well rounded. Slight wear on high points only.
Reverse: All feathers clear. Wear on claws and tops of wings.

LETTERED EDGE

DATE	MINTAGE	AG-3	G-6	VG-10	F-15	VF-30	EF-45	AU-50	UNC-60
1807 Sm Stars ..		27.50	45.00	50.00	75.00	125.00	225.00	700.00	1350.00
1807 Lg Stars ...	750,500	25.00	40.00	45.00	60.00	100.00	170.00	500.00	1175.00
1807 50 over 20 ..		25.00	40.00	45.00	60.00	95.00	165.00	500.00	1175.00
1808	1,368,600	20.00	35.00	40.00	50.00	65.00	120.00	375.00	1075.00
1808 over 7		25.00	40.00	45.00	55.00	65.00	120.00	375.00	1125.00
1809	1,405,810	25.00	40.00	45.00	55.00	75.00	120.00	375.00	1075.00
1810	1,276,276	20.00	35.00	40.00	50.00	60.00	90.00	275.00	1075.00
1811 Small 8		20.00	35.00	40.00	50.00	60.00	90.00	275.00	1075.00
1811 Large 8	1,203,644	20.00	35.00	40.00	50.00	60.00	90.00	275.00	1075.00
1811 Period between 18 and 11		25.00	40.00	50.00	75.00	110.00	175.00	475.00	1300.00
1812		20.00	35.00	40.00	50.00	55.00	80.00	250.00	1075.00
1812 over 11 Small 8	1,628,059	20.00	35.00	55.00	65.00	80.00	110.00	325.00	1100.00
1812 over 11 Large 8		20.00	35.00	55.00	65.00	80.00	110.00	325.00	1100.00

HALF DOLLARS

DATE	MINTAGE	AG-3	G-6	VG-10	F-15	VF-30	EF-45	AU-50	UNC-60
1813		20.00	35.00	40.00	50.00	60.00	80.00	250.00	1075.00
1813 50¢ over UNI	1,241,903	25.00	40.00	45.00	80.00	120.00	225.00	700.00	— —
1814		20.00	35.00	40.00	50.00	65.00	135.00	300.00	1075.00
1814 over 13 . .	1,039,075	25.00	40.00	50.00	65.00	100.00	150.00	425.00	1125.00
1815 over 12 . .	47,150	180.00	300.00	375.00	500.00	600.00	1200.00	2750.00	3250.00
1817		20.00	35.00	40.00	45.00	60.00	110.00	275.00	1050.00
1817 over 13 . .	1,215,567	25.00	40.00	50.00	65.00	90.00	135.00	425.00	1300.00
1818		20.00	35.00	40.00	45.00	60.00	125.00	275.00	1075.00
1818 over 7 Small 8	1,960,322	20.00	35.00	40.00	45.00	60.00	125.00	275.00	1125.00
1818 over 7 Large 8		20.00	35.00	40.00	45.00	60.00	125.00	275.00	1125.00
1819		20.00	35.00	40.00	45.00	60.00	125.00	275.00	1075.00
1819 over 18 Small 9	2,208,000	20.00	35.00	40.00	45.00	60.00	125.00	275.00	1125.00
1819 over 18 Large 9		20.00	35.00	40.00	45.00	60.00	110.00	275.00	1125.00
1820		20.00	35.00	45.00	55.00	70.00	125.00	325.00	1200.00
1820 over 19 . .	751,122	20.00	35.00	45.00	55.00	70.00	125.00	325.00	1150.00
1821	1,305,797	20.00	35.00	40.00	50.00	65.00	115.00	275.00	1050.00
1822		20.00	35.00	40.00	45.00	60.00	115.00	275.00	1075.00
1822 over 21 . .	1,559,573	32.50	55.00	70.00	90.00	135.00	200.00	600.00	1175.00
1823	1,694,200	20.00	35.00	40.00	45.00	60.00	110.00	275.00	1100.00
1824	3,504,954	17.50	30.00	35.00	45.00	60.00	115.00	275.00	1075.00
1824 over 21 . .		17.50	30.00	35.00	45.00	60.00	115.00	275.00	1175.00
1824 over 4 . . .		17.50	30.00	35.00	45.00	60.00	115.00	275.00	1175.00
1825	2,943,166	17.50	30.00	35.00	40.00	60.00	110.00	275.00	1000.00
1826	4,004,180	17.50	30.00	35.00	40.00	55.00	110.00	275.00	1000.00
1827		17.50	30.00	35.00	40.00	55.00	110.00	275.00	1100.00
1827 over 26 . .	5,493,400	20.00	35.00	40.00	50.00	65.00	115.00	275.00	1125.00
1828		17.50	30.00	35.00	40.00	55.00	110.00	230.00	1100.00
1828 Small 8 . .	3,075,200	17.50	30.00	35.00	40.00	55.00	110.00	230.00	1175.00
1828 Large 8 . .		17.50	30.00	35.00	40.00	55.00	100.00	225.00	1000.00
1829		17.50	30.00	35.00	40.00	55.00	100.00	225.00	1000.00
1829 over 27 . .	3,712,156	20.00	35.00	40.00	45.00	60.00	110.00	250.00	1100.00
1830 Small O . .	4,764,800	17.50	30.00	35.00	40.00	55.00	100.00	225.00	1000.00
1830 Large O . .		17.50	30.00	35.00	40.00	55.00	100.00	225.00	1000.00
1831	5,873,660	17.50	30.00	35.00	40.00	55.00	100.00	225.00	1000.00
1832 Small Letters	4,797,000	17.50	30.00	35.00	40.00	55.00	100.00	225.00	1000.00
1832 Large Letters		17.50	30.00	35.00	40.00	55.00	100.00	225.00	1000.00
1833	5,206,000	17.50	30.00	35.00	40.00	55.00	100.00	225.00	1000.00
1834	6,412,004	17.50	30.00	35.00	40.00	55.00	100.00	225.00	1000.00
1835	5,352,006	17.50	30.00	35.00	40.00	55.00	100.00	225.00	1000.00
1836		17.50	30.00	35.00	40.00	55.00	100.00	225.00	1000.00
1836 over 00 . .	6,545,000	32.50	55.00	75.00	85.00	125.00	200.00	525.00	— —

HALF DOLLARS

IN 1836 THE MOTTO ABOVE THE EAGLE
WAS REMOVED AND THE WORD CENTS WAS
PLACED UNDER THE EAGLE.

DATE	MINTAGE	G-6	VG-10	F-15	VF-30	EF-45	AU-50	UNC-60	UNC-65
1836	1,200	300.00	425.00	500.00	1000.00	1750.00	3500.00	4750.00	— —
1837	3,629,820	50.00	60.00	75.00	100.00	235.00	575.00	2250.00	— —

IN 1838 THE 50 CENTS WAS REMOVED AND
HALF DOL. WAS PUT ON THE REVERSE UNDER
THE EAGLE.
THE MINT MARK FOR 1838 0 AND 1839 0 IS LOCATED
ON THE OBVERSE ABOVE THE DATE

DATE	MINTAGE	G-6	VG-10	F-15	VF-30	EF-45	AU-50	UNC-60	UNC-65
1838	3,546,000	50.00	55.00	75.00	100.00	250.00	600.00	2400.00	— —
1838 0	20			RARE					
1939	1,362,160	50.00	55.00	75.00	100.00	250.00	600.00	2350.00	— —
1839 0	162,976	85.00	115.00	175.00	350.00	450.00	1200.00	3600.00	— —

HALF DOLLARS

Seated Liberty
1839-1891
Designer, Christian Gobrecht

AG-Obverse: Rim worn down into stars.
    Reverse: At least half of letters and eagle show.

G-Obverse: All stars show but tops touching rim.
    Reverse: All letters show some touching rim. Eagle outline complete.

VG-Obverse: At least three complete letters of "LIBERTY" in shield visible.
    Reverse: Letters clear and separated from rim.

F-Obverse: "LIBERTY" in shield complete but weak.
    Reverse: Some of the eagle's feathers show in the wings.

VF-Obverse: "LIBERTY" sharp. Some details in gown show.
    Reverse: Most of the feathers in both wings show.

EF-Obverse: Most details show. Wear on knees and breast.
    Reverse: All details show. Wear on the high points only.

**MINT MARKS
ON REVERSE**

DATE	MINTAGE	G-6	VG-10	F-15	VF-30	EF-45	AU-50	UNC-60	UNC-65
1839 No Drapery		50.00	60.00	75.00	165.00	500.00	1700.00	11000.00	45000.00
1839 Drapery From . Elbow	1,972,400	27.50	30.00	38.50	75.00	150.00	275.00	900.00	6750.00
1840 Small Letters	1,435,008	27.50	30.00	38.50	75.00	140.00	300.00	900.00	7000.00
1840 Large Letters		45.00	70.00	100.00	200.00	325.00	900.00	1650.00	18500.00
1840 0	855,100	25.00	32.50	39.50	75.00	150.00	275.00	950.00	6750.00
1841	310,000	40.00	55.00	95.00	140.00	225.00	400.00	1000.00	8750.00
1841 0	401,000	30.00	35.00	45.00	95.00	150.00	300.00	1000.00	7000.00
1842 Sm Date .	2,012,764	27.50	30.00	55.00	110.00	175.00	325.00	950.00	7500.00
1842 Lg Date ..		27.50	30.00	38.50	75.00	140.00	300.00	950.00	6750.00
1842 0 Sm. Date	957,000	250.00	300.00	450.00	900.00	2100.00	3500.00	— —	— —
1842 0 Lg. Date		27.50	30.00	38.50	75.00	150.00	300.00	900.00	6750.00
1843	3,844,000	27.50	30.00	38.50	75.00	140.00	200.00	900.00	6750.00
1843 0	2,268,000	27.50	30.00	38.50	75.00	150.00	275.00	950.00	6750.00

HALF DOLLARS

DATE	MINTAGE	G-6	VG-10	F-15	VF-30	EF-45	AU-50	UNC-60	UNC-65
1844	1,766,000	27.50	30.00	38.50	75.00	140.00	200.00	900.00	6250.00
1844 0	2,005,000	27.50	30.00	38.50	75.00	150.00	275.00	950.00	6750.00
1845	580,000	45.00	65.00	100.00	160.00	250.00	400.00	1050.00	8500.00
1845 0		27.50	30.00	38.50	95.00	175.00	275.00	1250.00	6750.00
1845 0 No	2,094,000								
Drapery		40.00	60.00	90.00	110.00	175.00	650.00	975.00	12500.00
1846 Sm Date .		27.50	30.00	38.50	75.00	140.00	200.00	900.00	6250.00
1846 Tall Date	2,210,000	27.50	30.00	38.50	75.00	140.00	200.00	900.00	6250.00
1846 over									
side 6		50.00	60.00	100.00	140.00	200.00	600.00	975.00	12500.00
1846 0 Sm.									
Date	2,304,000	27.50	30.00	38.50	70.00	140.00	200.00	900.00	6250.00
1846 0 Tall									
Date		90.00	110.00	160.00	280.00	400.00	275.00	1350.00	6750.00
1847	1,156,000	27.50	30.00	38.50	70.00	140.00	200.00	900.00	6250.00
1847 0	2,584,000	27.50	30.00	38.50	70.00	140.00	200.00	900.00	6250.00
1848	580,000	50.00	65.00	90.00	150.00	250.00	400.00	1000.00	8750.00
1848 0	3,180,000	27.50	30.00	38.50	70.00	140.00	250.00	900.00	6750.00
1849	1,252,000	27.50	30.00	38.50	70.00	140.00	275.00	900.00	7000.00
1849 0	2,310,000	27.50	30.00	38.50	70.00	140.00	250.00	900.00	6750.00
1850	227,000	55.00	85.00	150.00	225.00	350.00	500.00	900.00	10000.00
1850 0	2,456,000	27.50	30.00	38.50	70.00	150.00	400.00	900.00	8750.00
1851	200,750	55.00	85.00	120.00	235.00	360.00	600.00	1150.00	10000.00
1851 0	402,000	35.00	55.00	75.00	95.00	175.00	475.00	950.00	10000.00
1852	77,130	110.00	210.00	320.00	450.00	725.00	1200.00	1550.00	— —
1852 0	144,000	55.00	90.00	160.00	235.00	375.00	750.00	950.00	— —
1853 0						Rare			

ARROWS PLACED ON BOTH SIDES OF DATE
AND RAYS AROUND EAGLE. THE RAYS WERE
REMOVED IN 1854.

DATE	MINTAGE	G-6	VG-10	F-15	VF-30	EF-45	AU-50	UNC-60	UNC-65
1853	3,532,000	32.50	37.50	45.00	95.00	300.00	950.00	5000.00	— —
1853 0	1,328,000	32.50	37.50	45.00	95.00	300.00	1000.00	5000.00	— —
1854	2,982,000	27.50	35.00	40.00	75.00	125.00	375.00	1450.00	8750.00
1854 0	5,240,000	27.50	35.00	40.00	75.00	125.00	375.00	1450.00	8750.00
1855	759,500	32.50	37.50	45.00	75.00	125.00	375.00	1600.00	12000.00
1855 over 54 ..		75.00	125.00	175.00	350.00	700.00	1750.00	2450.00	17500.00
1855 0	3,688,000	27.50	35.00	40.00	75.00	125.00	375.00	1450.00	8500.00
1855S	129,950	150.00	200.00	350.00	600.00	1100.00	1500.00	3000.00	12500.00

HALF DOLLARS

**IN 1856 THE ARROWS ON BOTH SIDES
OF THE DATE WERE REMOVED.**

DATE	MINTAGE	G-6	VG-10	F-15	VF-30	EF-45	AU-50	UNC-60	UNC-65	PROOF-65
1856	938,000	27.50	30.00	35.00	65.00	95.00	175.00	950.00	6200.00	
1856 0	2,658,000	27.50	30.00	35.00	65.00	95.00	175.00	950.00	6200.00	
1856S	211,000	35.00	50.00	65.00	170.00	300.00	450.00	1250.00	9500.00	
1857	1,988,000	27.50	30.00	35.00	65.00	95.00	175.00	900.00	6200.00	9000.00
1857 0	818,000	27.50	30.00	37.50	70.00	100.00	225.00	1000.00	6750.00	
1857S	158,000	40.00	60.00	80.00	200.00	350.00	450.00	1250.00	9500.00	
1858	4,226,000	27.50	30.00	35.00	65.00	95.00	175.00	900.00	6200.00	8000.00
1858 0	7,294,000	27.50	30.00	35.00	65.00	95.00	175.00	900.00	6200.00	
1858S	476,000	30.00	40.00	50.00	125.00	180.00	325.00	1050.00	7500.00	
1859	748,000	27.50	35.00	45.00	75.00	110.00	300.00	900.00	7250.00	8000.00
1859 0	2,834,000	27.50	30.00	35.00	65.00	95.00	175.00	925.00	6200.00	
1859S	566,000	30.00	40.00	50.00	125.00	150.00	425.00	1000.00	8750.00	
1860	303,700	40.00	55.00	75.00	100.00	215.00	300.00	950.00	7250.00	8000.00
1860 0	1,290,000	27.50	30.00	37.50	65.00	95.00	175.00	925.00	6200.00	
1860S	472,000	27.50	35.00	45.00	70.00	125.00	225.00	950.00	6750.00	8000.00
1861 .	2,888,400	27.50	32.50	37.50	65.00	100.00	175.00	900.00	6200.00	8000.00
1861 0	2,532,633	27.50	32.50	37.50	65.00	100.00	175.00	900.00	6200.00	
1861S	939,500	30.00	35.00	40.00	65.00	100.00	175.00	925.00	6200.00	
1862	253,550	40.00	55.00	80.00	110.00	240.00	350.00	1000.00	7750.00	8000.00
1862S	1,352,000	27.50	30.00	35.00	65.00	95.00	175.00	900.00	6200.00	
1863	503,660	32.50	40.00	55.00	90.00	185.00	425.00	1000.00	8750.00	8000.00
1863S	916,000	27.50	32.50	40.00	70.00	110.00	200.00	900.00	6200.00	
1864	379,570	32.50	40.00	55.00	90.00	185.00	425.00	1000.00	8750.00	8000.00
1864S	658,000	30.00	37.50	40.00	75.00	120.00	225.00	900.00	6200.00	
1865	511,900	37.50	42.50	60.00	115.00	200.00	425.00	1000.00	8750.00	6000.00
1865S	675,000	32.50	37.50	47.50	80.00	115.00	200.00	850.00	6200.00	
1866					Rare					

**IN 1866 THE MOTTO "IN GOD WE TRUST"
WAS ADDED ON THE REVERSE ABOVE THE EAGLE.**

DATE	MINTAGE	G-6	VG-10	F-15	VF-30	EF-45	AU-50	UNC-60	UNC-65	PROOF-65
1866 . . .	745,625	30.00	40.00	60.00	90.00	175.00	275.00	1000.00	8750.00	6000.00
1866S	1,054,000	27.50	32.50	35.00	65.00	100.00	175.00	900.00	6200.00	
1867	449,925	35.00	50.00	80.00	125.00	175.00	350.00	1200.00	– –	6000.00
1867S	1,196,000	25.00	30.00	35.00	65.00	95.00	165.00	900.00	6200.00	
1868	418,200	45.00	65.00	90.00	120.00	250.00	400.00	1100.00	– –	6000.00
1868S	1,160,000	25.00	30.00	35.00	60.00	95.00	175.00	900.00	6200.00	

HALF DOLLARS

DATE	MINTAGE	G-6	VG-10	F-15	VF-30	EF-45	AU-50	UNC-60	UNC-65	PROOF-65
1869	795,900	27.50	30.00	35.00	65.00	100.00	200.00	900.00	6500.00	6000.00
1869S	656,000	32.50	40.00	50.00	75.00	120.00	225.00	900.00	6750.00	
1870	634,900	30.00	40.00	50.00	75.00	120.00	225.00	900.00	6750.00	6000.00
1870CC . . .	54,617	225.00	300.00	800.00	1000.00	1700.00	5500.00	— —	— —	
1870S	1,004,000	35.00	40.00	50.00	80.00	125.00	225.00	950.00	6750.00	
1871	1,204,560	25.00	30.00	35.00	60.00	95.00	150.00	900.00	6200.00	6000.00
1871CC . . .	153,950	60.00	85.00	175.00	275.00	525.00	1850.00	3750.00	— —	
1871S	2,178,000	25.00	27.50	35.00	60.00	90.00	140.00	900.00	6200.00	
1872	881,550	25.00	30.00	37.50	65.00	95.00	150.00	900.00	6200.00	6000.00
1872CC . . .	257,000	40.00	65.00	100.00	200.00	300.00	1200.00	1650.00	— —	
1872S	580,000	32.50	40.00	50.00	115.00	165.00	220.00	900.00	6200.00	
1873 Close/3	801,800	35.00	45.00	70.00	130.00	240.00	350.00	900.00	6250.00	6250.00
1873 Open/3		110.00	210.00	525.00	1500.00	3000.00	— —	— —	— —	
1873CC . . .	122,500	50.00	75.00	130.00	225.00	400.00	1250.00	— —	— —	

IN 1873 ARROWS WERE ADDED TO BOTH
SIDES OF THE DATE. THEY WERE REMOVED
IN 1875.

DATE	MINTAGE	G-6	VG-10	F-15	VF-30	EF-45	AU-50	UNC-60	UNC-65	PROOF-65
1873	1,815,700	35.00	40.00	47.50	95.00	275.00	525.00	2100.00	8500.00	10000.00
1873CC . . .	214,560	50.00	80.00	145.00	190.00	350.00	750.00	2300.00	11500.00	
1873S	228,000	35.00	45.00	65.00	100.00	290.00	700.00	2100.00	10500.00	
1874	2,360,300	37.50	42.50	50.00	100.00	275.00	525.00	2250.00	8500.00	10000.00
1874CC . . .	59,000	135.00	210.00	350.00	500.00	750.00	1250.00	2500.00	— —	
1874S	394,000	37.50	40.00	60.00	100.00	290.00	600.00	2100.00	9000.00	
1875	6,027,500	28.50	32.50	37.50	65.00	95.00	140.00	900.00	6000.00	
1875CC . . .	1,008,000	30.00	35.00	50.00	75.00	110.00	150.00	900.00	6000.00	
1875S	3,200,000	28.50	32.50	37.50	55.00	95.00	150.00	900.00	6000.00	
1876	8,419,150	28.50	30.00	35.00	55.00	95.00	150.00	900.00	6000.00	6250.00
1876CC . . .	1,956,000	30.00	35.00	40.00	60.00	110.00	160.00	900.00	8500.00	
1876S	4,528,000	28.50	30.00	35.00	55.00	95.00	150.00	900.00	6000.00	
1877	8,304,510	28.50	30.00	35.00	55.00	95.00	140.00	900.00	6000.00	6250.00
1877CC . . .	1,420,000	28.50	30.00	35.00	60.00	110.00	265.00	900.00	6700.00	
1877S	5,356,000	28.50	30.00	35.00	55.00	95.00	150.00	900.00	6000.00	
1878	1,378,400	28.50	30.00	35.00	55.00	95.00	140.00	900.00	6000.00	
1878CC . . .	62,000	200.00	300.00	400.00	525.00	900.00	2500.00	3000.00	— —	
1878S	12,000	2500.00	3500.00	4250.00	5500.00	7000.00	17500.00	— —	— —	
1879	5,900	165.00	200.00	250.00	300.00	400.00	750.00	1100.00	9500.00	6250.00
1880	9,755	110.00	130.00	185.00	250.00	350.00	700.00	1150.00	9000.00	6250.00
1881	10,975	110.00	130.00	185.00	235.00	325.00	700.00	1150.00	9000.00	6250.00
1882	5,500	165.00	200.00	250.00	310.00	425.00	775.00	1150.00	9500.00	6250.00
1883	9,039	110.00	130.00	190.00	250.00	350.00	700.00	1150.00	9000.00	6250.00
1884	5,275	165.00	200.00	250.00	310.00	425.00	775.00	1175.00	9500.00	6250.00
1885	6,130	110.00	165.00	230.00	280.00	375.00	700.00	1150.00	9000.00	6250.00
1886	5,886	165.00	200.00	265.00	310.00	425.00	700.00	1150.00	9000.00	6250.00
1887	5,710	165.00	200.00	265.00	310.00	425.00	700.00	1150.00	9000.00	6250.00
1888	12,833	100.00	130.00	165.00	215.00	310.00	700.00	1150.00	9000.00	6250.00
1889	12,711	100.00	130.00	165.00	210.00	325.00	700.00	1100.00	9000.00	6250.00
1890	12,590	100.00	130.00	165.00	210.00	325.00	700.00	1100.00	9000.00	6250.00
1891	200,600	30.00	35.00	50.00	65.00	125.00	250.00	900.00	8500.00	6250.00

HALF DOLLARS

Barber Half Dollars
1892-1915
Designer, Charles E. Barber

AG-Obverse: Outline of head visible. Letters evident but worn well into rim.
    Reverse: Most of eagle outline visible.

G-Obverse: All stars complete. Motto readable.
    Reverse: Tops of some letters run into rim.

VG-Obverse: At least the equivalent of three letters in "LIBERTY" show.
    Reverse: Some letters in "E PLURIBUS UNUM" can be seen.

F-Obverse: "LIBERTY" is complete but weak.
    Reverse: "E PLURIBUS UNUM" is complete but weak.

VF-Obverse: Complete wreath outline with considerable details in top part.
    Reverse: Most of the feathers will show.

EF-Obverse: Wear only on high points of forehead and leaves.
    Reverse: All detail show, with slight wear on wing edges.

THIS IS A LIBERTY HEAD HALF DOLLAR
BUT HAS COMMONLY BEEN NAMED BARBER
HALF DOLLARS AFTER ITS DESIGNER
CHARLES E. BARBER, CHIEF ENGRAVER OF THE MINT.

DATE	MINTAGE	G-6	VG-10	F-15	VF-30	EF-45	AU-50	UNC-60	UNC-65	PROOF-65
1892	935,245	24.50	30.00	45.00	80.00	200.00	325.00	1200.00	5850.00	5550.00
1892 O	390,000	150.00	200.00	250.00	350.00	475.00	725.00	2500.00	7825.00	
1892S	1,029,028	155.00	175.00	200.00	300.00	425.00	675.00	2000.00	8400.00	
1893	1,826,792	22.00	30.00	45.00	90.00	200.00	325.00	1200.00	6400.00	5550.00
1893 O	1,389,000	35.00	45.00	60.00	125.00	275.00	450.00	1550.00	8775.00	
1893S	740,000	80.00	115.00	160.00	265.00	350.00	575.00	1850.00	9350.00	
1894	1,148,972	20.00	27.50	50.00	90.00	210.00	350.00	1275.00	5900.00	5550.00
1894 O	2,138,000	20.00	30.00	50.00	100.00	250.00	375.00	1425.00	8500.00	
1894S	4,048,690	20.00	25.00	40.00	85.00	225.00	325.00	1350.00	7750.00	
1895	1,835,218	20.00	25.00	40.00	80.00	190.00	300.00	1300.00	7250.00	5550.00
1895 O	1,766,000	20.00	30.00	45.00	95.00	210.00	400.00	1550.00	9000.00	
1895S	1,108,086	30.00	37.50	60.00	115.00	250.00	375.00	1275.00	6650.00	
1896	950,762	22.50	30.00	50.00	100.00	225.00	375.00	1275.00	5650.00	5550.00
1896 O	924,000	28.50	37.50	60.00	125.00	310.00	575.00	2850.00	12500.00	
1896S	1,140,948	65.00	85.00	110.00	200.00	360.00	625.00	2850.00	12500.00	
1897	2,480,731	18.75	21.50	35.00	70.00	165.00	300.00	1100.00	5400.00	5550.00
1897 O	632,000	65.00	80.00	115.00	230.00	475.00	950.00	3650.00	15000.00	
1897S	933,900	130.00	140.00	185.00	250.00	410.00	675.00	3000.00	14000.00	

HALF DOLLARS

DATE	MINTAGE	G-0	VG-10	F-15	VF-30	EF-45	AU-50	UNC-60	UNC-65	PROOF-65
1898	2,956,735	18.75	20.00	35.00	65.00	160.00	300.00	1100.00	5400.00	5550.00
1898 O	874,000	27.50	35.00	75.00	160.00	350.00	500.00	1800.00	10850.00	
1898S	2,358,550	20.00	25.00	40.00	75.00	210.00	400.00	1600.00	9000.00	
1899	5,538,846	18.75	20.00	35.00	65.00	160.00	300.00	1100.00	5400.00	5550.00
1899 O	1,724,000	20.00	24.50	40.00	90.00	250.00	450.00	1700.00	11500.00	
1899S	1,686,411	20.00	25.00	40.00	70.00	210.00	350.00	1400.00	8000.00	
1900	4,762,912	18.75	20.00	35.00	70.00	160.00	300.00	1100.00	5400.00	5550.00
1900 O	2,744,000	20.00	23.50	40.00	75.00	270.00	475.00	1950.00	13800.00	
1900S	2,560,322	20.00	23.50	40.00	70.00	200.00	375.00	1425.00	8900.00	
1901	4,268,813	18.75	20.00	35.00	70.00	155.00	300.00	1100.00	5400.00	5550.00
1901 O	1,124,000	21.50	25.00	45.00	110.00	300.00	600.00	2600.00	13800.00	
1901S	847,044	24.50	30.00	65.00	165.00	475.00	950.00	3150.00	13800.00	
1902	4,922,777	18.75	20.00	35.00	48.50	150.00	300.00	1100.00	5400.00	5550.00
1902 O	2,526,000	19.50	21.50	40.00	60.00	200.00	400.00	1675.00	11500.00	
1902S	1,460,670	19.50	21.50	40.00	65.00	210.00	435.00	1550.00	8500.00	
1903	2,278,755	18.75	20.00	35.00	48.50	150.00	300.00	1100.00	5400.00	5550.00
1903 O	2,100,000	19.50	21.50	40.00	60.00	200.00	400.00	1550.00	9000.00	
1903S	1,920,772	19.50	21.50	40.00	65.00	210.00	425.00	1475.00	7500.00	
1904	2,992,670	18.75	20.00	35.00	48.50	150.00	300.00	1100.00	5400.00	5550.00
1904 O	1,117,600	22.50	23.50	45.00	85.00	300.00	600.00	2600.00	14000.00	
1904S	553,038	23.50	28.50	60.00	135.00	375.00	750.00	2600.00	11400.00	
1905	662,727	23.75	25.00	46.50	95.00	250.00	450.00	1675.00	7850.00	5550.00
1905 O	505,000	22.50	26.50	52.50	110.00	290.00	500.00	1950.00	10000.00	
1905S	2,494,000	18.75	20.00	40.00	65.00	210.00	390.00	1550.00	10000.00	
1906	2,638,675	18.75	20.00	35.00	48.50	150.00	300.00	1100.00	5400.00	5550.00
1906D	4,028,000	18.75	20.00	40.00	55.00	165.00	325.00	1200.00	6000.00	
1906 O	2,446,000	18.75	20.00	40.00	65.00	180.00	350.00	1425.00	6850.00	
1906S	1,740,154	18.75	21.50	40.00	70.00	210.00	365.00	1500.00	7000.00	
1907	2,598,575	18.75	20.00	35.00	48.50	150.00	300.00	1100.00	5400.00	5550.00
1907D	3,856,000	18.75	20.00	40.00	55.00	165.00	325.00	1200.00	6000.00	
1907 O	3,946,600	18.75	20.00	40.00	55.00	165.00	335.00	1275.00	6350.00	
1907S	1,250,000	18.75	22.50	42.50	70.00	215.00	390.00	1750.00	8500.00	
1908	1,354,545	18.75	20.00	35.00	48.50	150.00	300.00	1100.00	5400.00	5550.00
1908D	3,280,000	18.75	20.00	38.50	55.00	160.00	325.00	1200.00	6000.00	
1908 O	5,360,000	18.75	20.00	38.50	55.00	165.00	350.00	1200.00	6000.00	
1908S	1,644,828	18.75	21.50	40.00	65.00	210.00	360.00	1425.00	7000.00	
1909	2,368,650	18.75	20.00	35.00	48.50	150.00	300.00	1100.00	5400.00	5550.00
1909 O	925,400	19.50	22.50	42.50	80.00	270.00	575.00	2100.00	10250.00	
1909S	1,764,000	18.75	20.00	40.00	65.00	200.00	360.00	1500.00	7550.00	
1910	418,551	22.50	25.00	42.50	75.00	260.00	475.00	1600.00	7500.00	5550.00
1910S	1,948,000	18.75	20.00	38.50	90.00	265.00	350.00	1425.00	6500.00	
1911	1,406,543	18.75	20.00	35.00	48.50	150.00	300.00	1100.00	5400.00	5550.00
1911D	695,080	18.75	23.50	40.00	60.00	180.00	325.00	1175.00	5850.00	
1911S	1,272,000	18.75	20.00	38.50	65.00	185.00	330.00	1300.00	6500.00	
1912	1,550,700	18.75	20.00	35.00	48.50	150.00	300.00	1100.00	5400.00	5550.00
1912D	2,300,800	18.75	21.00	38.50	55.00	160.00	310.00	1200.00	6000.00	
1912S	1,370,000	18.75	21.00	38.50	60.00	180.00	350.00	1300.00	6500.00	
1913	188,627	32.50	36.50	55.00	115.00	275.00	500.00	1950.00	8500.00	5500.00
1913D	534,000	19.00	21.50	38.50	80.00	180.00	365.00	1350.00	5500.00	
1913S	604,000	19.00	21.50	40.00	75.00	200.00	375.00	1425.00	7500.00	
1914	124,610	38.50	45.00	75.00	175.00	350.00	650.00	2100.00	7800.00	7500.00
1914S	992,000	21.50	23.50	40.00	70.00	190.00	375.00	1425.00	7000.00	
1915	138,450	35.00	40.00	60.00	120.00	280.00	550.00	1975.00	9200.00	7500.00
1915D	1,170,400	18.75	20.00	35.00	55.00	160.00	310.00	1100.00	5250.00	
1915S	1,604,000	18.75	20.00	37.50	60.00	165.00	325.00	1125.00	5800.00	

HALF DOLLARS

Walking Liberty
1916-1947
Designer, Adolph A. Weinman

AG-Obverse: Liberty outline complete. Letters worn into rim.
   Reverse: Most of eagle's outline shows. Letters worn into rim.

G-Obverse: All letters complete with tops touching the rim.
   Reverse: Just the tops of the letters are worn into the rim.

VG-Obverse: Some of the skirt details show. Rim full.
   Reverse: Letters separated from rim.

F-Obverse: Most of the skirt details are evident.
   Reverse: some of the feathers show.

VF-Obverse: All the skirt lines will show.
   Reverse: The wing feathers are complete.

EF-Obverse: All details sharp with slight wear on head, breast and left leg.
   Reverse: Eagle's feathers complete with wear on breast.

**EXCEPT AS NOTED BELOW, THE MINT MARKS ARE
LOCATED ON THE INSIDE RIM OF THE REVERSE
JUST UNDER THE LEAVES.**

DATE	MINTAGE	G-6	VG-10	F-15	VF-30	EF-45	AU-50	UNC-60	UNC-65
1916	608,000	30.00	45.00	70.00	150.00	280.00	400.00	900.00	4000.00
1916D Mint									
Mark Obverse .	1,104,400	26.50	40.00	50.00	85.00	200.00	315.00	750.00	3750.00
1916S Mint									
Mark Obverse .	508,000	45.00	60.00	150.00	315.00	475.00	800.00	1875.00	7000.00
1917	12,292,000	18.00	20.00	22.50	35.00	50.00 `	100.00	350.00	1450.00
1917D Mint									
Mark Reverse .	1,940,000	20.00	25.00	30.00	62.50	180.00	415.00	1050.00	5250.00
1917D Mint									
Mark Obverse .	765,400	25.00	30.00	50.00	110.00	230.00	425.00	900.00	4350.00
1917S Mint									
Mark Reverse .	5,554,000	18.00	21.50	25.00	40.00	67.50	140.00	575.00	4000.00
1917S Mint									
Mark Obverse .	952,000	20.00	34.00	60.00	215.00	500.00	775.00	2175.00	9000.00
1918	6,634,000	17.50	22.50	30.00	60.00	180.00	360.00	725.00	3750.00
1918D	3,853,040	19.00	22.00	32.50	80.00	190.00	415.00	1850.00	3650.00
1918S	10,282,000	19.50	21.50	27.50	42.50	80.00	160.00	575.00	4000.00

HALF DOLLARS

DATE	MINTAGE	G 6	VG-10	F-15	VF-30	EF-45	AU-50	UNC-60	UNC-65	PROOF-65
1919	962,000	20.00	28.50	45.00	150.00	450.00	850.00	2175.00	8000.00	
1919D	1,165,000	19.50	27.50	46.50	180.00	575.00	1000.00	4250.00	25000.00	
1919S	1,552,000	19.00	23.00	35.00	130.00	475.00	1000.00	4000.00	27500.00	
1920	6,372,000	15.75	20.00	22.50	35.00	85.00	150.00	450.00	2800.00	
1920D	1,551,000	16.75	25.00	35.00	135.00	325.00	750.00	2750.00	10500.00	
1920S	4,624,000	17.00	21.50	26.50	60.00	150.00	475.00	2100.00	6500.00	
1921	246,000	95.00	115.00	230.00	550.00	1400.00	2150.00	4650.00	11500.00	
1921D	208,000	125.00	180.00	325.00	675.00	1600.00	2375.00	5000.00	14000.00	
1921S	548,000	26.00	37.50	60.00	290.00	1800.00	5600.00	16000.00	40000.00	
1923S	2,178,000	18.50	23.50	26.50	60.00	190.00	500.00	2175.00	11000.00	
1927S	2,392,000	17.00	21.50	24.50	40.00	115.00	325.00	1750.00	9000.00	
1928S	1,940,000	18.00	20.00	25.00	45.00	135.00	360.00	1850.00	11000.00	
1929D	1,001,200	19.50	23.50	26.50	35.00	100.00	200.00	725.00	3600.00	
1929S	1,902,000	18.00	20.00	22.50	32.50	90.00	200.00	750.00	3900.00	
1933S	1,786,000		18.50	20.00	30.00	80.00	175.00	725.00	4100.00	
1934	6,964,000		15.00	20.00	25.00	36.50	60.00	240.00	800.00	
1934D	2,361,400		16.50	21.50	27.50	70.00	150.00	450.00	1350.00	
1934S	3,652,000		16.00	20.00	26.50	48.00	160.00	725.00	2300.00	
1935	9,162,000		15.75	20.00	25.00	32.50	50.00	140.00	400.00	
1935D	3,003,800		16.50	20.00	27.50	70.00	150.00	450.00	1350.00	
1935S	3,854,000		16.50	20.00	26.50	60.00	160.00	550.00	1500.00	
1936	12,617,901		15.75	20.00	25.00	32.50	55.00	140.00	375.00	2650.00
1936D	4,252,400		16.00	21.00	30.00	52.50	86.50	325.00	875.00	
1936S	3,884,000		16.50	21.50	27.50	55.00	95.00	400.00	1150.00	
1937	9,527,728		15.75	20.00	26.50	35.00	55.00	140.00	375.00	1700.00
1937D	1,676,000		17.50	22.00	45.00	80.00	175.00	975.00	1350.00	
1937S	2,090,000		16.50	21.50	35.00	60.00	125.00	425.00	1200.00	
1938	4,118,152		15.00	20.00	30.00	38.50	70.00	325.00	850.00	1150.00
1938D	491,600		45.00	50.00	65.00	125.00	375.00	1100.00	5500.00	
1939	6,820,808		14.75	19.50	25.00	37.50	60.00	185.00	675.00	1000.00
1939D	4,267,800		15.00	20.00	27.50	37.50	60.00	225.00	625.00	
1939S	2,552,000		16.00	21.00	30.00	42.00	80.00	375.00	850.00	
1940	9,167,279		16.50	21.50	25.00	32.50	45.00	115.00	350.00	1050.00
1940S	4,550,000		17.50	22.50	27.50	35.00	55.00	350.00	900.00	
1941	24,207,412		14.50	19.50	22.50	24.50	26.50	70.00	210.00	1000.00
1941D	11,248,400		15.50	20.00	25.00	35.00	55.00	160.00	375.00	
1941S	8,098,000		16.50	21.50	27.50	45.00	90.00	375.00	725.00	
1942	47,839,120		14.50	19.50	22.50	24.50	26.50	70.00	210.00	1000.00
1942D	10,973,800		15.50	20.00	25.00	35.00	55.00	160.00	375.00	
1942S	12,708,000		15.00	20.00	25.00	40.00	75.00	315.00	625.00	
1943	53,190,000		14.50	19.50	22.50	24.50	26.50	70.00	210.00	
1943D	11,346,000		16.00	21.00	25.00	35.00	55.00	175.00	450.00	
1943S	13,450,000		15.75	20.00	30.00	40.00	70.00	275.00	525.00	
1944	28,206,000		14.75	19.50	22.50	24.50	26.50	70.00	210.00	
1944D	9,769,000		16.50	21.50	25.00	30.00	50.00	140.00	325.00	
1944S	8,904,000		16.50	21.50	27.50	40.00	65.00	275.00	600.00	
1945	31,502,000		14.75	19.50	22.50	24.50	26.50	75.00	210.00	
1945D	9,966,800		16.50	21.50	25.00	30.00	50.00	130.00	300.00	
1945S	10,156,000		16.50	21.50	25.00	35.00	60.00	275.00	475.00	
1946	12,118,000		16.50	21.50	25.00	27.50	32.50	82.50	225.00	
1946D	2,151,100		17.50	22.50	27.50	45.00	85.00	150.00	235.00	
1946S	3,724,000		17.00	22.00	25.00	40.00	60.00	250.00	425.00	
1947	4,094,000		16.50	19.50	22.50	30.00	70.00	160.00	400.00	
1947D	3,900,600		17.00	21.50	22.50	25.00	60.00	130.00	325.00	

HALF DOLLARS

Franklin Head
1948-1963
Designer, John R. Sinnock

VG-Obverse: Rim and letters are full.
          (This coin usually is not seen below the grade VG)
  Reverse: No details in the bell. Tops of letters run into rim.

F-Obverse: Some hair details show at the back of the neck and behind the ear.
  Reverse: Letters just touching rim.

VF-Obverse: All the hair details show with wear quite evident around ear.
  Reverse: Some of the horizontal lines on the upper and lower parts of the bell show.

EF-Obverse: All hair details will show slight wear on the high points only.
  Reverse: Most of the bells horizontal lines will show.

DATE	MINTAGE	VG-10	F-15	VF-30	EF-45	AU-50	UNC-60	UNC-65	PROOF-65
1948	3,006,814	22.00	23.50	25.00	27.50	30.00	50.00	70.00	
1948D	4,028,600	20.00	22.50	24.50	26.50	27.50	30.00	45.00	
1949	5,614,000	18.50	19.50	21.50	22.50	25.00	100.00	275.00	
1949D	4,120,600	20.00	25.00	29.50	30.00	35.00	75.00	250.00	
1949S	3,744,000	21.50	30.00	40.00	65.00	100.00	350.00	625.00	
1950	7,793,509	17.50	18.50	19.50	20.00	22.50	60.00	125.00	550.00
1950D	8,031,600	17.50	18.50	19.50	20.00	22.50	40.00	85.00	
1951	16,859,602	16.75	17.50	18.50	19.50	21.50	23.50	38.50	450.00
1951D	9,475,200	17.00	18.50	20.00	22.50	25.00	125.00	250.00	
1951S	13,696,000	16.50	17.50	18.50	19.50	21.50	65.00	130.00	
1952	21,274,073	15.00	16.00	17.00	18.00	20.00	22.50	37.50	275.00
1952D	25,395,600	15.00	16.00	17.00	18.00	20.00	22.50	37.50	
1952S	5,526,000	18.50	19.50	21.50	22.50	25.00	50.00	100.00	
1953	2,796,920	25.00	26.00	27.50	30.00	32.50	40.00	78.50	160.00
1953D	20,900,400	15.00	16.50	17.50	18.50	19.50	21.50	30.00	
1953S	4,148,000	20.00	21.50	22.50	23.50	25.00	30.00	45.00	
1954	13,421,503	16.50	17.50	18.50	19.50	21.50	22.50	25.00	90.00
1954D	25,445,580	15.00	16.00	17.00	18.00	19.00	21.50	26.50	
1954S	4,993,400	18.75	19.50	21.00	22.00	23.50	25.00	38.50	
1955	2,876,381	20.00	22.00	25.00	27.50	30.00	32.50	35.00	75.00
1956	4,701,384	20.00	21.50	22.50	23.50	25.00	26.50	27.50	35.00
1957	6,361,952	18.75	19.00	19.50	20.00	21.00	22.50	25.00	30.00
1957D	19,966,850	15.00	16.00	17.00	17.50	18.50	20.00	23.50	30.00
1958	4,917,652	19.50	20.00	21.50	22.00	23.00	24.00	25.00	27.50
1958D	23,962,412	14.50	15.50	16.50	17.50	18.50	19.00	20.00	

HALF DOLLARS

DATE	MINTAGE	F-15	VF-30	EF-45	AU-50	UNC-60	UNC-65	PROOF-65
1959	7,349,291	17.50	18.00	18.50	19.50	20.00	22.50	
1959D	13,053,750	16.50	17.50	18.50	19.50	22.50	25.00	
1960	7,716,602	17.50	18.00	18.50	19.00	19.50	20.00	22.00
1960D	18,215,812	15.00	16.00	16.50	17.00	17.50	18.50	
1961	8,290,000	14.75	15.50	16.00	16.50	17.00	18.50	20.00
1961D	20,276,442	14.50	15.00	15.50	16.00	17.00	18.50	
1962	12,932,019	15.00	15.50	16.00	16.50	17.00	17.50	18.50
1962D	35,473,281	14.50	15.00	15.50	16.00	17.00	17.50	
1963	25,239,645	14.50	15.00	15.50	16.00	17.00	17.50	18.50
1963D	67,069,292	14.50	15.00	15.50	16.00	17.00	17.50	

Kennedy Head
1964-To Date
Designers: Obverse, Gilroy Roberts
Reverse, Frank Gasparro

DATE	MINTAGE	UNC-65	PROOF-65
1964	277,254,766	15.50	18.50
1964D	156,205,446	16.50	

IN 1965 THE COMPOSITION OF THE HALF DOLLAR CHANGED TO A CLAD SANDWICH TYPE COIN. FROM 1965 THROUGH 1970 THE TWO OUTER LAYERS CONTAINED 80 PERCENT SILVER, 20 PERCENT COPPER WITH A CORE OF 21 PERCENT SILVER AND 79 PERCENT COPPER.
*THE 1970D WAS ISSUED ONLY IN MINT SETS.

DATE	MINTAGE		UNC-65	PROOF-65
1965	65,879,366		10.50	
1966	108,984,932		10.50	
1967	295,046,978		17.50	
1968D	246,951,930		7.50	
1968S	3,041,506	Proof only		15.00
1969D	129,881,800		8.50	
1969S	2,934,631	Proof only		15.00
1970D* . . .	2,150,000		75.00	
1970S	2,632,810	Proof only		30.00

IN 1971 THE COMPOSITION CHANGED TO AN INNER CORE OF PURE COPPER AND THE TWO OUTER LAYERS OF 75 PERCENT COPPER, 25 PERCENT NICKEL.

DATE	MINTAGE		UNC-65	PROOF-65
1971	155,164,000		2.50	
1971D	302,097,424		2.50	
1971S	3,220,733	Proof only		8.25
1972	153,180,000		2.75	
1972D	141,890,000		2.25	
1972S	3,260,996	Proof only		8.25

HALF DOLLARS

DATE	MINTAGE		EF-45	UNC-65	PROOF-65
1973	64,964,000			2.25	
1973D	83,171,400			2.25	
1973S	2,760,339	Proof only			8.75
1974	201,596,000			2.00	
1974D	79,066,300			2.25	
1974S	2,612,568	Proof only			8.75

Bicentennial Half Dollars
1976

ALL DATED 1776-1976 AND COINED IN 1975 AND 1976.

DATE	MINTAGE		EF-45	UNC-65	PROOF-65
1976	234,308,000			2.00	
1976D	287,565,248			2.00	
1976S	7,059,099	Proof only			4.25

A BICENTENNIAL SILVER CLAD COIN WAS STRUCK IN 1976 WITH THE SAME COMPOSITION AS THE 1965-1970 ISSUES.

1976S ..SILVER CLAD MINTAGE FIGURES NOT RELEASED					12.50

RETURN TO REGULAR KENNEDY HALF DOLLAR. SAME DESIGN AND COMPOSITION AS THE 1971 ISSUE.

DATE	MINTAGE		EF-45	UNC-65	PROOF-65
1977	43,598,000			2.00	
1977D	31,449,106			2.00	
1977S	3,251,152	Proof only			8.00
1978	14,350,000			2.25	
1978D	13,765,799			3.75	
1978S	3,127,781	Proof only			16.00
1979	68,312,000			1.75	
1979D	15,815,422			2.00	
1979S	3,677,175	Proof only			14.50
1980P	44,134,000			1.75	
1980D	33,456,449			1.75	
1980S	2,144,231	Proof only			13.00
1981P				1.75	
1981D				1.75	
1981S		Proof only			13.00

COMMEMORATIVE HALF DOLLARS 1892-1954

Columbian Exposition
1892-1893

Authorized on August 5, 1892. This is the first commemorative coin by the United States. Issued and sold at the Columbian Exposition in Chicago.
Weight 192.9 grains, .900 fine.

COLUMBUS

THE SANTA MARIA

DATE	ISSUED QUANTITY	VF-30	EF-45	AU-50	UNC-60	UNC-65
1892	950,000	19.50	25.00	27.50	40.00	225.00
1893	1,550,000	18.75	22.50	25.00	35.00	225.00

COMMEMORATIVE HALF DOLLARS

Pan-Pacific Exposition
1915

Authorized on January 16, 1915. The Exposition celebrated the opening of the Panama Canal. Made at the San Francisco Mint.
Weight 192.9 grains, .900 fine.

DATE	ISSUED QUANTITY	VF-30	EF-45	AU-50	UNC-60	UNC-65
1915S	27,134	175.00	275.00	300.00	1200.00	9750.00

Illinois Centennial
1918

Authorized on June 1, 1918. Issued to commemorate the One Hundredth Anniversary of Illinois admission into the Union.
Weight 192.9 grains, .900 fine.

A. LINCOLN   ILLINOIS STATE SEAL

1918	100,058	36.50	55.00	60.00	135.00	400.00

COMMEMORATIVE HALF DOLLARS

Maine Centennial
1920

Authorized on May 10, 1920. Issued to commemorate the One Hundredth Anniversary of Maine. The coins arrived too late for the Centennial celebration. They were sold by the state treasurer.
Weight 192.9 grains, .900 fine.

DATE	ISSUED QUANTITY	VF-30	EF-45	AU-50	UNC-60	UNC-65
1920	50,028	60.00	67.50	75.00	165.00	700.00

Pilgrim Tercentenary
1920-1921

Authorized on May 12, 1920. Issued to commemorate the Three Hundredth Anniversary of the Landing of the Pilgrims at Plymouth, Massachusetts.
Weight 192.9 grains, .900 fine.

		GOVERNOR BRADFORD		THE MAYFLOWER		
1920	152,112	45.00	55.00	60.00	100.00	375.00
1921	20,053	77.50	85.00	95.00	275.00	1050.00

COMMEMORATIVE HALF DOLLARS

Alabama Centennial
1921

Authorized on May 10, 1920. The Centennial was celebrated in 1919. The coins were not struck until 1921. This is the first time the portrait of a living person was used on a U.S. coin.
Weight 192.9 grains, .900 fine.

W. W. BIBB
FIRST GOVERNOR
OF ALABAMA AND
T. E. KILBY GOVERNOR
1919

EAGLE

DATE	ISSUED QUANTITY	VF-30	EF-45	AU-50	UNC-60	UNC-65
1921 with 2x2	6,002	135.00	150.00	160.00	625.00	2175.00
1921 No. 2x2	59,038	75.00	82.50	90.00	575.00	1600.00

THE 2x2 IS JUST ABOVE THE STARS ON THE OBVERSE.

Missouri Centennial
1921

Authorized on May 4, 1921. Issued for the One Hundredth Anniversary of the admission of Missouri into the Union.
Weight 192.9 grains, .900 fine.

FRONTIERSMAN

FRONTIERSMAN WITH AN INDIAN

1921 2 ☆ 4	5,000	365.00	400.00	435.00	1200.00	3150.00
1921 No. 2 ☆ 4	15,428	340.00	375.00	400.00	1150.00	2950.00

THE 2 ☆ 4 IS LOCATED JUST ABOVE THE DATE ON OBVERSE

COMMEMORATIVE HALF DOLLARS

Grant Memorial
1922

Authorized on February 2, 1922. Issued to commemorate the centenary of Ulysses S. Grant's Birth.
Weight 192.9 grains, .900 fine.

ULYSSES GRANT

GRANT'S BOYHOOD LOG CABIN

DATE	ISSUED QUANTITY	VF-30	EF-45	AU-50	UNC-60	UNC-65
1922 with Star	4,256	— —	475.00	525.00	1350.00	5400.00
1922 No Star	67,405	28.50	55.00	65.00	150.00	575.00

STAR IS LOCATED JUST ABOVE THE "N" IN GRANT ON THE OBVERSE.

Monroe Doctrine Centennial
1923

Authorized on January 24, 1923. Issued in conjunction with a motion picture exposition.
Weight 192.9 grains, .900 fine.

JAMES MONROE AND
JOHN QUINCY ADAMS.

TWO FEMALE FIGURES FOR
THE WESTERN HEMISPHERE.

1923	274,077	22.50	32.50	37.50	85.00	300.00

COMMEMORATIVE HALF DOLLARS

Huguenot-Walloon Tercentenary
1924

Authorized February 26, 1924. Issued to commemorate the settlings of the Huguenots and Walloons in New Netherlands, now called New York.
Weight 192.9 grains, .900 fine.

ADMIRAL COLIGNY
AND
WILLIAM THE SILENT

THE VESSEL
NIEU NEDERLAND

DATE	ISSUED QUANTITY	VF-30	EF-45	AU-50	UNC-60	UNC-65
1924	142,080	45.00	70.00	75.00	160.00	575.00

Lexington-Concord Sesquicentennial
1925

Authorized January 14, 1925. Issued to commemorate the One Hundred Fiftieth Anniversary of the Battles of Lexington and Concord.
Weight 192.9 grains, .900 fine.

MINUTE MAN

THE BELFRY

1925	162,013	30.00	60.00	65.00	115.00	375.00

COMMEMORATIVE HALF DOLLARS

Stone Mountain Memorial
1925

Authorized March 17, 1924. Issued to raise funds to have figures of the Confederate Leaders carved on Stone Mountain in Georgia.

GENERALS LEE AND JACKSON   AMERICAN EAGLE

DATE	ISSUED QUANTITY	VF-30	EF-45	AU-50	UNC-60	UNC-65
1925	1,314,709	30.00	35.00	38.50	50.00	135.00

California Diamond Jubilee
1925

Authorized on February 24, 1925. Issued to commemorate the Seventy-Fifth Anniversary of California's admission to the Union.
Weight 192.9 grains, .900 fine.

GOLD PROSPECTOR   GRIZZLY BEAR

1925S	86,594	40.00	80.00	90.00	250.00	900.00

COMMEMORATIVE HALF DOLLARS

Fort Vancouver Centennial
1925

Authorized on February 24, 1925. Issued to raise funds for the pageant for the celebration.
Weight 192.9 grains, .900 fine.

DR. JOHN McLAUGHLIN   FRONTIERSMAN WITH MUSKET

DATE	ISSUED QUANTITY	VF-30	EF-45	AU-50	UNC-60	UNC-65
1925S	14,994	135.00	275.00	300.00	800.00	2100.00

COINED AT THE SAN FRANCISCO MINT BUT MINT MARK WAS OMITTED.

Sesquicentennial of American Independence
1926

Authorized on March 3, 1925. Issued to commemorate the One Hundred Fiftieth Anniversary of the Declaration of Independence.
Weight 192.9 grains, .900 fine.

PRESIDENTS COOLIDGE AND WASHINGTON   LIBERTY BELL

1926	141,120	28.50	36.50	40.00	85.00	300.00

COMMEMORATIVE HALF DOLLARS

Oregon Trail Memorial
1926-1939

Authorized on May 17, 1926. Issued to commemorate the Oregon Trail. Coined at the Philadelphia, Denver, and San Francisco Mints.
Weight 192.9 grains, .900 fine.

INDIAN

WAGON ON OREGON TRAIL

DATE	ISSUED QUANTITY	VF-30	EF-45	AU-50	UNC-60	UNC-65
1926	47,955	65.00	72.50	80.00	190.00	365.00
1926S	83,055	65.00	72.50	80.00	190.00	365.00
1928	6,028	100.00	115.00	125.00	425.00	850.00
1933D	5,008	150.00	160.00	175.00	475.00	1050.00
1934D	7,006	82.50	90.00	100.00	350.00	775.00
1936	10,006	72.50	76.50	80.00	225.00	575.00
1936S	5,006	90.00	100.00	110.00	325.00	900.00
1937D	12,008	67.50	75.00	80.00	200.00	425.00
1938	6,006					
1938D	6,005	In sets of 3 only			800.00	1650.00
1938S	6,006					
1939	3,004					
1939D	3,004	In sets of 3 only			1300.00	2275.00
1939S	3,005					

COMMEMORATIVE HALF DOLLARS

Vermont Sesquicentennial
1927

Authorized on March 3, 1925. Issued to commemorate the One Hundred Fiftieth anniversary of Vermont's Independence and the Battle of Bennington.

IRA ALLEN
FOUNDER OF VERMONT

DATE	ISSUED QUANTITY	VF-30	EF-45	AU-50	UNC-60	UNC-65
1927	28,162	100.00	115.00	125.00	400.00	1075.00

Hawaiian Sesquicentennial
1928

Authorized on March 7, 1928. Issued to commemorate the rediscovery of the Islands by Captain Cook.

CAPTAIN JAMES COOK   **HAWAIIAN NATIVE CHIEF**

DATE	ISSUED QUANTITY	VF-30	EF-45	AU-50	UNC-60	UNC-65
1928	10,008	900.00	1000.00	1100.00	2100.00	5450.00

COMMEMORATIVE HALF DOLLARS

Daniel Boone Bicentennial
1934-1938

Authorized on May 26, 1934. Issued to commemorate the Two Hundredth Anniversary of Daniel Boone's Birth.

DANIEL BOONE   **BOONE WITH
CHIEF BLACK FISH**

DATE	ISSUED QUANTITY	VF-30	EF-45	AU-50	UNC-60	UNC-65
1934	10,007	67.50	75.00	80.00	175.00	350.00
1935 No						
1934	10,010					
1935D No						
1934	5,005	Set of 3			465.00	800.00
1935S No						
1934	5,005					
1935 with						
1934	10,008					
1935D with						
1934	2,003	Set of 3			2250.00	3250.00
1935S with						
1934	2,004					

**THE 1934 ADDED ON 1935 COINS IS LOCATED
JUST ABOVE THE WORD PIONEER ON THE REVERSE.**

COMMEMORATIVE HALF DOLLARS

DATE	ISSUED QUANTITY	VF-30	EF-45	AU-50	UNC-60	UNC-65
1936	12,012					
1936D	5,005	Set of 3			465.00	800.00
1936S	5,006					
1937	9,810					
1937D	2,506	Set of 3			1000.00	1875.00
1937S	2,506					
1938	2,100					
1938D	2,100	Set of 3			2000.00	3150.00
1938S	2,100					

Maryland Tercentenary
1934

Authorized on May 9, 1934. Issued to commemorate the Three Hundredth Anniversary of the founding of the Maryland Colony.

CECIL CALVERT
(LORD BALTIMORE)

ARMS OF
MARYLAND

DATE	ISSUED QUANTITY	VF-30	EF-45	AU-50	UNC-60	UNC-65
1934	25,015	50.00	75.00	90.00	250.00	750.00

COMMEMORATIVE HALF DOLLARS

Texas Centennial
1934-1938

Authorized on June 15, 1933. Issued to commemorate Texas independence. Coined at the Philadelphia, Denver and San Francisco Mints.

DATE	ISSUED QUANTITY	VF-30	EF-45	AU-50	UNC-60	UNC-65
1934	61,350	100.00	110.00	120.00	275.00	600.00
1935	9,994					
1935D	10,007	Set of 3			425.00	725.00
1935S	10,008					
1936	8,911					
1936D	9,039	Set of 3			425.00	725.00
1936S	9,064					
1937	6,571					
1937D	6,605	Set of 3			525.00	775.00
1937S	6,637					
1938	3,780					
1938D	3,775	Set of 3			950.00	1500.00
1938S	3,816					

COMMEMORATIVE HALF DOLLARS

Arkansas Centennial
1935-1939

Authorized on Mary 14, 1934. Issued to commemorate the One Hundredth Anniversary of the admission of Arkansas into the Union. The centennial year was 1936 but the first issue was brought out in 1935.

**AMERICAN WOMAN
AND INDIAN CHIEF**

EAGLE

DATE	ISSUED QUANTITY	VF-30	EF-45	AU-50	UNC-60	UNC-65
1935	13,012					
1935D	5,505	Set of 3			400.00	765.00
1935S	5,506					
1936	9,660					
1936D	9,660	Set of 3			400.00	765.00
1936S	9,662					
1937	5,505					
1937D	5,505	Set of 3			425.00	800.00
1937S	5,506					
1938	3,156					
1938D	3,155	Set of 3			775.00	1650.00
1938S	3,156					
1939	2,104					
1939D	2,104	Set of 3			2175.00	3375.00
1939S	2,105					

COMMEMORATIVE HALF DOLLARS

Connecticut Tercentenary
1935

Authorized on June 1, 1934. Issued to commemorate the Three Hundredth Anniversary of the founding of the Connecticut Colony.

CHARTER OAK TREE   EAGLE

DATE	ISSUED QUANTITY	VF-30	EF-45	AU-50	UNC-60	UNC-65
1935	25,018	145.00	165.00	180.00	350.00	1000.00

Hudson, N.Y. Sesquicentennial
1935

Authorized on May 2, 1935. Issued to commemorate the One Hundred Fiftieth Anniversary of the founding of Hudson by the explorer Hendrik Hudson.

SHIP, HALF MOON   SEAL OF HUDSON

1935	10,008	500.00	600.00	650.00	1050.00	2250.00

COMMEMORATIVE HALF DOLLARS

San Diego, California-Pacific Exposition
1935-1936

Authorized on May 3, 1935. Issued for the California-Pacific International Exposition. Coined at the San Francisco Mint in 1935 and at the Denver Mint in 1936.

SEATED WOMAN
WITH SPEAR

OBSERVATION TOWER
AND CALIFORNIA
EXPOSITION BUILDING

DATE	ISSUED QUANTITY	VF-30	EF-45	AU-50	UNC-60	UNC-65
1935S.....	70,132	39.50	43.50	46.50	110.00	300.00
1936D.....	30,092	47.50	52.50	57.50	180.00	400.00

Old Spanish Trail
1935

Authorized on June 5, 1935. Issued to commemorate the Four Hundredth Anniversary of the Cabeza De Vaca Exposition in 1535.

HEAD OF COW

OLD SPANISH
TRAIL AND
YUCCA TREE

DATE	ISSUED QUANTITY	VF-30	EF-45	AU-50	UNC-60	UNC-65
1935......	10,008	– –	675.00	750.00	1275.00	3000.00

COMMEMORATIVE HALF DOLLARS

Albany, New York Charter
1936

Authorized on June 16, 1936. Issued to commemorate the Two Hundred Fiftieth Anniversary of Albany, N.Y.

BEAVER   GOVERNOR DONGAN
WITH ROBERT LIVINGSTON
AND PETER SCHUYLER

DATE	ISSUED QUANTITY	VF-30	EF-45	AU-50	UNC-60	UNC-65
1936	17,671	– –	190.00	210.00	450.00	725.00

Bridgeport, Connecticut Centennial
1936

Authorized on May 15, 1936. Issued to commemorate the One Hundredth Anniversary of Bridgeport.

P. T. BARNUM   EAGLE

1936	25,015	75.00	85.00	95.00	230.00	475.00

COMMEMORATIVE HALF DOLLARS

Cincinnati Musical Center
1936

Authorized on March 31, 1936. Issued to commemorate the Fiftieth Anniversary of Cincinnati as a music center.

STEPHEN FOSTER

DATE	ISSUED QUANTITY	VF-30	EF-45	AU-50	UNC-60	UNC-65
1936	5,005					
1936D	5,005	Set of 3			2100.00	2950.00
1936S	5,006					

Cleveland, Great Lakes Exposition
1936

Authorized on May 5, 1936. Issued for the centennial celebration of Cleveland, Ohio, at the Great Lakes Exposition. Part of the coins were struck in 1937 but dated 1936.

MOSES CLEVELAND   **MAP OF THE GREAT LAKES**

1936	50,030	36.50	40.00	45.00	110.00	210.00

COMMEMORATIVE HALF DOLLARS

Columbia, S.C. Sesquicentennial
1936

Authorized on March 18, 1936. Issued to commemorate the One Hundred Fiftieth Anniversary of the founding of Columbia. Coined at the Philadelphia, Denver and San Francisco Mints.

JUSTICE

STATE EMBLEM

DATE	ISSUED QUANTITY		UNC-60	UNC-65
1936	9,007			
1936D	8,009	Set of 3	1450.00	2250.00
1936S	8,007			

COMMEMORATIVE HALF DOLLARS

Delaware Tercentenary
1936

Authorized on May 15, 1936. Issued to commemorate the Three Hundredth Anniversary of the Landing of the Swedes at Wilmington, Delaware. The Celebration took place in Sweden and Delaware in 1938. Sweden issued a two kronor coin to commemorate the celebration.

CHURCH BUILT
BY SWEDES

SWEDISH SHIP
KALMAR NYCKEL

DATE	ISSUED QUANTITY	VF-30	EF-45	AU-50	UNC-60	UNC-65
1936	20,993	— —	165.00	180.00	375.00	700.00

Elgin, Illinois Centennial
1936

Authorized on June 16, 1936. Issued to commemorate the One Hundredth Anniversary of the founding of Elgin.

PIONEER
MEMORIAL

1936	20,015	95.00	110.00	125.00	325.00	775.00

131

COMMEMORATIVE HALF DOLLARS

Battle of Gettysburg
1936

Authorized on June 16, 1936. Issued to commemorate the Seventy-Fifth Anniversary of the Battle of Gettysburg.

UNION AND CONFEDERATE
VETERANS

SHIELDS OF THE
UNION AND CONFEDERATE
ARMIES

DATE	ISSUED QUANTITY	VF-30	EF-45	AU-50	UNC-60	UNC-65
1936	26,928	140.00	150.00	165.00	450.00	900.00

Long Island Tercentenary
1936

Authorized on April 13, 1936. Issued to commemorate the Three Hundredth Anniversary of the Landing on Long Island by the Dutch at Jamaica Bay.

DUTCHMAN
AND INDIAN

DUTCH SHIP

1936	81,826	47.50	52.50	57.50	100.00	260.00

COMMEMORATIVE HALF DOLLARS

Lynchburg, Virginia Sesquicentennial
1936

Authorized on May 26, 1936. Issued to commemorate the One Hundred Fiftieth Anniversary of Lynchburg.

SENATOR CARTER GLASS   **LIBERTY AND
                                            COURTHOUSE**

DATE	ISSUED QUANTITY	VF-30	EF-45	AU-50	UNC-60	UNC-65
1936	20,013	110.00	125.00	135.00	300.00	700.00

Norfolk, Virginia Bicentennial
1936

Authorized on June 28, 1937. Issued to commemorate the Tercentennial of the Norfolk Land Grant and the Two Hundredth Anniversary of the city.

SEAL OF THE CITY   **ROYAL MACE
                                        OF NORFOLK**

1936	16,936	245.00	275.00	300.00	625.00	1275.00

COMMEMORATIVE HALF DOLLARS

Providence, Rhode Island Tercentenary
1936

ROGER WILLIAMS
WITH INDIAN

ANCHOR OF
HOPE

DATE	ISSUED QUANTITY	VF-30	EF-45	AU-50	UNC-60	UNC-65
1936	20,013					
1936D	15,010	Set of 3			800.00	1275.00
1936S	15,011					

Arkansas Centennial (Robinson)
1936

Authorized on June 26, 1936. Issued to commemorate the One Hundredth Anniversary of Arkansas into the Union. This is a change in design from the 1935 issue. Only the obverse of the coin changed. The reverse is the same as the 1935 issue.

SENATOR JOSEPH T. ROBINSON

1936	25,265	82.50	90.00	100.00	200.00	560.00

COMMEMORATIVE HALF DOLLARS

San Francisco-Oakland Bay Bridge
1936

Authorized on June 26, 1936. Issued to commemorate the opening of the San Francisco-Oakland Bay Bridge.

GRIZZLY BEAR **BAY BRIDGE**

DATE	ISSUED QUANTITY	VF-30	EF-45	AU-50	UNC-60	UNC-65
1936S	71,424	62.50	70.00	76.50	150.00	325.00

Wisconsin Centennial
1936

Authorized on May 15, 1936. Issued to commemorate the One Hundredth Anniversary of Wisconsin.

BADGER **STATE SEAL**

1936	25,015	100.00	110.00	125.00	250.00	725.00

COMMEMORATIVE HALF DOLLARS

York County, Maine Tercentenary
1936

Authorized on June 26, 1936. Issued to commemorate the Three Hundredth Anniversary of the Founding of York County.

YORK COUNTY SEAL

STOCKADE

DATE	ISSUED QUANTITY	VF-30	EF-45	AU-50	UNC-60	UNC-65
1936	25,015	100.00	115.00	125.00	250.00	725.00

Battle of Antietam
1937

Authorized on June 24, 1937. Issued to commemorate the Seventy-Fifth Anniversary of the Battle of Antietam, during the Civil War.

GENERALS LEE
AND McCLELLAN

THE BURNSIDE
BRIDGE

1937	18,028	200.00	250.00	275.00	575.00	1050.00

COMMEMORATIVE HALF DOLLARS

Roanoke Island, N.C.
1937

Authorized on June 24, 1936. Issued to commemorate the Three Hundred Fiftieth Anniversary of Roanoke Island and Virginia Dare the first white child born on the American Continent.

SIR WALTER RALEIGH — ELEANOR DARE HOLDING VIRGINIA

DATE	ISSUED QUANTITY	VF-30	EF-45	AU-50	UNC-60	UNC-65
1937	29,030	80.00	90.00	100.00	250.00	775.00

New Rochelle, New York
1938

Authorized on May 15, 1936. Issued to commemorate the Two Hundred Fiftieth Anniversary of the Founding of New Rochelle by the French Huguenots.

JOHN PRELL AND CALF — SEAL OF THE CITY

1938	15,266	200.00	265.00	290.00	600.00	1125.00

COMMEMORATIVE HALF DOLLARS

Iowa Centennial
1946

Authorized on August 7, 1946. Issued to commemorate the One Hundredth Anniversary of the admission of Iowa into the Union.

**IOWA CAPITOL
BUILDING**

STATE SEAL

DATE	ISSUED QUANTITY	VF-30	EF-45	AU-50	UNC-60	UNC-65
1946	100,057	45.00	52.50	60.00	125.00	275.00

Booker T. Washington Memorial
1946-1951

Authorized on August 7, 1946. Issued to commemorate Booker T. Washington, a black American educator.

**BOOKER T. WASHINGTON, OBVERSE AND
HIS BIRTHPLACE LOG CABIN LOWER REVERSE.**

138

COMMEMORATIVE HALF DOLLARS

DATE	ISSUED QUANTITY	VF-30	EF-45	AU-50	UNC-60	UNC-65
1946	1,000,546	17.50	22.00	25.00	30.00	35.00
1946D	200,113	17.50	22.00	25.00	30.00	35.00
1946S	500,279	17.50	22.00	25.00	30.00	35.00
1946-D-S . .		Set of 3			75.00	82.50
1947	100,017					
1947D	100,017	Set of 3			97.50	155.00
147S	100,017					
1948	8,005					
1948D	8,005	Set of 3			160.00	400.00
1948S	8,005					
1949	6,004					
1949D	6,004	Set of 3			300.00	575.00
1949S	6,004					
1950	6,004	42.50	47.50	50.00	100.00	200.00
1950D	6,004	42.50	47.50	50.00	100.00	200.00
1950S	512,091	17.50	22.00	25.00	30.00	35.00
1950-D-S . .		Set of 3			240.00	500.00
1951	510,082	17.50	22.00	25.00	30.00	35.00
1951D	7,004	32.50	37.50	40.00	75.00	140.00
1951S	7,004	32.50	37.50	40.00	75.00	140.00
1951-D-S . .		Set of 3			190.00	400.00

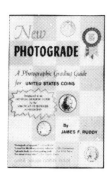

COMMEMORATIVE HALF DOLLARS

Washington Carver
1951-1954

Authorized on September 21, 1951. Issued to commemorate two outstanding black Americans, George Washington Carver, Agricultural Chemist and Booker T. Washington, Educator. This series is the last of the commemorative coins struck by the United States.

**GEORGE WASHINGTON CARVER
AND BOOKER T. WASHINGTON**

MAP of U.S.A.

DATE	ISSUED QUANTITY	VF-30	EF-45	AU-50	UNC-60	UNC-65
1951	110,018	17.50	22.00	25.00	30.00	35.00
1951D	10,004	25.00	30.00	35.00	50.00	75.00
1951S	10,004	25.00	30.00	35.00	50.00	75.00
1951-D-S . .		Set of 3			110.00	165.00
1952	2,006,292	17.50	22.00	25.00	30.00	35.00
1952D	8,006	35.00	40.00	45.00	75.00	175.00
1952S	8,006	35.00	40.00	45.00	75.00	175.00
1952-D-S . .		Set of 3			160.00	350.00
1953	8,003	45.00	50.00	60.00	100.00	225.00
1953D	8,003	45.00	50.00	60.00	100.00	225.00
1953S	108,020	25.00	30.00	35.00	40.00	50.00
1953-D-S . .		Set of 3			250.00	425.00
1954	12,006	25.00	30.00	35.00	50.00	75.00
1954D	12,006	25.00	30.00	35.00	50.00	75.00
1954S	122,024	17.50	22.00	25.00	30.00	35.00
1954-D-S . .		Set of 3			110.00	165.00

SILVER DOLLARS
1794-1935

Authorized on April 2, 1792. From 1794 through 1845 they were coined at the Philadelphia Mint. The Philadelphia Mint was assisted in 1846 by the New Orleans Mint, in 1859 by the San Francisco Mint, in 1870 by the Carson City Mint, and in 1921 by the Denver Mint.

All Silver dollars through 1935 were made of approximately 90 percent silver, 10 percent copper.

Flowing Hair
1794-1795
Designer, Robert Scot

AG-Obverse: Head outline is faint. Few stars visible.
   Reverse: Some letters visible. Eagle outline faint.

  G-Obverse: Head outline clear. All stars and letters show.
   Reverse: Complete eagle outline but worn smooth.

VG-Obverse: Some hair details show at the back of the neck.
   Reverse: Evidence of feathers on tail and left wing.

  F-Obverse: Some details show on face and hair.
   Reverse: Some feathers show in both wings.

VF-Obverse: Most of hair details show.
   Reverse: Leaves in wreath are distinct. Most of feathers show in both wings.

 EF-Obverse: All the hair details show with little wear on top of the head.
   Reverse: All of the wing feathers show. Wear evident on breast and edges of wings.

THREE LEAVES UNDER EACH WING

DATE	MINTAGE	AG-3	G-6	VG-10	F-15	VF-30	EF-45	AU-50	UNC-60
1794	1,758	2100.00	3500.00	5500.00	7500.00	13500.00	17500.00	— —	— —
1795 2 leaves									
under wings ...	160,295	1675.00	2800.00	3150.00	4200.00	6500.00	10000.00	27500.00	30000.00
1795 3 leaves ..		1675.00	2800.00	3150.00	4200.00	6500.00	10000.00	27500.00	30000.00

SILVER DOLLARS

Draped Bust, Small Eagle
1796-1798
Designer, Robert Scot

AG-Obverse: Outline of head and few stars show.
    Reverse: Parts of eagle and some letters visible.

G-Obverse: "LIBERTY" clear. Tops of stars run into rim.
    Reverse: Eagle outline complete but no details.

VG-Obverse: All stars and lettering clear and separated from rim.
    Reverse: Rim is full. Part of "E PLURIBUS UNUM" shows.

F-Obverse: Some hair details show. Ear lobe clear.
    Reverse: Some wing feathers show. Most of "E PLURIBUS UNUM" visible.

VF-Obverse: Most details in hair and face show clearly.
    Reverse: Most of the feathers show. "E PLURIBUS UNUM" is complete.

EF-Obverse: All details show clearly with slight wear on high hairlines at forehead.
    Reverse: All feathers visible. Edges of wings show slight wear.

DATE	MINTAGE	AG-3	G-6	VG-10	F-15	VF-30	EF-45	AU-50	UNC-60
1795	42,738	1700.00	2850.00	3000.00	3250.00	4250.00	7000.00	10500.00	27500.00
1796	72,920	1850.00	3100.00	3250.00	3650.00	4600.00	7500.00	12000.00	23000.00
1797 Sm. letters		1850.00	3100.00	3250.00	3650.00	4600.00	7500.00	12000.00	23000.00
1797 Lg. letters	7,776	1850.00	3100.00	3250.00	3650.00	4600.00	7500.00	12000.00	25000.00
1797 10 Stars left 6 Stars right		1850.00	3100.00	3250.00	3650.00	4600.00	7500.00	12000.00	25000.00
1798 13 Stars . .	*327,536	1850.00	3100.00	3250.00	3650.00	4600.00	7500.00	12000.00	23000.00
1798 15 Stars . .		1850.00	3100.00	3250.00	3650.00	4600.00	7500.00	12000.00	23000.00

*Mintage for 1798 includes total of Small and Large Eagle types.

SILVER DOLLARS

Draped Bust, Large Eagle
1798-1804
Designer, Robert Scot

DATE	MINTAGE	AG-3	G-6	VG-10	F-15	VF-30	EF-45	AU-50	UNC-60
1798	Included	350.00	575.00	650.00	850.00	1150.00	2000.00	3750.00	12500.00
1798 10 arrows	in above	350.00	575.00	650.00	850.00	1150.00	2000.00	3750.00	12500.00
1798 13 arrows		350.00	575.00	650.00	850.00	1150.00	2000.00	3750.00	12500.00
1799		350.00	575.00	650.00	850.00	1150.00	2000.00	3750.00	15000.00
1799 over 98 13 Stars		350.00	575.00	650.00	850.00	1150.00	2000.00	3750.00	15000.00
1799 over 98 15 Stars	423,515	350.00	575.00	650.00	850.00	1150.00	2000.00	3750.00	15000.00
1799 8 Stars left 5 Stars right		350.00	575.00	650.00	850.00	1150.00	2000.00	3750.00	12500.00
1800		350.00	575.00	650.00	850.00	1150.00	2000.00	3750.00	12500.00
1800 10 arrows	220,920	350.00	575.00	650.00	850.00	1150.00	2000.00	3750.00	12500.00
1800 12 arrows		350.00	575.00	650.00	850.00	1150.00	2000.00	3750.00	12500.00
1801	54,454	375.00	600.00	675.00	875.00	1200.00	2150.00	4000.00	13000.00
1802		375.00	600.00	675.00	875.00	1200.00	2150.00	4000.00	13000.00
1802 over 01	41,650	375.00	600.00	675.00	875.00	1200.00	2150.00	4000.00	13000.00
1803	85,634	350.00	575.00	650.00	850.00	1150.00	2000.00	3750.00	12500.00

SILVER DOLLARS

1804 ORIGINAL

THE 1804 SILVER DOLLAR IS ONE OF THE MOST VALUED COINS IN AMERICA. THERE ARE ONLY EIGHT ORIGINALS AND SEVEN RESTRIKES KNOWN. ESTIMATED VALUE WOULD BE WELL OVER $250,000.00.

Gobrecht Pattern Dollars
1836-1839

GOBRECHT PATTERN DOLLARS WERE STRUCK IN THESE THREE YEARS AS WELL AS SOME RESTRIKES IN LATER YEARS. TOTAL QUANTITIES STRUCK ARE UNKNOWN. TEN OR MORE VARIETIES EXIST, SOME WITH THE DESIGNER'S NAME AND SOME WITHOUT. SOME HAVE STARS ON THE REVERSE AND SOME WITHOUT. ALL ARE SCARCE.

SILVER DOLLARS

Seated Liberty
1840-1873
Designer, Christian Gobrecht

AG-Obverse: Rim worn down into stars.
   Reverse: At least half of letters and eagle show.

 G-Obverse: All stars show but tops touching rim.
   Reverse: All letters show, some touching rim. Eagle outline complete.

VG-Obverse: At least three complete letters of "LIBERTY" in shield visible.
   Reverse: Letters clear and separated from rim.

 F-Obverse: "LIBERTY" in shield complete but very weak.
   Reverse: Some of the eagle's feathers show in both wings.

VF-Obverse: "LIBERTY" sharp. Some details in gown show.
   Reverse: Most of the feathers show.

EF-Obverse: Most details show. Evidence of wear on knees.
   Reverse: All feathers show. Slight wear on wing edges and claws.

MINT MARK
BELOW EAGLE

DATE	MINTAGE	G-6	VG-10	F-15	VF-30	EF-45	AU-50	UNC-60	UNC-65	PROOF-65
1840	61,005	120.00	140.00	185.00	250.00	450.00	750.00	1700.00	— —	— —
1841	173,000	90.00	110.00	165.00	215.00	375.00	550.00	1750.00	6500.00	— —
1842	184,618	90.00	110.00	165.00	215.00	375.00	550.00	1700.00	6300.00	— —
1843	165,100	90.00	110.00	165.00	215.00	375.00	550.00	1700.00	6300.00	— —
1844	20,000	150.00	185.00	275.00	300.00	500.00	800.00	1800.00	— —	— —
1845	24,500	140.00	180.00	275.00	300.00	550.00	850.00	1800.00	— —	— —
1846	110,600	95.00	110.00	165.00	215.00	375.00	550.00	1750.00	6500.00	— —
1846 0	59,000	130.00	160.00	275.00	325.00	550.00	850.00	— —	— —	— —
1847	140,750	95.00	110.00	165.00	215.00	375.00	550.00	1750.00	6300.00	— —
1848	15,000	125.00	150.00	225.00	325.00	550.00	850.00	1800.00	6500.00	— —
1849	62,600	105.00	130.00	175.00	250.00	400.00	600.00	1750.00	6300.00	— —
1850	7,500	175.00	200.00	400.00	550.00	750.00	1500.00	1700.00	— —	— —
1850 0	40,000	150.00	190.00	275.00	500.00	900.00	1400.00	3500.00	— —	— —
1851	1,300	SCARCE								
1852	1,100	SCARCE								
1853	46,110	120.00	140.00	200.00	350.00	500.00	750.00	1750.00	— —	— —

SILVER DOLLARS

DATE	MINTAGE	G-6	VG-10	F 15	VF 00	EF-40	AU-50	UNC-60	UNC-65	PROOF-65
1854	33,140	145.00	190.00	300.00	450.00	750.00	1250.00	1750.00	— —	— —
1855	26,000	220.00	300.00	450.00	600.00	750.00	1500.00	1900.00	— —	15000.00
1856	63,500	140.00	170.00	300.00	525.00	750.00	1500.00	1800.00	— —	9500.00
1857	94,000	135.00	160.00	225.00	400.00	650.00	1200.00	1700.00	— —	9500.00
1858	80	Proof only								9500.00
1859	256,500	110.00	130.00	225.00	275.00	350.00	525.00	1700.00	6300.00	9500.00
1859 0	360,000	90.00	110.00	165.00	225.00	350.00	525.00	1700.00	6300.00	— —
1859S	20,000	125.00	165.00	300.00	450.00	600.00	1200.00	— —	— —	— —
1860	218,930	110.00	130.00	175.00	225.00	375.00	550.00	1700.00	6300.00	9500.00
1860 0	515,000	90.00	110.00	165.00	225.00	350.00	525.00	1700.00	6300.00	— —
1861	78,500	100.00	125.00	175.00	275.00	400.00	750.00	1750.00	6500.00	9500.00
1862	12,090	240.00	300.00	500.00	750.00	950.00	2000.00	2500.00	— —	9500.00
1863	27,660	145.00	180.00	300.00	425.00	675.00	1250.00	1950.00	6300.00	9500.00
1864	31,170	145.00	180.00	300.00	425.00	675.00	1250.00	1750.00	6300.00	9500.00
1865	47,000	140.00	170.00	300.00	425.00	650.00	1200.00	1800.00	6300.00	9500.00

THE MOTTO WAS ADDED TO THE REVERSE.

"IN GOD WE TRUST"

DATE	MINTAGE	G-6	VG-10	F-15	VF-30	EF-45	AU-50	UNC-60	UNC-65	PROOF-65
1866	49,625	125.00	165.00	275.00	400.00	625.00	1250.00	1900.00	6300.00	9500.00
1867	47,525	130.00	165.00	275.00	400.00	625.00	1250.00	1900.00	6300.00	9500.00
1868	162,700	115.00	160.00	275.00	375.00	550.00	1000.00	1800.00	6300.00	9500.00
1869	424,300	95.00	130.00	170.00	225.00	375.00	550.00	1700.00	6300.00	9500.00
1870	416,000	95.00	130.00	170.00	225.00	375.00	550.00	1700.00	6300.00	9500.00
1870CC . . .	12,462	165.00	250.00	375.00	500.00	900.00	1750.00	— —	— —	— —
1870S	UNKNOWN	SCARCE								
1871	1,074,760	90.00	110.00	170.00	225.00	375.00	550.00	1700.00	6300.00	9500.00
1871CC . . .	1,376	450.00	550.00	1000.00	1500.00	2750.00	5750.00	6000.00	— —	— —
1872	1,106,450	90.00	115.00	170.00	225.00	375.00	550.00	1700.00	6300.00	9500.00
1872CC . . .	3,150	250.00	300.00	575.00	800.00	1500.00	3250.00	— —	— —	— —
1872S	9,000	145.00	175.00	325.00	600.00	1250.00	2750.00	3000.00	6300.00	9500.00
1873	293,600	90.00	125.00	170.00	225.00	375.00	550.00	— —	— —	— —
1873CC . . .	2,300	550.00	675.00	1500.00	1800.00	3500.00	7500.00	— —	— —	— —

SILVER DOLLARS

Morgan Dollars
1878-1921
Designer, George T. Morgan

Silver dollars were resumed by the Bland-Allison Act of February 28, 1878. George T. Morgan designed the new dollars which were produced from 1878 to 1921.

In 1904 the silver bullion supply became exhausted and the silver dollar was suspended until 1921 when an additional 86 million plus were struck before a new design was adopted.

The large number of Morgan Dollars that were struck caused a pile up in the Treasury vaults because they were not needed for commerce. The only place they circulated to any extent was in the western states. As a result, The Pittman Act of April 23, 1918, had over 270 million of the coins melted down.

AG-Obverse: Few letters show. Date legible.
    Reverse: Letters worn down smooth with rim.

G-Obverse: Complete outline of head. All letters show but worn at tops.
    Reverse: Just the tops of letters worn into rim.

VG-Obverse: All letters and stars worn but complete.
    Reverse: Details of feathers in deepest parts of wings show.

F-Obverse: Some of the hair details show. Letters and stars strong.
    Reverse: Most of the wing feathers show.

VF-Obverse: Ear clear. Most hair detail show.
    Reverse: All feathers on wings show.

EF-Obverse: All hair details show. Wear only around ear only.
    Reverse: Wear on only the high points of breast feathers.

THIS IS A LIBERTY HEAD DOLLAR BUT
HAS COMMONLY BEEN NAMED MORGAN
DOLLAR AFTER IT'S DESIGNER GEORGE T. MORGAN.

SILVER DOLLARS

DATE	MINTAGE	G-8	VG-10	F-15	VF-30	EF-45	AU-50	UNC-60	UNC-65	PROOF-65
1878 7 tail feathers ...			26.50	42.50	45.00	47.50	50.00	110.00	325.00	9500.00
1878 8 tail feathers ...			30.00	40.00	42.50	55.00	85.00	115.00	400.00	7000.00
1878 7 over 8 feathers .			30.00	45.00	55.00	70.00	75.00	135.00	700.00	
1878CC ...	2,212,000		37.50	55.00	65.00	75.00	80.00	165.00	300.00	
1878S	9,774,000		26.50	37.50	40.00	42.50	45.00	80.00	125.00	
1879	14,807,100		26.00	37.50	40.00	42.50	45.00	90.00	400.00	7000.00
1879CC ...	756,000		50.00	76.50	120.00	350.00	650.00	1400.00	7000.00	
1879 0.....	2,887,000		26.00	37.50	40.00	42.50	47.50	110.00	1000.00	
1879S	9,110,000		26.50	37.50	38.00	40.00	42.50	80.00	120.00	
1880	12,601,355		26.50	37.50	40.00	42.50	45.00	95.00	340.00	7000.00
1880CC ...	591,000	50.00	60.00	90.00	110.00	130.00	165.00	360.00	450.00	
1880 0.....	5,305,000		26.50	40.00	42.50	45.00	50.00	150.00	1300.00	
1880S	8,900,000		26.50	37.50	40.00	42.50	45.00	80.00	115.00	
1881	9,163,975		26.50	40.00	42.50	45.00	47.50	90.00	340.00	9500.00
1881CC ...	296,000	85.00	100.00	125.00	140.00	165.00	185.00	360.00	475.00	
1881 0.....	5,708,000		26.50	37.50	40.00	42.50	45.00	87.50	450.00	
1881S	12,760,000		26.50	36.50	37.50	40.00	42.50	80.00	115.00	
1882	11,101,100		26.50	37.50	40.00	42.50	45.00	90.00	340.00	7000.00
1882CC	1,133,000		38.00	55.00	65.00	75.00	80.00	150.00	225.00	
1882 0.....	6,090,000		26.50	40.00	42.50	45.00	47.50	77.50	425.00	
1882S	9,250,000		26.50	37.50	40.00	45.00	47.50	80.00	120.00	
1883	12,291,039		26.50	37.50	40.00	42.50	45.00	85.00	325.00	7000.00
1883CC ...	1,204,000		38.50	55.00	65.00	75.00	80.00	150.00	175.00	
1883 0.....	8,725,000		26.50	37.50	40.00	42.50	45.00	70.00	150.00	
1883 S	6,250,000		26.50	40.00	45.00	60.00	225.00	700.00	4200.00	
1884	14,070,875		26.50	37.50	38.50	40.00	42.50	125.00	375.00	8200.00
1884CC ...	1,136,000		55.00	70.00	75.00	87.50	95.00	150.00	175.00	
1884 0.....	9,730,000		26.50	37.50	40.00	42.50	45.00	70.00	150.00	
1884S	3,200,000		26.50	40.00	45.00	65.00	375.00	1650.00	— —	
1885	17,787,767		26.50	37.50	40.00	42.50	45.00	70.00	150.00	9500.00
1855CC ...	228,000	230.00	245.00	275.00	300.00	325.00	350.00	385.00	475.00	
1885 0.....	9,185,000		26.50	37.50	40.00	42.50	45.00	70.00	150.00	
1885S	1,497,000		26.50	40.00	45.00	60.00	85.00	280.00	1000.00	
1886	19,963,886		26.50	37.50	40.00	42.50	45.00	70.00	115.00	9000.00
1886 0.....	10,710,000		26.50	40.00	42.50	45.00	75.00	725.00	8650.00	
1886S	750,000		37.50	55.00	65.00	85.00	95.00	425.00	1175.00	
1887	20,290,710		26.50	37.50	40.00	42.50	45.00	70.00	115.00	8000.00
1887 0.....	11,550,000		26.50	40.00	42.50	45.00	47.50	80.00	800.00	
1887S	1,771,000		26.50	40.00	45.00	47.50	50.00	200.00	550.00	
1888	19,183,833		26.50	37.50	40.00	42.50	45.00	75.00	275.00	8000.00
1880 0.....	12,150,000		26.50	37.50	40.00	45.00	47.50	85.00	350.00	
1888S	657,000		40.00	60.00	85.00	110.00	120.00	425.00	1250.00	
1889	21,726,811		26.50	40.00	45.00	47.50	50.00	80.00	265.00	8000.00
1889CC ...	350,000	200.00	240.00	350.00	525.00	950.00	2500.00	8100.00	30000.00	
1889 0.....	11,875,000		26.50	37.50	40.00	42.50	45.00	225.00	1950.00	
1889S	700,000		40.00	65.00	87.50	100.00	110.00	265.00	750.00	
1890	16,802,590		26.50	40.00	42.50	45.00	47.50	90.00	400.00	8000.00
1890CC ...	2,309,041		38.50	55.00	65.00	80.00	95.00	310.00	825.00	
1890 0.....	10,701,000		26.50	37.50	40.00	45.00	47.50	140.00	900.00	
1890S	8,230,373		26.50	40.00	45.00	50.00	55.00	120.00	340.00	
1891	8,694,206		26.50	40.00	42.50	45.00	65.00	275.00	875.00	8000.00
1891CC ...	1,618,000		38.00	55.00	65.00	80.00	90.00	240.00	725.00	
1891 0.....	7,954,529		26.50	40.00	42.50	45.00	65.00	265.00	2950.00	
1891S	5,296,000		27.50	40.00	42.50	45.00	47.50	135.00	450.00	
1892	1,037,245		27.50	45.00	50.00	55.00	65.00	290.00	1750.00	8000.00

SILVER DOLLARS

DATE	MINTAGE	G-6	VG-10	F-15	VF-30	EF-45	AU-50	UNC-60	UNC-65	PROOF-65
1892CC ...	1,352,000		50.00	75.00	90.00	135.00	265.00	525.00	1500.00	
1892 O	2,744,000		26.50	40.00	50.00	55.00	70.00	400.00	3950.00	
1892S	1,200,000		32.50	60.00	110.00	280.00	1200.00	8100.00	26450.00	
1893	378,792	50.00	60.00	100.00	120.00	185.00	300.00	825.00	3500.00	10000.00
1893CC ...	677,000	52.50	62.50	125.00	250.00	575.00	750.00	1500.00	5750.00	
1893 O	300,000	55.00	65.00	125.00	190.00	375.00	575.00	1675.00	21000.00	
1893S	100,000	1150.00	1450.00	1850.00	2950.00	5000.00	13500.00	27500.00	68500.00	
1894	110,972	350.00	450.00	500.00	675.00	875.00	1200.00	2000.00	8450.00	14000.00
1894 O	1,723,000		26.50	45.00	50.00	70.00	115.00	825.00	10000.00	
1894S	1,260,000		34.00	60.00	115.00	170.00	300.00	750.00	2750.00	
1895	12,880		— —	— —	— —	— —	— —	— —	— —	45000.00
1895 O	450,000	62.50	77.50	120.00	235.00	525.00	1100.00	4000.00	53000.00	
1895S	400,000	77.50	95.00	145.00	260.00	725.00	1275.00	2350.00	6000.00	
1896	9,976,762		26.50	40.00	42.50	45.00	47.50	80.00	265.00	8500.00
1896 O	4,900,000		26.50	40.00	45.00	50.00	140.00	1250.00	14500.00	
1896S	5,000,000		33.00	55.00	90.00	170.00	375.00	1225.00	3300.00	
1897	2,822,731		26.50	40.00	42.50	45.00	47.50	110.00	325.00	8500.00
1897 O	4,004,000		26.50	40.00	45.00	50.00	87.50	775.00	8500.00	
1897S	5,825,000		26.50	40.00	45.00	50.00	55.00	135.00	525.00	
1898	5,884,735		26.50	37.50	40.00	42.50	45.00	90.00	265.00	8500.00
1898 O	4,440,000		26.50	37.50	40.00	42.50	45.00	70.00	160.00	
1898S	4,102,000		27.50	40.00	45.00	55.00	85.00	500.00	1275.00	
1899	330,846		57.50	100.00	110.00	125.00	130.00	180.00	600.00	8500.00
1899 O	12,290,000		26.50	37.50	40.00	42.50	45.00	70.00	200.00	
1899S	2,562,000		28.50	40.00	55.00	60.00	100.00	650.00	1375.00	
1900	8,830,912		26.50	37.50	40.00	42.50	45.00	70.00	240.00	8500.00
1900 O	13,320,000		26.50	37.50	40.00	42.50	45.00	75.00	230.00	
1900S	3,540,000		26.50	40.00	45.00	55.00	70.00	425.00	1075.00	
1901	6,962,813		38.00	60.00	65.00	85.00	330.00	1575.00	14750.00	17500.00
1901 O	13,320,000		26.50	40.00	42.50	45.00	47.50	80.00	425.00	
1901S	2,284,000		27.50	45.00	55.00	70.00	110.00	650.00	2350.00	
1902	7,994,777		26.50	40.00	42.50	45.00	55.00	120.00	850.00	12500.00
1902 O	8,636,000		26.50	37.50	40.00	42.50	45.00	70.00	170.00	
1902S	1,530,000		45.00	75.00	115.00	170.00	265.00	725.00	1875.00	
1903	4,652,755		26.50	40.00	45.00	50.00	55.00	130.00	650.00	12500.00
1903 O	4,450,000	280.00	310.00	365.00	425.00	500.00	535.00	575.00	825.00	
1903S	1,241,000		30.00	60.00	95.00	260.00	875.00	3800.00	9750.00	
1904	2,788,650		26.50	38.50	40.00	45.00	75.00	475.00	3100.00	13000.00
1904 O	3,720,000		26.50	37.50	40.00	42.50	45.00	70.00	150.00	
1904S	2,304,000		40.00	80.00	100.00	190.00	775.00	2175.00	7600.00	
1921	44,690,000		26.50	35.00	37.50	38.50	40.00	45.00	115.00	
1921D	20,345,000		26.50	35.00	37.50	38.50	40.00	65.00	550.00	
1921S	21,695,000		26.50	36.50	38.50	40.00	42.50	100.00	1275.00	

SILVER DOLLARS

Peace Dollars
1921-1935
Designer, Anthony DeFrancisci

The new Peace Dollars designed by Anthony De Francisci, were struck in December 1921 and released to the public on January 3, 1922. They were minted until 1935 but not continuously, as no pieces were struck from 1929 to 1933.

VG-Obverse: Head worn smooth. (This coin is generally not found in grades under Very Good)
Reverse: The lettering very weak. No feather details.

F-Obverse: Some hair details show.
Reverse: Right wing outline complete with some feathers showing.

VF-Obverse: Most hair details show. Hair worn flat only on forehead and over ear.
Reverse: Wear on right wing and head otherwise most feathers show.

EF-Obverse: All hair details show. Slight wear on hair over ear and forehead.
Reverse: All feathers show, some may be weak.

AU-Obverse: Slight trace of wear on high points of cheek and hair.
Reverse: Slight evidents of wear on high points of neck and right wing.

DATE	MINTAGE	G-6	VG-10	F-15	VF-30	EF-45	AU-50	UNC-60	UNC-65
1921	1,006,473		50.00	65.00	70.00	90.00	140.00	900.00	4750.00
1922	51,737,000		26.50	30.00	36.50	37.50	40.00	45.00	92.50
1922D	15,063,000		26.50	30.00	32.50	35.00	37.50	95.00	650.00
1922S	17,475,000		26.50	30.00	32.50	35.00	37.50	100.00	975.00
1923	30,800,000		26.50	30.00	32.50	35.00	37.50	45.00	92.50
1923D	6,811,000		26.50	30.00	33.00	36.50	40.00	90.00	875.00
1923S	19,020,000		26.50	30.00	32.50	35.00	37.50	170.00	1150.00
1924	11,811,000		26.50	30.00	32.50	35.00	37.50	62.50	275.00
1924S	1,728,000		27.50	32.50	35.00	47.50	70.00	425.00	2450.00
1925	10,198,000		26.50	30.00	32.50	35.00	37.50	62.50	200.00
1925S	1,610,000		27.50	32.50	35.00	45.00	65.00	400.00	2150.00
1926	1,939,000		27.50	32.50	34.00	40.00	55.00	100.00	550.00
1926D	2,348,700		27.50	32.50	35.00	47.50	70.00	250.00	1175.00
1926S	6,980,000		27.50	32.50	35.00	40.00	55.00	115.00	550.00

SILVER DOLLARS

DATE	MINTAGE	G-6	VG-10	F-15	VF-30	EF-45	AU-50	UNC-60	UNC-65
1927	848,000		33.00	40.00	50.00	60.00	85.00	200.00	1100.00
1927D	1,268,900		26.50	32.00	35.00	60.00	145.00	500.00	3650.00
1927S	866,000		27.50	35.00	40.00	50.00	100.00	600.00	2050.00
1928	360,649	190.00	215.00	230.00	275.00	325.00	385.00	575.00	2350.00
1928S	1,632,000		26.50	30.00	35.00	40.00	85.00	450.00	2050.00
1934	954,057		33.00	35.00	45.00	55.00	100.00	225.00	1150.00
1934D	1,569,500		26.50	32.00	35.00	47.50	90.00	300.00	2175.00
1934S	1,011,000		27.50	37.50	70.00	275.00	800.00	3900.00	13500.00
1935	1,576,000		26.50	30.00	32.50	45.00	70.00	160.00	800.00
1935S	1,964,000		26.50	30.00	34.00	47.50	95.00	375.00	2175.00

Eisenhower Clad Dollars
1971 To 1978
Designer, Frank Gasparro

The new Eisenhower dollars, engraved by Frank Gasparro, was prompted by the West as a need in gambling casinos.

From 1971 through 1976 the clad dollars were made of two different compositions. The first type is a silver clad made of two outer layers of 80% silver, 20 percent copper with an inner core of 21 percent silver, 79 percent copper. These were used for proofs and collectors. The second type is a copper clad made of two outer layers of 25 percent nickel, 75 percent copper with a pure copper core.

PRESIDENT DWIGHT
D. EISENHOWER

APOLLO II
INSIGNIA

DATE		MINTAGE		UNC-65	PROOF-65
1971	CN	47,799,000		5.95	
1971D	CN	68,587,424		6.50	
1971S Silver Clad		6,868,530		18.50	20.00
1972	CN	75,890,000		6.25	
1972D	CN	92,548,511		5.95	
1972S Silver Clad		2,193,056		30.00	60.00
1973	CN	2,000,056		30.00	
1973D	CN	2,000,000		30.00	
1973S	CN	2,760,399	Proof only		20.00
1973S Silver Clad		1,883,140			200.00
1974	CN	27,366,000		3.75	
1974D	CN	45,517,000		3.75	
1974S	CN	2,612,568	Proof only		13.50
1974S Silver Clad		1,900,000		30.00	62.50

CLAD DOLLARS

Bicentennial Dollars
1976

ALL DATED 1776-1976 AND COINED IN 1975-1976.

HIGH RELIEF **LOW RELIEF**

TYPE II **TYPE I**

DATE		MINTAGE		UNC-65	PROOF-65
1976	Type I CN	4,019,000		7.25	
1976	Type II CN ...	113,318,000		3.75	
1976D	Type I CN....	21,048,710		4.25	
1976D	Type II CN ...	82,179,564		3.75	
1976S	Type I CN	2,845,450	Proof only		20.00
1976S	Type II CN ...	4,149,730	Proof only		8.50
1976S Silver Clad		(Approx 3,300,000)		20.00	22.50

Return to the regular Eisenhower dollar. Same design obverse and reverse as the 1971 issue. All are of clad copper nickel composition.

1977		12,596,000		5.25	
1977D		32,983,006		5.50	
1977S		3,251,152	Proof only		10.75
1978		25,702,000		3.75	
1978D		23,012,890		4.00	
1978S		3,127,781	Proof only		25.00

CLAD DOLLARS

Susan B. Anthony
1979 To Date
Designer, Frank Gasparro

A major change in the size of the dollar. The Susan B. Anthony dollar, designed by Frank Gasparro, is about one half inch smaller, in diameter, then the previous Eisenhower Dollar. All are of clad copper nickel composition.

DATE	MINTAGE	UNC-65	PROOF-65
1979	360,222,000	2.00	
1979D	288,015,744	2.00	
1979S	109,576,000	2.00	24.00
1980P	27,610,000	2.00	
1980D	41,628,708	2.00	
1980S	20,422,000	2.00	24.00
1981P		2.00	
1981D		2.00	
1981S		2.00	24.00

TRADE DOLLARS
1873-1883
Designer, William Barber

Authorized on February 12, 1873. This coin was used for trade with the Orient. Trade Dollars were coined at the Philadelphia, Carson City, and San Francisco Mints.
Composition, 90 percent silver, 10 percent copper.

AG-Obverse: Outline of Liberty is worn smooth but complete.
    Reverse: Some letters touch rim. Eagle outline complete.

G-Obverse: Outline of Liberty more distinct. The seat of bales is visible.
    Reverse: Letters are clear of rim.

VG-Obverse: A part of motto, "IN GOD WE TRUST" is visible.
    Reverse: A part of "E PLURIBUS UNUM" shows.

F-Obverse: "IN GOD WE TRUST" and "LIBERTY" will be complete but rather weak. Some gown details show.
    Reverse: "E PLURIBUS UNUM" is complete but weak. Some wing feathers visible.

VF-Obverse: Motto and "LIBERTY" sharp. Most gown details show.
    Reverse: Motto strong. Most eagle's feathers show.

EF-Obverse: All details show. Slight wear on breast and knees.
    Reverse: All feathers show. Slight wear on breast and legs.

TRADE DOLLARS

DATE	MINTAGE	G-6	VG-10	F-15	VF-30	EF-45	AU-50	UNC-60	UNC-65	PROOF-65
1873	397,500	70.00	80.00	90.00	110.00	175.00	330.00	1050.00	5950.00	10000.00
1873CC . . .	124,500	80.00	90.00	95.00	115.00	180.00	340.00	1150.00	5950.00	
1873S	703,000	70.00	80.00	90.00	110.00	175.00	330.00	1050.00	5950.00	
1874	987,800	65.00	75.00	85.00	100.00	165.00	325.00	1050.00	5950.00	10000.00
1874CC . . .	1,373,200	80.00	90.00	95.00	115.00	180.00	340.00	1100.00	5950.00	
1874S	2,549,000	70.00	80.00	90.00	110.00	175.00	330.00	1050.00	5950.00	
1875	218,900	90.00	110.00	135.00	200.00	300.00	450.00	1250.00	5950.00	10000.00
1875CC . . .	1,573,700	80.00	90.00	95.00	115.00	180.00	340.00	1150.00	5950.00	
1875S	4,487,000	70.00	80.00	90.00	110.00	175.00	330.00	1050.00	5950.00	
1876	456,150	70.00	80.00	90.00	110.00	175.00	330.00	1050.00	5950.00	10000.00
1876CC . . .	509,000	80.00	90.00	100.00	125.00	175.00	330.00	1150.00	5950.00	
1876S	5,227,000	70.00	80.00	90.00	110.00	175.00	330.00	1050.00	5950.00	
1877	3,039,710	70.00	80.00	90.00	110.00	175.00	330.00	1050.00	5950.00	10000.00
1877CC . . .	534,000	80.00	90.00	125.00	165.00	195.00	425.00	1250.00	5950.00	
1877S	9,519,000	70.00	80.00	90.00	110.00	175.00	330.00	1050.00	5950.00	
1878	900	Proof only								10000.00
1878CC . . .	97,000	120.00	165.00	200.00	250.00	450.00	1250.00	2650.00	– –	
1878S	4,162,000	70.00	80.00	90.00	110.00	175.00	330.00	2500.00	5950.00	
1879	1,541	Proof only								10000.00
1880	1,987	Proof only								10000.00
1881	960	Proof only								10000.00
1882	1,097	Proof only								10000.00
1883	979	Proof only								10000.00

There are ten 1884 and five 1885 trade dollars known. However, the Mint report shows none made in these two years. They are believed to be struck at the mint by an unknown person for private distribution.

COMMEMORATIVE DOLLARS

Lafayette
1900
Designer, Charles E. Barber

Authorized on March 3, 1899. Issued to commemorate General Lafayette. The Lafayette Memorial Commission sold this coin for $2.00 each.

		GEORGE WASHINGTON AND LAFAYETTE		GENERAL LAFAYETTE MONUMENT			

DATE	MINTAGE			EF-45	AU-50	UNC-60	UNC-65
1900	36,026			525.00	875.00	1950.00	9375.00

PROOF SETS

Modern proof sets have been issued by the mint from 1936 to 1942, 1950 to 1964 and 1968 to date. Proof sets were temporarily suspended between 1943 and 1949 and again between 1965 and 1967. Those issued from 1936 thru 1964 were struck at Philadelphia and those issued from 1968 to date have been struck at San Francisco. Proof sets from 1973 to date have included dollar coins.

DATE	MINTAGE	PROOF-65
1936	3,837	8250.00
1937	5,542	5000.00
1938	8,045	2350.00
1939	8,795	2275.00
1940	11,246	1800.00
1941	15,287	1675.00
1942 . . . . . . }	21,120	1675.00
1942 Ty. II . }		2000.00
1950	51,386	775.00
1951	57,500	550.00
1952	81,980	325.00
1953	128,800	200.00
1954	233,300	125.00
1955	378,200	87.50
1956	669,384	47.50
1957	1,247,952	27.50
1958	875,652	38.50
1959	1,149,291	27.50
1960 . . . . . . }	1,691,602	21.00
1960 Sm. . }		60.00
1961	3,028,244	20.00
1962	3,218,019	20.00
1963	3,075,645	20.00
1964	3,950,762	20.00
1968S	3,041,509	10.00
1969S	2,934,631	10.00
1970S . . . . }	2,632,810	21.00
1970S Sm. }		210.00
1971S	3,220,733	10.00
1972S	3,260,996	10.00
1973S	2,760,339	17.50
1974S	2,612,568	16.00
1975S	2,845,450	22.50
1976S	4,123,056	11.00
1976S		
3 piece	3,295,666	25.00
1977S	3,251,152	12.50
1978S	3,127,781	25.00
1979S . . . . }	3,677,175	25.00
1979S Ty.II }		225.00
1980S	2,144,231	25.00

GOLD DOLLARS
1849-1889

Authorized on March 3, 1849. They were coined at the Philadelphia Mint, Charlotte, North Carolina Mint, Dahlonega, Georgia Mint, the New Orleans Mint and the San Francisco Mint.
All Gold Dollars were made of 90 percent gold, 10 percent copper.

Liberty Head
1849-1854
Designer, James B. Longacre

F-Obverse: "LIBERTY" is fully visible but weak.
  Reverse: Leaves are clear but no fine details show.

VF-Obverse: "LIBERTY" is strong. Some fine hair details show.
  Reverse: Leaves show some details.

EF-Obverse: All details show. Wear only on high points of hair.
  Reverse: All details show. Wear only on tips of leaves.

CLOSED WREATH

DATE	MINTAGE	F-15	VF-30	EF-45	AU-50	UNC-60	UNC-65
1849 Open Wreath ...	688,567	300.00	550.00	825.00	1250.00	1500.00	8000.00
1849 Closed Wreath ...		300.00	550.00	825.00	1250.00	1500.00	8000.00
1849C	11,634	425.00	750.00	1250.00	1750.00	2275.00	— —
1849D	21,588	350.00	650.00	1000.00	1500.00	2750.00	— —
1849 0	215,000	325.00	600.00	850.00	1250.00	1600.00	— —
1850	481,953	300.00	525.00	650.00	850.00	1475.00	9500.00
1850C	6,966	450.00	750.00	1250.00	1750.00	2750.00	— —
1850D	8,382	400.00	700.00	1200.00	1750.00	2250.00	— —
1850 0	14,000	325.00	600.00	850.00	1250.00	1450.00	8800.00
1851	3,317,671	300.00	525.00	650.00	850.00	1350.00	7800.00
1851C	41,267	350.00	650.00	1000.00	1500.00	1900.00	9500.00
1851D	9,882	425.00	750.00	1250.00	1750.00	1950.00	10000.00
1851 0	290,000	300.00	525.00	650.00	850.00	1200.00	8500.00
1852	2,045,351	300.00	525.00	650.00	850.00	1350.00	7800.00
1852C	9,434	375.00	700.00	1250.00	1750.00	2000.00	14000.00
1852D	6,360	375.00	700.00	1250.00	1750.00	1975.00	— —
1852 0	140,000	300.00	525.00	650.00	850.00	1475.00	8550.00
1853	4,076,051	300.00	525.00	650.00	850.00	1375.00	7850.00
1853C	11,515	425.00	700.00	1000.00	1500.00	2750.00	— —
1853D	6,583	375.00	700.00	1200.00	1750.00	2000.00	— —
1853 0	290,000	300.00	525.00	650.00	850.00	1250.00	8550.00

GOLD DOLLARS

DATE	MINTAGE	F-15	VF-30	EF-45	AU-50	UNC-60	UNC-65
1854	736,709	300.00	525.00	650.00	850.00	1350.00	7850.00
1854D	2,935	600.00	1000.00	1750.00	2500.00	4000.00	— —
1854S	14,632	300.00	525.00	900.00	2250.00	2250.00	15000.00

Indian Small Head
1854-1856

DATE	MINTAGE	F-15	VF-30	EF-45	AU-50	UNC-60	UNC-65
1854	902,736	455.00	750.00	1350.00	2500.00	6500.00	27500.00
1855	758,269	455.00	750.00	1350.00	2500.00	6250.00	27500.00
1855C	9,803	750.00	950.00	3500.00	7500.00	— —	— —
1855D	1,811	2500.00	4000.00	7500.00	15000.00	— —	— —
1855 0	55,000	650.00	1250.00	2500.00	5000.00	6975.00	— —
1856S	24,600	600.00	1000.00	2000.00	4000.00	7000.00	— —

Indian Large Head
1856-1889

DATE	MINTAGE	F-15	VF-30	EF-45	AU-50	UNC-60	UNC-65	PROOF 65
1856 straight 5 .	1,762,936	350.00	525.00	675.00	950.00	1500.00	7500.00	
1856 slant 5		350.00	500.00	650.00	950.00	1200.00	6500.00	— —
1856D	1,460	3500.00	5000.00	7000.00	10000.00	— —	— —	
1857	774,789	350.00	500.00	750.00	1000.00	1200.00	6500.00	— —
1857C	13,280	550.00	800.00	1000.00	1500.00	— —	— —	
1857D	3,533	1250.00	2000.00	2500.00	3500.00	5000.00	— —	
1857S	10,000	550.00	900.00	1400.00	1900.00	— —	— —	
1858	117,995	375.00	500.00	750.00	1000.00	1350.00	6500.00	— —
1858D	3,477	750.00	1500.00	2250.00	3500.00	— —	— —	
1858S	10,000	525.00	775.00	1200.00	1700.00	— —	— —	
1859	168,244	400.00	500.00	750.00	1000.00	1200.00	6850.00	— —
1859C	5,235	750.00	1250.00	2000.00	3250.00	4000.00	— —	
1859D	4,952	800.00	1500.00	2250.00	4000.00	4750.00	— —	
1859S	15,000	500.00	700.00	1250.00	1750.00	— —	— —	

GOLD DOLLARS

DATE	MINTAGE	F-15	VF-30	EF-45	AU-50	UNC-60	UNC-65	PROOF-65
1860	36,668	350.00	525.00	775.00	1000.00	1200.00	7000.00	13500.00
1860D	1,566	3500.00	5000.00	7000.00	12500.00	15000.00	— —	
1860S	13,000	525.00	700.00	1000.00	1500.00	2000.00	7500.00	
1861	527,499	350.00	500.00	750.00	1000.00	1200.00	6500.00	13500.00
1861D	*	5950.00	7500.00	13500.00	18000.00	19500.00	— —	
1862	1,361,390	350.00	500.00	750.00	1000.00	1200.00	6500.00	13500.00
1863	6,250	650.00	875.00	1500.00	2500.00	3250.00	— —	16000.00
1864	5,950	625.00	800.00	1400.00	2400.00	3000.00	— —	16000.00
1865	3,725	625.00	800.00	1400.00	2400.00	3000.00	— —	16000.00
1866	7,130	625.00	800.00	1400.00	2400.00	3000.00	9000.00	16000.00
1867	5,250	650.00	850.00	1500.00	2500.00	3150.00	— —	13500.00
1868	10,525	550.00	750.00	1400.00	2400.00	3000.00	9000.00	13500.00
1869	5,925	625.00	775.00	1400.00	2400.00	3000.00	9000.00	13500.00
1870	6,335	600.00	750.00	1400.00	2400.00	2900.00	9000.00	13500.00
1870S	3,000	750.00	1250.00	1750.00	2250.00	2850.00	9500.00	
1871	3,900	600.00	775.00	1400.00	2400.00	3000.00	9000.00	13500.00
1872	3,530	625.00	775.00	1400.00	2400.00	3000.00	— —	13500.00
1873 Open 3 ...	125,125	350.00	500.00	750.00	1000.00	1200.00	6850.00	
1873 Closed 3 ..		425.00	725.00	1250.00	2250.00	— —	— —	13500.00
1874	198,820	350.00	500.00	750.00	1000.00	1200.00	6850.00	12000.00
1875	420	3750.00	5250.00	8250.00	12500.00	15000.00	35000.00	— —
1876	3,245	210.00	700.00	1250.00	1750.00	2000.00	7000.00	12000.00
1877	3,920	475.00	775.00	1400.00	2000.00	2250.00	7500.00	12000.00
1878	3,020	525.00	775.00	1400.00	2000.00	2750.00	7500.00	12000.00
1879	3,030	475.00	775.00	1400.00	2000.00	2750.00	7500.00	12000.00
1880	1,636	400.00	700.00	1400.00	2000.00	2750.00	7500.00	10000.00
1881	7,707	425.00	550.00	850.00	1250.00	1750.00	6500.00	10000.00
1882	5,125	425.00	575.00	850.00	1250.00	1750.00	6500.00	10000.00
1883	11,007	400.00	525.00	850.00	1250.00	1750.00	6500.00	10000.00
1884	6,236	400.00	525.00	850.00	1250.00	1750.00	6500.00	10000.00
1885	12,261	400.00	525.00	800.00	1250.00	1750.00	6500.00	10000.00
1886	6,016	400.00	525.00	850.00	1250.00	1750.00	6500.00	10000.00
1887	8,543	400.00	525.00	850.00	1250.00	1750.00	6500.00	10000.00
1888	16,580	400.00	525.00	800.00	1250.00	1750.00	6500.00	10000.00
1889	30,729	400.00	525.00	800.00	1250.00	1750.00	6500.00	10000.00

*The U. S. Mint report shows no 1861D gold dollars made by the Dahlonega mint. It is believed that the small quantities in existence were made after the Confederate States took over and placed the mint under the management of the local government.

$2.50 GOLD DOLLARS
Quarter Eagles
1796-1929

Authorized on April 2, 1792. They were coined at the Philadelphia Mint, Charlotte, North Carolina Mint, Dahlonega, Georgia Mint, the New Orleans Mint, the San Francisco Mint, and starting in 1911 at the Denver Mint.

The metal composition from 1796 to 1834, 91.67 percent gold, 8.33 percent copper. From 1834 to 1839, 89.92 percent gold, 10.08 percent copper and from 1840 to 1929, 90 percent gold, 10 percent copper.

Liberty Cap Small Head
1796-1807
Designer, Robert Scot

F-Obverse: Some faint details in Liberty's cap are evident.
Some hair details at back of head and neck show.
Reverse: "E PLURIBUS UNUM" is legible but weak.

VF-Obverse: Most cap and hair details show. Wear very evident on hair over ear.
Reverse: "E PLURIBUS UNUM" is sharp. Most of feathers show.

EF-Obverse: All details show with slight wear only on the high points of cap and curls.
Reverse: All details show with slight wear on head and wing edges.

STARS ON
OBVERSE

DATE	MINTAGE	F-15	VF-30	EF-45	AU-50	UNC-60	UNC-65
1796 NO STARS ..	963	9000.00	13500.00	25000.00	40000.00	50000.00	— —
1796 STARS	432	7000.00	12000.00	17500.00	30000.00	40000.00	— —
1797	427	5000.00	7500.00	11500.00	17500.00	25000.00	— —
1798	1,094	3750.00	6000.00	9000.00	15000.00	22000.00	— —
1802 over 01	3,035	2250.00	3750.00	6000.00	9500.00	13000.00	— —
1804 13 Stars reverse	3,327	3500.00	5500.00	12500.00	25000.00	35000.00	— —
1804 14 Stars reverse		2000.00	3000.00	5250.00	7500.00	10000.00	— —
1805	1,781	1750.00	3250.00	5500.00	7500.00	10000.00	— —
1806 over 04	1,616	2250.00	3750.00	6000.00	9500.00	13000.00	— —
1806 over 05		2500.00	5000.00	7500.00	10500.00	15000.00	— —
1807	6,812	1750.00	3000.00	5250.00	7500.00	10000.00	— —

$2.50 GOLD DOLLARS
QUARTER EAGLES

Liberty Cap Large Head
1808-1834
Designer, John Reich

F-Obverse: "LIBERTY" on headband legible but weak. Some hair and cap details evident.
    Reverse: "E PLURIBUS UNUM" readable but weak. Some feathers show.

VF-Obverse: "LIBERTY" sharp. Most details show.
    Reverse: "E PLURIBUS UNUM" clear. Most feathers show.

EF-Obverse: All details show with slight wear on the high points of cap and curls.
    Reverse: All details show with slight wear on head and wing edges.

DATE	MINTAGE	F-15	VF-30	EF-45	AU-50	UNC-60	UNC-65
1808	2,710	7500.00	12500.00	25000.00	40000.00	50000.00	— —
1821	6,448	2250.00	3750.00	6750.00	9000.00	14000.00	— —
1824 over							
21	2,600	2250.00	3750.00	6750.00	9000.00	14000.00	— —
1825	4,434	2250.00	3750.00	6750.00	9000.00	14000.00	— —
1826 over							
25	760	4000.00	8000.00	12000.00	25000.00	35000.00	— —
1827	2,800	2250.00	3750.00	6750.00	9000.00	14000.00	— —

In 1829 the coin was made about 1.5mm. smaller in diameter. Composition stayed the same.

DATE	MINTAGE	F-15	VF-30	EF-45	AU-50	UNC-60	UNC-65
1829	3,403	1750.00	3000.00	5000.00	7500.00	10000.00	— —
1830	4,540	1750.00	3000.00	5000.00	7500.00	10000.00	— —
1831	4,520	1750.00	3000.00	5000.00	7500.00	10000.00	— —
1832	4,400	1750.00	3000.00	5000.00	7500.00	10000.00	— —
1833	4,160	1750.00	3000.00	5000.00	7500.00	10000.00	— —
1834	4,000	7000.00	9000.00	17500.00	35000.00	45000.00	— —

$2.50 GOLD DOLLARS
QUARTER EAGLES

Liberty Head No Motto
1834-1839
Designer, William Kneass

F-Obverse: "LIBERTY" is complete with only one or two letters weak.
Reverse: Some of the eagle's feathers in both wings show.

VF-Obverse: "LIBERTY" sharp. Most of the details show. Wear very evident on hair around ear and forehead.

Reverse: Most of the feathers show.

EF-Obverse: All details show. Slight wear on high points of hair only.
Reverse: Wear on the tip of each feather, otherwise all feathers show.

**MOTTO REMOVED
FROM ABOVE EAGLE**

DATE	MINTAGE	F-15	VF-30	EF-45	AU-50	UNC-60	UNC-65
1834	112,234	400.00	475.00	750.00	1250.00	5150.00	22000.00
1835	131,402	400.00	475.00	750.00	1250.00	5150.00	22000.00
1836	547,986	400.00	475.00	750.00	1250.00	5150.00	22000.00
1837	45,080	425.00	500.00	850.00	1500.00	5350.00	25000.00
1838	47,030	425.00	500.00	850.00	1500.00	5350.00	25000.00
1838C	7,880	650.00	750.00	1250.00	2000.00	7500.00	— —
1839	27,021	425.00	500.00	850.00	1500.00	5750.00	25000.00
1839C	18,140	450.00	550.00	950.00	1750.00	6750.00	27500.00
1839D	13,674	450.00	575.00	950.00	1750.00	6750.00	27500.00
1839 0	17,781	425.00	525.00	850.00	1500.00	5850.00	25000.00

Coronet Type
1840-1907
Designer: Christian Gobrecht

1840	18,859	300.00	375.00	450.00	550.00	2100.00	6600.00
1840C	12,822	350.00	450.00	650.00	950.00	— —	11000.00
1840D	3,532	400.00	550.00	1250.00	1750.00	— —	— —
1840 0	33,580	325.00	400.00	500.00	650.00	1300.00	8250.00

$2.50 GOLD DOLLARS
QUARTER EAGLES

DATE	MINTAGE	F-15	VF-30	EF-45	AU-50	UNC-60	UNC-65	PROOF-65
1841		Proof only						165000.00
1841C	10,281	325.00	425.00	600.00	675.00	1675.00	8750.00	
1841D	4,164	375.00	475.00	750.00	950.00	2000.00	10500.00	
1842	2,823	375.00	475.00	675.00	850.00	— —	— —	
1842C	6,737	375.00	475.00	850.00	1000.00	1750.00	9350.00	
1842D	4,643	350.00	525.00	750.00	900.00	— —	— —	
1842 0	19,800	325.00	425.00	525.00	675.00	2000.00	8750.00	
1843	100,546	300.00	375.00	450.00	550.00	800.00	5500.00	
1843C Sm. date	26,054	1500.00	2250.00	4000.00	7500.00	— —	— —	
1843C Lg. date		350.00	450.00	650.00	850.00	1500.00	8000.00	
1843D	36,209	400.00	550.00	750.00	1000.00	1575.00	10000.00	
1843 0	368,002	300.00	375.00	450.00	550.00	800.00	6600.00	
1844	6,784	375.00	475.00	675.00	850.00	2000.00	8250.00	
1844C	11,622	375.00	450.00	625.00	750.00	2500.00	7150.00	
1844D	17,332	375.00	450.00	625.00	750.00	1500.00	7500.00	
1845	91,051	275.00	350.00	425.00	500.00	625.00	5500.00	
1845D .,......	19,460	375.00	450.00	675.00	850.00	1750.00	8750.00	
1845 0	4,000	450.00	600.00	1500.00	3750.00	— —	— —	
1846	21,598	300.00	375.00	450.00	550.00	800.00	5500.00	
1846C	4,808	500.00	850.00	1250.00	1750.00	2000.00	11000.00	
1846D	19,303	400.00	550.00	750.00	1250.00	1650.00	10000.00	
1846 0	62,000	350.00	450.00	650.00	850.00	1050.00	5500.00	
1847	29,814	300.00	375.00	450.00	550.00	700.00	5500.00	
1847C	23,226	400.00	550.00	750.00	1250.00	1600.00	8250.00	
1847D	15,784	400.00	550.00	750.00	1250.00	1600.00	8250.00	
1847 0	124,000	300.00	375.00	450.00	550.00	1000.00	5500.00	
1848	7,497	450.00	675.00	1000.00	1350.00	1850.00	8250.00	
1848 CAL.	1,389	5000.00	7500.00	12500.00	17500.00	— —	45000.00	
1848C	16,788	450.00	650.00	950.00	1500.00	1850.00	9350.00	
1848D	13,771	500.00	700.00	1000.00	1750.00	2250.00	10500.00	
1849	23,294	300.00	375.00	450.00	550.00	675.00	5500.00	
1849C	10,220	350.00	475.00	650.00	850.00	1750.00	9350.00	
1849D	10,945	350.00	475.00	650.00	850.00	1650.00	9350.00	
1850	252,923	300.00	375.00	450.00	550.00	700.00	4400.00	
1850C	9,148	350.00	450.00	625.00	775.00	1750.00	9350.00	
1850D	12,148	350.00	450.00	625.00	775.00	1750.00	9350.00	
1850 0	84,000	300.00	375.00	450.00	550.00	825.00	5500.00	
1851	1,372,748	300.00	375.00	450.00	550.00	700.00	4400.00	
1851C	14,923	400.00	550.00	700.00	950.00	1775.00	8500.00	
1851D	11,264	400.00	550.00	700.00	1250.00	1800.00	9350.00	
1851 0	148,000	325.00	395.00	475.00	550.00	675.00	5500.00	
1852	1,159,681	300.00	375.00	450.00	550.00	700.00	4400.00	
1852C	9,772	400.00	550.00	700.00	950.00	1850.00	8500.00	
1852D	4,078	450.00	650.00	850.00	1250.00	1900.00	10500.00	
1852 0	140,000	300.00	375.00	450.00	550.00	675.00	5500.00	
1853	1,404,668	300.00	375.00	450.00	550.00	700.00	4400.00	
1853D	3,178	600.00	800.00	1000.00	1250.00	2700.00	— —	

$2.50 GOLD DOLLARS
QUARTER EAGLES

DATE	MINTAGE	F-15	VF-30	EF-45	AU-50	UNC-60	UNC-65	PROOF-65
1854	596,258	300.00	375.00	450.00	550.00	700.00	4400.00	
1854C	7,295	400.00	550.00	700.00	950.00	1650.00	8500.00	
1854D	1,760	2500.00	3500.00	5000.00	7500.00	— —	— —	
1854 0	153,000	300.00	375.00	450.00	550.00	700.00	6600.00	
1854S	246	15000.00	20000.00	27500.00	— —	— —	— —	
1855	235,480	300.00	375.00	450.00	550.00	700.00	6600.00	
1855C	3,677	625.00	1000.00	1750.00	2600.00	3350.00	— —	
1855D	1,123	900.00	1500.00	2750.00	5000.00	— —	— —	
1856	384,240	300.00	375.00	450.00	550.00	750.00	4400.00	
1856C	7,913	500.00	650.00	950.00	1200.00	— —	— —	
1856D	874	3000.00	5000.00	7500.00	12500.00	— —	— —	
1856 0	21,100	400.00	550.00	700.00	950.00	1100.00	9350.00	
1856S	72,120	350.00	450.00	600.00	750.00	950.00	9350.00	
1857	214,130	300.00	375.00	450.00	550.00	725.00	4400.00	
1857D	2,364	550.00	750.00	1250.00	2500.00	3350.00	— —	
1857 0	34,000	300.00	375.00	450.00	550.00	800.00	6600.00	
1857S	69,200	300.00	375.00	450.00	550.00	1500.00	8350.00	
1858	47,377	300.00	375.00	550.00	750.00	900.00	4650.00	
1858C	9,056	350.00	450.00	650.00	800.00	1600.00	10000.00	
1859	39,444	300.00	375.00	550.00	700.00	900.00	5500.00	
1859D	2,244	450.00	625.00	1250.00	2000.00	2750.00	10500.00	
1859S	15,200	300.00	375.00	725.00	925.00	1500.00	8000.00	
1860	22,675	300.00	400.00	550.00	850.00	1100.00	6000.00	22000.00
1860C	7,469	400.00	550.00	900.00	1500.00	2400.00	9350.00	
1860S	35,600	300.00	375.00	550.00	750.00	1700.00	8350.00	
1861	1,283,878	300.00	375.00	475.00	650.00	775.00	4400.00	22000.00
1861S	24,000	450.00	550.00	900.00	1200.00	— —	8350.00	
1862	98,543	300.00	400.00	550.00	850.00	1050.00	4400.00	22000.00
1862 over 1		1250.00	2000.00	2750.00	3500.00	— —	— —	
1862S	8,000	500.00	650.00	1125.00	1600.00	3250.00	— —	
1863	30	Proof only						82500.00
1863S	10,800	400.00	550.00	900.00	1500.00	1875.00	— —	
1864	2,874	1700.00	2750.00	3950.00	4750.00	— —	— —	38500.00
1865	1,545	1200.00	1650.00	2750.00	4000.00	— —	— —	38500.00
1865S	23,376	300.00	450.00	750.00	1250.00	2000.00	10000.00	
1866	3,110	500.00	750.00	1100.00	1875.00	2500.00	9350.00	27500.00
1866S	38,960	300.00	450.00	750.00	1250.00	2100.00	10000.00	
1867	3,250	350.00	525.00	750.00	950.00	1850.00	9350.00	22000.00
1867S	28,000	300.00	450.00	700.00	1000.00	2000.00	8250.00	
1868	3,625	400.00	550.00	750.00	1250.00	1600.00	7150.00	22000.00
1868S	34,000	300.00	450.00	650.00	850.00	1450.00	7150.00	
1869	4,345	300.00	450.00	650.00	850.00	1150.00	6600.00	22000.00
1869S	29,500	300.00	450.00	650.00	850.00	1500.00	6850.00	
1870	4,555	325.00	500.00	700.00	925.00	1275.00	7150.00	22000.00
1870S	16,000	325.00	550.00	750.00	1000.00	1350.00	7750.00	

$2.50 GOLD DOLLARS
QUARTER EAGLES

DATE	MINTAGE	F-15	VF-30	EF-45	AU-50	UNC-60	UNC-65	PROOF-65
1871	5,350	350.00	600.00	850.00	1250.00	1500.00	8250.00	22000.00
1871S	22,000	325.00	550.00	750.00	950.00	1100.00	7750.00	
1872	3,030	300.00	450.00	650.00	850.00	1175.00	10500.00	22000.00
1872S	18,000	300.00	450.00	600.00	750.00	1475.00	6850.00	
1873	178,025	300.00	450.00	600.00	750.00	900.00	4400.00	22000.00
1873S	27,000	300.00	450.00	675.00	900.00	1300.00	5500.00	
1874	3,940	400.00	550.00	700.00	950.00	1350.00	8750.00	27500.00
1875	420	2500.00	5000.00	8500.00	15000.00	– –	30000.00	55000.00
1875S	11,600	300.00	450.00	600.00	750.00	1250.00	6600.00	
1876	4,221	350.00	600.00	800.00	1150.00	2000.00	8250.00	19000.00
1876S	5,000	350.00	475.00	600.00	900.00	1300.00	8750.00	
1877	1,652	500.00	650.00	850.00	1250.00	1600.00	10500.00	27500.00
1877S	35,400	300.00	450.00	600.00	850.00	1050.00	4400.00	
1878	286,260	300.00	450.00	600.00	850.00	1050.00	2750.00	22000.00
1878S	178,000	300.00	450.00	600.00	850.00	1050.00	2750.00	
1879	88,990	300.00	450.00	600.00	850.00	1050.00	2750.00	19000.00
1879S	43,500	300.00	450.00	600.00	850.00	1050.00	2750.00	
1880	2,996	350.00	550.00	700.00	950.00	1425.00	8250.00	22000.00
1881	691	1250.00	1750.00	3000.00	4500.00	– –	13750.00	27500.00
1882	4,067	300.00	450.00	600.00	850.00	1200.00	8250.00	19000.00
1883	2,002	300.00	450.00	600.00	850.00	1200.00	7150.00	19000.00
1884	2,023	300.00	450.00	600.00	850.00	1200.00	7150.00	19000.00
1885	887	650.00	1250.00	2000.00	3500.00	4500.00	13750.00	27500.00
1886	4,088	300.00	450.00	600.00	850.00	1200.00	8250.00	16500.00
1887	6,282	300.00	450.00	600.00	850.00	1175.00	5500.00	15500.00
1888	16,098	300.00	450.00	550.00	750.00	1050.00	3000.00	15500.00
1889	17,648	300.00	450.00	575.00	750.00	1050.00	3000.00	15500.00
1890	8,813	300.00	450.00	575.00	750.00	1175.00	4400.00	15500.00
1891	11,040	300.00	450.00	575.00	750.00	1075.00	3850.00	15500.00
1892	2,545	350.00	550.00	750.00	900.00	1250.00	7150.00	15500.00
1893	30,106	300.00	450.00	575.00	750.00	975.00	3000.00	15500.00
1894	4,122	300.00	450.00	575.00	750.00	1000.00	6000.00	15500.00
1895	6,119	300.00	450.00	525.00	700.00	975.00	4400.00	15500.00
1896	19,202	275.00	350.00	425.00	500.00	675.00	2750.00	13750.00
1897	29,904	275.00	350.00	425.00	500.00	675.00	2750.00	13750.00
1898	24,165	275.00	350.00	425.00	500.00	675.00	2750.00	13750.00
1899	27,350	275.00	350.00	425.00	500.00	675.00	2750.00	13750.00
1900	67,205	275.00	350.00	425.00	500.00	675.00	2750.00	13750.00
1901	91,323	275.00	350.00	425.00	500.00	675.00	2750.00	13750.00
1902	133,733	275.00	350.00	425.00	500.00	675.00	2750.00	13750.00
1903	201,257	275.00	350.00	425.00	500.00	675.00	2750.00	13750.00
1904	160,960	275.00	350.00	425.00	500.00	675.00	2750.00	13750.00
1905	217,944	275.00	350.00	425.00	500.00	675.00	2750.00	13750.00
1906	176,490	275.00	350.00	425.00	500.00	675.00	2750.00	13750.00
1907	336,448	275.00	350.00	425.00	500.00	675.00	2750.00	13750.00

$2.50 GOLD DOLLARS
QUARTER EAGLES

Indian Head
1908-1929
Designer, Bela Lyon Pratt

F-Obverse: The band on the forehead has no design. The knot in hair cord is very faint.
Reverse: Some feathers show. The upper part of wing shows definite wear.

VF-Obverse: A part of the design in the band on forehead is visible. Hair cord knot is sharp.
Reverse: Most feathers show.

EF-Obverse: Forehead band shows complete design. Slight wear shows on cheek and high points of bonnet.
Reverse: All feathers show. Wear only on wing edge at neckline.

DATE	MINTAGE	F-15	VF-30	EF-45	AU-50	UNC-60	UNC-65	PROOF-65
1908	565,057	325.00	350.00	400.00	525.00	650.00	3850.00	13750.00
1909	441,899	325.00	350.00	400.00	525.00	650.00	4850.00	13750.00
1910	492,682	325.00	350.00	400.00	525.00	650.00	5250.00	13750.00
1911	704,191	325.00	350.00	400.00	525.00	650.00	4450.00	13750.00
1911D	55,680	950.00	1450.00	1750.00	3500.00	8500.00	29500.00	
1912	616,197	325.00	350.00	400.00	525.00	650.00	4350.00	13750.00
1913	722,165	325.00	350.00	400.00	525.00	650.00	4350.00	13750.00
1914	240,117	325.00	350.00	400.00	525.00	1300.00	6250.00	13750.00
1914D	448,000	325.00	350.00	400.00	525.00	650.00	3850.00	
1915	606,100	325.00	350.00	400.00	525.00	650.00	3850.00	13750.00
1925D	578,000	325.00	350.00	400.00	525.00	650.00	3500.00	
1926	446,000	325.00	350.00	400.00	525.00	650.00	3500.00	
1927	388,000	325.00	350.00	400.00	525.00	650.00	3500.00	
1928	416,000	325.00	350.00	400.00	525.00	650.00	3500.00	
1929	532,000	325.00	350.00	400.00	525.00	650.00	3500.00	

THREE DOLLAR GOLD
1854-1889
Designer: James B. Longacre

Authorized on February 21, 1853 and designed by James B. Longacre. They were unpopular which led to little demand. Because of the low quantity struck in each year they are considered scarce today. All Three Dollar Gold pieces were made of 90 percent gold, 10 percent copper.

F-Obverse: "LIBERTY" complete. Feather tops of headdress are worn smooth.
Reverse: Some details in wreath show but definite wear is visible. "3 DOLLARS" and date are bold.

VF-Obverse: Some faint details show in tops of the headdress feathers.
Reverse: Most wreath details show.

EF-Obverse: All details show. Slight wear on high points of feathers and hair.
Reverse: All wreath details show. Slight wear on knot of bow and high points of wreath.

DATE	MINTAGE	F-15	VF-30	EF-45	AU-50	UNC-60	UNC-65	PROOF-65
1854	138,618	850.00	1350.00	1700.00	2350.00	5000.00	14000.00	
1854D	1,120	6000.00	9500.00	16500.00	21000.00	— —	— —	
1854 0	24,000	900.00	1400.00	1950.00	2750.00	5550.00	17500.00	
1855	50,555	875.00	1350.00	1900.00	2700.00	5000.00	17000.00	
1855S	6,600	925.00	1400.00	1950.00	2750.00	— —		
1856	26,010	875.00	1350.00	1900.00	2700.00	5000.00	17000.00	— —
1856S	34,500	875.00	1350.00	1950.00	2750.00	6500.00	— —	
1857	20,891	875.00	1350.00	1950.00	2750.00	5000.00	17000.00	— —
1857S	14,000	975.00	1400.00	2250.00	3250.00	— —	— —	
1858	2,133	1100.00	1600.00	2500.00	3750.00	6600.00	22500.00	— —
1859	15,638	875.00	1350.00	1900.00	2700.00	5000.00	17000.00	— —
1860	7,155	900.00	1400.00	2250.00	3250.00	5350.00	20000.00	30000.00
1860S	7,000	925.00	1400.00	1900.00	2700.00	— —	— —	
1861	6,072	900.00	1400.00	2250.00	3250.00	5350.00	20000.00	30000.00
1862	5,785	900.00	1400.00	2250.00	3250.00	5500.00	20000.00	31000.00
1863	5,039	1000.00	1500.00	2500.00	3750.00	7000.00	22500.00	32500.00
1864	2,680	1100.00	1600.00	2350.00	3500.00	7500.00	21250.00	31000.00
1865	1,165	1250.00	1750.00	3500.00	5750.00	8250.00	35000.00	40000.00
1866	4,030	1250.00	1750.00	2500.00	3750.00	6250.00	22500.00	32500.00
1867	2,650	1100.00	1600.00	2750.00	4000.00	6250.00	25000.00	31000.00
1868	4,875	1000.00	1500.00	2750.00	4000.00	6250.00	25000.00	32500.00
1869	2,525	1250.00	1750.00	2900.00	4250.00	6350.00	27500.00	32500.00
1870	3,535	1050.00	1500.00	2900.00	4250.00	6250.00	27500.00	32500.00
1870S	2					— —	— —	
1871	1,330	1200.00	1700.00	2750.00	4000.00	6750.00	25000.00	32500.00

THREE DOLLAR GOLD

DATE	MINTAGE	F-15	VF-30	EF-45	AU-50	UNC-60	UNC-65	PROOF-65
1872	2,030	1050.00	1500.00	2500.00	3750.00	6250.00	22500.00	32500.00
1873 Open 3	25	Proof only				— —		75000.00
1873 Closed 3		2000.00	5000.00	6500.00	9500.00	— —	— —	40000.00
1874	41,820	875.00	1350.00	1950.00	2750.00	5000.00	17000.00	35000.00
1875	20	Proof only				— —		150000.00
1876	45	Proof only				— —		75000.00
1877	1,488	1500.00	2000.00	3750.00	6500.00	7750.00	— —	40000.00
1878	82,324	875.00	1350.00	1750.00	2500.00	4950.00	15000.00	35000.00
1879	3,030	1000.00	1500.00	1900.00	2700.00	5000.00	17000.00	30000.00
1880	1,036	1000.00	1500.00	1900.00	2700.00	5100.00	17000.00	30000.00
1881	554	1400.00	1900.00	3500.00	5750.00	7000.00	22500.00	31000.00
1882	1,576	1250.00	1750.00	2900.00	4250.00	5350.00	20000.00	30000.00
1883	989	1400.00	1900.00	3000.00	4500.00	5500.00	21000.00	30000.00
1884	1,106	1250.00	1750.00	3000.00	4500.00	5350.00	21000.00	27500.00
1885	910	1400.00	1900.00	3250.00	5000.00	6000.00	21000.00	27500.00
1886	1,142	1250.00	1750.00	2900.00	4250.00	5750.00	21000.00	27500.00
1887	6,160	950.00	1350.00	2500.00	3750.00	5000.00	15000.00	25000.00
1888	5,291	950.00	1350.00	2500.00	3750.00	5000.00	15000.00	25000.00
1889	2,429	950.00	1350.00	2500.00	3750.00	5000.00	15000.00	25000.00

$5.00 GOLD
HALF EAGLES
1795-1929

Authorized on April 2, 1792. The half eagle was the first gold coin struck at the Philadelphia Mint and later struck at all of the seven U.S. Mints. From 1795 to 1834, Liberty Cap type, the composition was .9167 gold, .0833 copper. The composition changed with the 1834 Liberty head through 1838 to .8992 gold, .1008 copper. Again it changed , in 1839 through 1929, to 90% gold, 10% copper.

Liberty Cap Small Eagle
1795-1807
Designer, Robert Scot

DATE	MINTAGE	F-15	VF-30	EF-45	AU-50	UNC-60	UNC-65
1795	8,707	4500.00	6000.00	9000.00	20000.00	25000.00	— —
1796 over 5	6,196	4500.00	6250.00	9000.00	22500.00	27500.00	— —
1797 15 Stars . .	3,609	6000.00	8250.00	15000.00	25000.00	30000.00	— —
1797 16 Stars . .		6000.00	8250.00	15000.00	25000.00	30000.00	— —
1798	*	EXTREMELY RARE					

$5.00 GOLD
HALF EAGLES

Liberty Cap Large Eagle
1795-1807
Designer, Robert Scot

F-Obverse: Some evidence of details in Liberty's cap and hair at back of neck.
Reverse: "E PLURIBUS UNUM" is legible but weak.

VF-Obverse: Most cap and hair details show. Wear very evident on hair over ear.
Reverse: "E PLURIBUS UNUM" is sharp. Most of feathers show.

EF-Obverse: All details show with slight wear only on the high points of cap and curls.
Reverse: All details show with slight wear on head and wing edges.

DATE	MINTAGE	F-15	VF-30	EF-45	AU-50	UNC-60	UNC-65
1795	*	6000.00	10000.00	15000.00	30000.00	35000.00	— —
1797 7 over 5	*	5250.00	7500.00	10500.00	20000.00	25000.00	— —
1798 13 Stars . .	*24,867	2500.00	4000.00	6000.00	11000.00	15000.00	— —
1798 14 Stars . .		2500.00	5000.00	7000.00	12000.00	16000.00	— —
1799	7,451	2250.00	3500.00	5500.00	10000.00	12500.00	— —
1800	37,628	2250.00	3500.00	5500.00	10000.00	12500.00	— —
1802 2 over 1	53,176	2000.00	3000.00	4500.00	8000.00	10000.00	— —
1803 3 over 2	33,506	2000.00	3000.00	4500.00	8000.00	10000.00	— —
1804	30,475	2000.00	3000.00	4500.00	8000.00	10000.00	— —

*THE MINT HAD BEEN CLOSED DUE TO YELLOW FEVER. LATE IN 1798 AN EMERGENCY STRIKING RESULTED IN THE MIXED DATES WITH QUANTITY FIGURES ALL INCLUDED IN THE MINTAGE FIGURES FOR 1798.

DATE	MINTAGE	F-15	VF-30	EF-45	AU-50	UNC-60	UNC-65
1805	33,183	2000.00	3000.00	4500.00	8000.00	10000.00	— .
1806	64,093	2000.00	3000.00	4500.00	7000.00	9000.00	— —
1807	32,488	2000.00	3000.00	4500.00	8000.00	10000.00	— —

$5.00 GOLD
HALF EAGLES

Liberty Cap Large Head
1807-1834
Designer, John Reich

F-Obverse: "LIBERTY" on headband legible but weak. Some hair and cap details evident.
Reverse: "E PLURIBUS UNUM" readable but weak. Some feathers show.

VF-Obverse: "LIBERTY" sharp. Most details show.
Reverse: "E PLURIBUS UNUM" clear. Most feathers show.

EF-Obverse: All details show with slight wear on the high points of cap and curls.
Reverse: All details show with slight wear on head and wing edges.

DATE	MINTAGE	F-15	VF-30	EF-45	AU-50	UNC-60	UNC-65
1807	51,605	2000.00	2750.00	4000.00	6500.00	8000.00	15000.00
1808	55,578	1750.00	2500.00	3500.00	6000.00	8000.00	15000.00
1808 over 7		1750.00	2500.00	3500.00	6000.00	8000.00	15000.00
1809 over 8	33,875	1750.00	2500.00	3500.00	6000.00	8000.00	15000.00
1810	100,287	1750.00	2500.00	3500.00	6000.00	8000.00	15000.00
1811	99,581	1750.00	2500.00	3500.00	6000.00	8000.00	15000.00
1812	58,087	1750.00	2500.00	3500.00	6000.00	8000.00	15000.00
1813	95,428	2000.00	3250.00	5000.00	7500.00	9000.00	17500.00
1814 over 3	15,454	3000.00	4000.00	5500.00	8500.00	10000.00	20000.00
1815	635	EXTREMELY RARE					
1818	48,588	2500.00	3500.00	5000.00	7000.00	8500.00	15000.00
1819	51,723	EXTREMELY RARE					
1820	263,806	2250.00	3500.00	4500.00	6500.00	7500.00	12500.00
1821	34,641	3500.00	6000.00	10000.00	22500.00	25000.00	— —
1822	17,796	EXTREMELY RARE					
1823	14,485	3000.00	4500.00	6500.00	8500.00	10000.00	17500.00
1824	17,340	6000.00	10000.00	17500.00	30000.00	32500.00	— —
1825 over 1	29,060	3500.00	6000.00	10000.00	17500.00	20000.00	— —
1825 over 4		EXTREMELY RARE					
1826	18,069	4000.00	6500.00	10000.00	20000.00	25000.00	— —
1827	24,913	6000.00	12500.00	20000.00	35000.00	40000.00	— —

$5.00 GOLD
HALF EAGLES

DATE	MINTAGE	F-15	VF-30	EF-45	AU-50	UNC-60	UNC-65
1828		6000.00	10000.00	20000.00	35000.00	40000.00	– –
1828 over 7	28,029	5000.00	7000.00	15000.00	27500.00	32000.00	– –
1829	57,442	EXTREMELY RARE					
1830	126,351	3500.00	5000.00	8000.00	15000.00	18500.00	– –
1831	140,594	3500.00	5000.00	8000.00	15000.00	18500.00	– –
1832							
12 Stars . .	157,487	EXTREMELY RARE					
1832							
13 Stars . .		5500.00	8000.00	12500.00	22500.00	27500.00	– –
1833	193,630	3000.00	4500.00	7000.00	14000.00	18000.00	38000.00
1834		3000.00	5000.00	8000.00	17500.00	20000.00	– –
1834 Serf 4	50,141	3000.00	5000.00	8000.00	17500.00	20000.00	– –

Liberty Head No Motto
1834-1838
Designer, William Kneass

F-Obverse: "LIBERTY" is complete with only one or two weak letters.
  Reverse: Some of the feathers in both wings show.

VF-Obverse: "LIBERTY" sharp. Most of the details show. Wear evident on hair around ear and forehead.
  Reverse: Most of the feathers show.

EF-Obverse: All details show. Slight wear on high points of hair only.
  Reverse: Wear on the tip of each feather, otherwise all feathers show.

DATE	MINTAGE	F-15	VF-30	EF-45	AU-50	UNC-60	UNC-65
1834		400.00	500.00	800.00	1600.00	6500.00	32000.00
1834 Serf 4	657,460	525.00	675.00	1400.00	3100.00	– –	– –
1835	371,534	400.00	500.00	800.00	1600.00	6750.00	32000.00
1836	553,174	400.00	500.00	800.00	1600.00	6500.00	32000.00
1837	207,121	450.00	550.00	900.00	2000.00	8250.00	35000.00
1838	286,588	400.00	500.00	800.00	1600.00	6500.00	32000.00
1838C	17,179	925.00	1500.00	3000.00	6000.00	– –	– –
1838D	20,583	925.00	1500.00	2850.00	5750.00	– –	– –

173

$5.00 GOLD
HALF EAGLES

Coronet Type
1839-1908
Designer, Christian Gobrecht

DATE	MINTAGE	F-15	VF-30	EF-45	AU-50	UNC-60	UNC-65
1839	118,143	350.00	400.00	600.00	900.00	2500.00	15000.00
1839C	17,205	600.00	750.00	1250.00	2500.00	5000.00	— —
1839D	18,939	600.00	750.00	1250.00	2500.00	4175.00	— —
1840	137,382	350.00	400.00	500.00	650.00	2500.00	15000.00
1840C	18,992	500.00	750.00	1250.00	2500.00	5000.00	— —
1840D	22,896	500.00	750.00	1400.00	3000.00	4750.00	— —
1840 0	40,120	375.00	500.00	650.00	1000.00	3250.00	— —
1841	15,833	350.00	450.00	600.00	900.00	3000.00	15000.00
1841C	21,467	450.00	750.00	900.00	1750.00	5000.00	— —
1841D	29,392	450.00	750.00	900.00	1750.00	4600.00	— —
1841 0	50	EXTREMELY RARE					
1842	27,578	350.00	500.00	600.00	900.00	3400.00	15000.00
1842C Sm. date	27,432	900.00	1250.00	2000.00	4500.00	— —	— —
1842C Lg. date		450.00	600.00	900.00	1750.00	— —	— —
1842D Sm. date	59,608	450.00	600.00	900.00	1750.00	— —	— —
1842D Lg. date		600.00	800.00	1250.00	2500.00	— —	— —
1842 0	16,400	375.00	550.00	850.00	1750.00	5000.00	— —
1843	611,205	350.00	400.00	850.00	1000.00	1500.00	15000.00
1843C	44,277	450.00	600.00	900.00	1750.00	4350.00	— —
1843D	98,452	450.00	600.00	900.00	1500.00	4150.00	— —
1843 0 Sm. Letters . . .	19,075	350.00	450.00	750.00	1500.00	4150.00	— —
1843 0 Lg. Letters . . .	82,000	350.00	450.00	900.00	1750.00	4250.00	— —
1844	340,330	350.00	400.00	500.00	650.00	1600.00	15000.00
1844C	23,631	550.00	650.00	1000.00	2000.00	4900.00	— —
1844D	88,982	450.00	600.00	750.00	1500.00	4250.00	— —
1844 0	364,600	375.00	600.00	750.00	1500.00	2750.00	— —
1845	417,099	350.00	400.00	500.00	650.00	1500.00	15000.00
1845D	90,629	450.00	600.00	900.00	1750.00	4250.00	— —
1845 0	41,000	375.00	575.00	750.00	1500.00	4300.00	— —
1846	395,942	350.00	400.00	500.00	650.00	1500.00	15000.00
1846C	12,995	550.00	700.00	1200.00	2500.00	5000.00	— —
1846D	80,294	550.00	650.00	900.00	1750.00	4250.00	— —
1846 0	58,000	375.00	600.00	700.00	1500.00	4150.00	— —
1847	915,981	350.00	400.00	500.00	650.00	1300.00	15000.00
1847C	84,151	450.00	600.00	900.00	1750.00	5750.00	— —

$5.00 GOLD
HALF EAGLES

DATE	MINTAGE	F-15	VF-30	EF-45	AU-50	UNC-60	UNC-65	PROOF-65
1847D	64,405	450.00	600.00	900.00	1750.00	4500.00	— —	
1847 O	12,000	450.00	600.00	900.00	1750.00	— —	— —	
1848	260,775	350.00	400.00	500.00	650.00	1600.00	15000.00	
1848C	64,472	450.00	600.00	900.00	1750.00	5000.00	— —	
1848D	47,465	450.00	600.00	900.00	1750.00	4000.00	— —	
1849	133,070	350.00	400.00	500.00	650.00	1500.00	15000.00	
1849C	64,823	450.00	700.00	900.00	1750.00	4500.00	— —	
1849D	39,036	450.00	700.00	900.00	1750.00	5000.00	— —	
1850	64,491	350.00	400.00	500.00	650.00	2000.00	15000.00	
1850C	63,591	450.00	600.00	900.00	1750.00	4500.00	— —	
1850D	43,984	450.00	600.00	900.00	1750.00	5250.00	— —	
1851	377,505	350.00	400.00	500.00	650.00	1500.00	1500.00	
1851C	49,176	450.00	600.00	900.00	1750.00	4750.00	— —	
1851D	62,710	450.00	600.00	900.00	1750.00	4500.00	— —	
1851 O	41,000	375.00	600.00	750.00	1400.00	4750.00	— —	
1852	573,901	350.00	400.00	500.00	650.00	1400.00	15000.00	
1852C	72,574	450.00	600.00	900.00	1750.00	4000.00	— —	
1852D	91,584	450.00	600.00	900.00	1750.00	4250.00	— —	
1853	305,770	350.00	400.00	500.00	650.00	1500.00	15000.00	
1853C	65,571	450.00	600.00	900.00	1750.00	4500.00	— —	
1853D	89,678	450.00	600.00	900.00	1750.00	4000.00	— —	
1854	160,675	350.00	400.00	500.00	650.00	1575.00	15000.00	
1854C	39,283	450.00	600.00	900.00	1750.00	5000.00	— —	
1854D	56,413	450.00	600.00	900.00	1750.00	4250.00	— —	
1854 O	46,000	450.00	600.00	750.00	1400.00	3500.00	— —	
1854S	268	EXTREMELY RARE						
1855	117,098	350.00	400.00	500.00	650.00	1600.00	15000.00	
1855C	39,788	450.00	600.00	900.00	1750.00	4800.00	— —	
1855D	22,432	450.00	600.00	900.00	1750.00	4600.00	— —	
1855 O	11,100	450.00	600.00	900.00	1750.00	5000.00	— —	
1855S	61,000	350.00	400.00	500.00	650.00	4150.00	— —	
1856	197,990	350.00	400.00	500.00	650.00	1400.00	15000.00	
1856C	28,457	450.00	600.00	900.00	1750.00	4850.00	— —	
1856D	19,786	450.00	600.00	900.00	1750.00	4850.00	— —	
1856 O	10,000	450.00	650.00	1250.00	2500.00	— —	— —	
1856S	105,100	350.00	400.00	500.00	650.00	4150.00	— —	
1857	98,188	350.00	400.00	500.00	650.00	1600.00	15000.00	
1857C	31,360	450.00	600.00	900.00	1750.00	4850.00	— —	
1857D	17,046	450.00	600.00	900.00	1750.00	4850.00	— —	
1857 O	13,000	450.00	675.00	900.00	1750.00	4900.00	— —	
1857S	87,000	350.00	400.00	500.00	650.00	4150.00	— —	
1858	15,136	400.00	450.00	600.00	1250.00	2500.00	18000.00	
1858C	38,856	450.00	600.00	900.00	1750.00	4900.00	— —	
1858D	15,362	450.00	600.00	950.00	1750.00	4900.00	— —	
1858S	18,600	450.00	600.00	750.00	1450.00	7500.00	— —	
1859	16,814	350.00	450.00	600.00	1250.00	3000.00	— —	
1859C	31,847	450.00	600.00	900.00	1750.00	4850.00	— —	
1859D	10,366	525.00	750.00	1000.00	1900.00	5000.00	— —	
1859S	13,220	450.00	600.00	750.00	1450.00	7500.00	— —	
1860	19,825	350.00	450.00	550.00	1100.00	2500.00	— —	— —
1860C	14,813	450.00	600.00	1000.00	1900.00	5000.00	— —	
1860D	14,635	450.00	600.00	1000.00	1900.00	4900.00	— —	
1860S	21,200	375.00	550.00	650.00	1250.00	— —	—	
1861	688,150	350.00	400.00	500.00	1000.00	1500.00	15000.00	— —
1861C	6,879	1250.00	2000.00	3250.00	5500.00	— —	— —	
1861D	1,597	3500.00	6000.00	9000.00	15000.00	— —	— —	
1861S	18,000	350.00	450.00	650.00	1250.00	— —	— —	

$5.00 GOLD
HALF EAGLES

DATE	MINTAGE	F-15	VF-30	EF-45	AU-50	UNC-60	UNC-65	PROOF-65
1862	4,465	450.00	600.00	900.00	1750.00	– –	– –	– –
1862S	9,500	450.00	600.00	800.00	1500.00	– –	– –	– –
1863	2,472	600.00	800.00	1350.00	2500.00	5750.00	– –	– –
1863S	17,000	375.00	500.00	650.00	1250.00	5750.00	– –	
1864	4,200	450.00	600.00	750.00	1450.00	4750.00	– –	– –
1864S	3,888	1500.00	3000.00	5000.00	– –	– –	– –	
1865	1,295	600.00	900.00	1350.00	2500.00	7500.00	– –	– –
1865S	27,612	350.00	450.00	600.00	1250.00	– –	– –	
1866S	9,000	350.00	550.00	750.00	1450.00	– –	– –	

IN 1866 THE MOTTO WAS PLACED ON REVERSE ABOVE THE EAGLE.

1866	6,730	450.00	600.00	1250.00	3250.00	3250.00	– –	30000.00
1866S	34,920	450.00	600.00	1100.00	2250.00	3500.00	3500.00	– –
1867	6,920	400.00	600.00	850.00	1600.00	2250.00	– –	30000.00
1867S	29,000	450.00	600.00	1500.00	2750.00	– –	– –	
1868	5,725	400.00	600.00	800.00	1500.00	2250.00	– –	30000.00
1868S	52,000	400.00	600.00	900.00	1750.00	– –	– –	
1869	1,785	600.00	900.00	1350.00	2750.00	3500.00	– –	30000.00
1869S	31,000	450.00	600.00	1100.00	2250.00	– –	– –	
1870	4,035	400.00	750.00	1200.00	2500.00	3000.00	– –	30000.00
1870CC . . .	7,675	2000.00	3000.00	6000.00	– –	– –	– –	
1870S	17,000	450.00	700.00	1250.00	2500.00	4250.00	– –	
1871	3,230	500.00	750.00	1200.00	2300.00	4000.00	– –	30000.00
1871CC . . .	20,770	600.00	1000.00	1800.00	3500.00	6500.00	– –	
1871S	25,000	350.00	600.00	1000.00	1900.00	4250.00	– –	
1872	1,690	600.00	900.00	1350.00	2500.00	3250.00	– –	30000.00
1872CC . . .	16,980	600.00	1000.00	2000.00	3750.00	5250.00	– –	
1872S	36,400	350.00	500.00	600.00	1250.00	5000.00	– –	
1873	112,505	350.00	400.00	500.00	600.00	750.00	7000.00	30000.00
1873CC . . .	7,416	900.00	1500.00	2750.00	4000.00	9750.00	– –	
1873S	31,000	450.00	650.00	1250.00	2500.00	– –	– –	
1874	3,508	450.00	750.00	1200.00	2500.00	4000.00	– –	30000.00
1874CC . . .	21,198	600.00	900.00	1800.00	3500.00	5000.00	– –	
1874S	16,000	450.00	700.00	1250.00	2500.00	– –	– –	
1875	220	EXTREMELY RARE					– –	
1875CC . . .	11,828	900.00	1500.00	2750.00	4250.00	8850.00	– –	
1875S	9,000	450.00	700.00	1250.00	2500.00	4250.00	– –	
1876	1,477	750.00	1250.00	2000.00	3750.00	4500.00	– –	30000.00
1876CC . . .	6,887	600.00	1000.00	2000.00	4000.00	6500.00	– –	
1876S	4,000	600.00	1000.00	2000.00	4000.00	6500.00	– –	
1877	1,152	750.00	1250.00	2000.00	3750.00	4600.00	– –	32000.00
1877CC . . .	8,680	600.00	1000.00	2000.00	4000.00	6500.00	– –	
1877S	26,700	350.00	400.00	500.00	600.00	2000.00	7000.00	

$5.00 GOLD
HALF EAGLES

DATE	MINTAGE	F-15	VF-30	EF-45	AU-50	UNC-60	UNC-65	PROOF-65
1878	131,740	350.00	400.00	500.00	600.00	750.00	4000.00	27000.00
1878CC . . .	9,054	1250.00	2500.00	4250.00	7500.00	– –	– –	
1878S	144,700	350.00	400.00	500.00	600.00	750.00	4000.00	
1879	301,950	350.00	400.00	500.00	600.00	725.00	4000.00	25000.00
1879CC . . .	17,281	400.00	600.00	1250.00	2500.00	3250.00	– –	
1879S	426,200	350.00	400.00	500.00	600.00	725.00	4000.00	
1880	3,166,436	350.00	400.00	500.00	600.00	725.00	4000.00	25000.00
1880CC . . .	51,017	350.00	500.00	900.00	1750.00	2250.00	7000.00	
1880S	1,348,900	350.00	400.00	500.00	600.00	725.00	4000.00	
1881	5,708,802	350.00	400.00	500.00	600.00	725.00	4000.00	25000.00
1881CC . . .	13,886	350.00	650.00	1350.00	2750.00	3250.00	– –	
1881S	969,000	350.00	400.00	500.00	600.00	725.00	4000.00	
1882	2,514,568	350.00	400.00	500.00	600.00	725.00	4000.00	25000.00
1882CC . . .	82,817	350.00	400.00	500.00	600.00	900.00	6000.00	
1882S	969,000	350.00	400.00	500.00	600.00	725.00	4000.00	
1883	233,461	350.00	400.00	500.00	600.00	850.00	4000.00	25000.00
1883CC . . .	12,958	350.00	600.00	1200.00	2250.00	2850.00	– –	
1883S	83,200	350.00	400.00	600.00	1000.00	1450.00	5000.00	
1884	191,078	350.00	400.00	500.00	600.00	850.00	4500.00	25000.00
1884CC . . .	16,402	400.00	600.00	1250.00	2350.00	3000.00	– –	
1884S	177,000	350.00	400.00	500.00	600.00	725.00	3800.00	
1885	601,506	350.00	400.00	500.00	600.00	725.00	3800.00	25000.00
1885S	1,211,500	350.00	400.00	500.00	600.00	725.00	3800.00	
1886	388,432	350.00	400.00	500.00	600.00	725.00	3800.00	25000.00
1886S	3,268,000	350.00	400.00	500.00	600.00	725.00	3800.00	
1887	87	Proof only						55000.00
1887S	1,912,000	350.00	400.00	500.00	600.00	725.00	3800.00	
1888	18,296	350.00	400.00	500.00	600.00	725.00	4500.00	20000.00
1888S	293,900	350.00	400.00	500.00	600.00	725.00	4000.00	
1889	7,565	450.00	600.00	1000.00	1750.00	2250.00	– –	20000.00
1890	4,328	450.00	850.00	1250.00	2400.00	3250.00	– –	20000.00
1890CC . . .	53,800	350.00	400.00	500.00	600.00	900.00	4750.00	
1891	61,413	350.00	450.00	500.00	600.00	850.00	4000.00	20000.00
1891CC . . .	208,000	350.00	450.00	550.00	650.00	775.00	4500.00	
1892	753,572	350.00	400.00	500.00	600.00	825.00	4000.00	20000.00
1892CC . . .	82,968	350.00	450.00	550.00	650.00	1000.00	5000.00	
1892 O	10,000	650.00	900.00	1200.00	2250.00	3750.00	– –	
1892S	298,400	350.00	400.00	500.00	600.00	850.00	4500.00	
1893	1,528,197	350.00	400.00	500.00	600.00	825.00	4000.00	20000.00
1893CC . . .	60,000	350.00	400.00	550.00	650.00	1000.00	5000.00	
1893 O	110,000	350.00	500.00	600.00	700.00	1200.00	4750.00	
1893S	224,000	350.00	400.00	500.00	600.00	850.00	4000.00	
1894	957,955	350.00	400.00	500.00	600.00	825.00	3750.00	20000.00
1894 O	16,600	350.00	400.00	650.00	750.00	1350.00	5000.00	
1894S	55,900	350.00	400.00	500.00	600.00	1450.00	5500.00	
1895	1,345,936	350.00	400.00	500.00	650.00	825.00	3750.00	20000.00
1895S	112,000	350.00	400.00	500.00	650.00	1000.00	4750.00	
1896	59,063	350.00	400.00	500.00	650.00	875.00	4500.00	20000.00
1896S	155,400	350.00	400.00	500.00	650.00	950.00	5500.00	
1897	867,883	350.00	400.00	500.00	650.00	825.00	3750.00	20000.00
1897S	354,000	350.00	400.00	500.00	650.00	950.00	4500.00	
1898	633,495	350.00	400.00	500.00	650.00	850.00	3750.00	20000.00
1898S	1,397,400	350.00	400.00	500.00	650.00	850.00	4500.00	
1899	1,710,729	350.00	400.00	500.00	650.00	850.00	3750.00	20000.00
1899S	1,545,000	350.00	400.00	500.00	650.00	850.00	4000.00	
1900	1,405,730	350.00	400.00	500.00	650.00	850.00	3750.00	20000.00
1900S	329,000	350.00	400.00	500.00	650.00	850.00	4500.00	

$5.00 GOLD
HALF EAGLES

DATE	MINTAGE	F-15	VF-30	EF-45	AU-50	UNC-60	UNC-65	PROOF-65
1901	616,040	350.00	400.00	500.00	650.00	850.00	3750.00	20000.00
1901S, 1 over 0	3,648,000	350.00	450.00	600.00	900.00	850.00	3750.00	
1901S		350.00	400.00	500.00	650.00	825.00	3750.00	
1902	172,562	350.00	400.00	500.00	650.00	825.00	3750.00	20000.00
1902S	939,000	350.00	400.00	500.00	650.00	825.00	3750.00	
1903	227,024	350.00	400.00	500.00	650.00	825.00	3750.00	20000.00
1903S	1,855,000	350.00	400.00	500.00	650.00	825.00	3750.00	
1904	392,136	350.00	400.00	500.00	650.00	825.00	3750.00	20000.00
1904S	97,000	350.00	400.00	500.00	650.00	825.00	4500.00	
1905	302,308	350.00	400.00	500.00	650.00	825.00	3750.00	20000.00
1905S	880,700	350.00	400.00	500.00	650.00	825.00	4500.00	
1906	348,820	350.00	400.00	500.00	650.00	825.00	3750.00	20000.00
1906D	320,000	350.00	400.00	500.00	650.00	825.00	4000.00	
1906S	598,000	350.00	400.00	500.00	650.00	825.00	3750.00	
1907	626,192	350.00	400.00	500.00	650.00	825.00	3750.00	20000.00
1907D	888,000	350.00	400.00	500.00	650.00	825.00	4000.00	
1908	421,874	350.00	400.00	500.00	650.00	825.00	3750.00	

Indian Head
1908-1929
Designer, Bela Lyon Pratt

F-Obverse: The band on the forehead has no design. The knot in the hair cord is very faint.
Reverse: Some feathers show. The upper part of the wing shows definite wear.

VF-Obverse: A part of the design in the headband is visible. Hair cord knot is sharp.
Reverse: Most of the feathers show.

EF-Obverse: Headband shows complete design. Slight wear shows on cheek and high points of bonnet.
Reverse: All feathers show. Wear only on wing edge at neckline.

1908	578,012	275.00	350.00	450.00	600.00	1050.00	6750.00	25000.00
1908D	148,000	275.00	350.00	450.00	600.00	1050.00	7750.00	
1908S	82,000	450.00	650.00	1000.00	1325.00	6750.00	20000.00	
1909	627,138	275.00	350.00	450.00	600.00	1100.00	8000.00	25000.00
1909D	3,423,560	275.00	350.00	450.00	600.00	1025.00	5750.00	
1909 0	34,200	950.00	1650.00	2500.00	3250.00	15000.00	— —	
1909S	297,200	300.00	400.00	525.00	950.00	4750.00	20000.00	
1910	604,250	275.00	350.00	450.00	600.00	1100.00	7750.00	25000.00
1910D	193,600	275.00	350.00	450.00	600.00	4000.00	12000.00	
1910S	770,200	300.00	400.00	525.00	700.00	4750.00	16500.00	
1911	915,139	275.00	350.00	450.00	600.00	1000.00	6500.00	25000.00
1911D	72,500	600.00	750.00	1000.00	1325.00	9000.00	— —	
1911S	1,416,000	700.00	850.00	1050.00	1575.00	3000.00	12000.00	
1912	790,144	275.00	350.00	450.00	600.00	1000.00	6500.00	25000.00
1912S	392,000	300.00	400.00	525.00	700.00	4000.00	19000.00	

$5.00 GOLD
HALF EAGLES

DATE	MINTAGE	F-15	VF-30	EF-45	AU-50	UNC-60	UNC-65	PROOF 65
1913	916,000	275.00	350.00	450.00	600.00	1000.00	6500.00	25000.00
1913S	408,000	475.00	575.00	875.00	1050.00	8750.00	— —	
1914	247,125	275.00	375.00	500.00	650.00	1000.00	6500.00	25000.00
1914D	247,000	275.00	375.00	500.00	650.00	1250.00	9500.00	
1914S	263,000	300.00	400.00	525.00	700.00	3250.00	12750.00	
1915	588,075	275.00	350.00	450.00	600.00	1000.00	6500.00	25000.00
1915S	164,000	300.00	400.00	525.00	700.00	6000.00	18500.00	
1916S	240,000	275.00	375.00	500.00	650.00	2750.00	15750.00	
1929	662,000	3500.00	4250.00	5250.00	8750.00	13500.00	— —	

$10.00 GOLD EAGLES 1795-1933

Authorized on April 2, 1792. From 1795 through 1804 the composition was .9167 gold, .0833 copper. It was changed in 1838 to 90% gold, 10% copper until it was discontinued in 1933.

Liberty Cap Small Eagle
1795-1797
Designer, Robert Scot

DATE	MINTAGE	F-15	VF-30	EF-45	AU-50	UNC-60	UNC-65
1795 9 Leaves under Eagle		5000.00	7500.00	12500.00	25000.00	30000.00	— —
1795 12 Leaves under Eagle	5,583	4000.00	7000.00	10000.00	20000.00	25000.00	— —
1796	4,146	4000.00	7000.00	10000.00	20000.00	25000.00	— —
1797	3,615	4500.00	7250.00	11000.00	22500.00	27500.00	— —

Liberty Cap Large Eagle
1797-1804
Designer, Robert Scot

F-Obverse: Some evidence of details in Liberty's cap and hair at back of neck.
Reverse: "E PLURIBUS UNUM" is legible but weak.

VF-Obverse: Most cap and hair details show. Wear very evident on hair over ear.
Reverse: "E PLURIBUS UNUM" is sharp. Most of feathers show.

EF-Obverse: All details show with slight wear on the high points of cap and curls.
Reverse: All details show with slight wear on head and wing edges.

$10.00 GOLD
EAGLES

DATE	MINTAGE	F-15	VF-30	EF-45	AU-50	UNC-60	UNC-65
1797	10,940	2000.00	4000.00	6000.00	15000.00	20000.00	— —
1798 4							
Stars right	900	5000.00	9000.00	14000.00	30000.00	35000.00	— —
1798 6							
Stars right	842	10500.00	25000.00	— —	— —	— —	— —
1799	37,449	2000.00	2750.00	5000.00	15000.00	20000.00	— —
1800	5,999	2250.00	3000.00	6000.00	17500.00	22000.00	— —
1801	44,344	2000.00	3000.00	5000.00	15000.00	20000.00	— —
1803	15,017	2250.00	3500.00	7000.00	20000.00	25000.00	— —
1804	3,757	3000.00	4500.00	10000.00	25000.00	30000.00	— —

Coronet Type
1838-1907S
No Motto
Designer, Christian Gobrecht

F-Obverse: "LIBERTY" is complete with only one or two weak letters.
Reverse: Some of the feathers show on both wings.

VF-Obverse: "LIBERTY" sharp. Most of the details show. Wear evident on hair around ear and forehead.
Reverse: Most of the eagle's feathers show.

EF-Obverse: All details show. Slight wear on high points of hair.
Reverse: Wear shows only on the tips of the feathers.

DATE	MINTAGE	F-15	VF-30	EF-45	AU-50	UNC-60	UNC-65
1838	7,200	1000.00	1750.00	3500.00	7500.00	9000.00	— —
1839 Lg.							
Letters . . .	25,801	750.00	1250.00	1750.00	4500.00	6000.00	— —
1839 Sm.							
Letters . . .	12,447	750.00	1250.00	1750.00	4500.00	6000.00	— —

$10.00 GOLD
EAGLES

DATE	MINTAGE	F-15	VF-30	EF-45	AU-50	UNC-60	UNC-65	PROOF-65
1840	47,338	500.00	600.00	800.00	2500.00	7000.00	25000.00	
1841	63,131	500.00	600.00	800.00	2500.00	7000.00	25000.00	
1841 0	2,500	750.00	1250.00	2000.00	5000.00	— —	— —	
1842	81,507	500.00	600.00	800.00	2500.00	7000.00	25000.00	
1842 0	27,400	500.00	600.00	800.00	2500.00	6750.00	25000.00	
1843	75,462	550.00	650.00	900.00	3000.00	— —	25000.00	
1843 0	175,162	600.00	700.00	1000.00	3250.00	5500.00	25000.00	
1844	6,361	750.00	1000.00	1500.00	4500.00	6500.00	— —	
1844 0	118,700	550.00	650.00	900.00	3000.00	5250.00	25000.00	
1845	26,153	500.00	600.00	800.00	2500.00	— —	25000.00	
1845 0	47,500	500.00	600.00	800.00	2500.00	6350.00	25000.00	
1846	20,095	500.00	600.00	800.00	2500.00	— —	— —	
1846 0	81,780	500.00	600.00	800.00	2500.00	6000.00	25000.00	
1847	862,258	500.00	600.00	800.00	2500.00	5350.00	25000.00	
1847 0	571,500	500.00	600.00	800.00	2500.00	5350.00	25000.00	
1848	145,484	500.00	600.00	800.00	2500.00	6000.00	25000.00	
1848 0	35,850	500.00	600.00	800.00	2500.00	— —	— —	
1849	653,618	500.00	600.00	800.00	2500.00	5500.00	25000.00	
1849 0	23,900	500.00	750.00	1250.00	4000.00	— —	27500.00	
1850	291,451	500.00	600.00	800.00	2500.00	5250.00	25000.00	
1850 0	57,500	500.00	600.00	800.00	2500.00	6250.00	25000.00	
1851	176,328	500.00	600.00	800.00	2500.00	5350.00	25000.00	
1851 0	263,000	500.00	600.00	800.00	2500.00	6000.00	25000.00	
1852	263,106	500.00	600.00	800.00	2500.00	5250.00	25000.00	
1852 0	18,000	600.00	750.00	1000.00	3500.00	— —	— —	
1853	201,253	500.00	600.00	800.00	2500.00	5250.00	25000.00	
1853 over 2		1000.00	1250.00	1750.00	5000.00	— —	— —	
1853 0	51,000	500.00	600.00	800.00	2500.00	5750.00	25000.00	
1854	54,250	500.00	600.00	800.00	2500.00	6250.00	25000.00	
1854 0	52,500	600.00	750.00	1000.00	3250.00	6500.00	— —	
1854S	123,826	500.00	700.00	950.00	3000.00	6750.00	— —	
1855	121,701	500.00	600.00	850.00	2750.00	5250.00	25000.00	
1855 0	18,000	500.00	650.00	900.00	2750.00	— —	— —	
1855S	9,000	750.00	1250.00	2000.00	4000.00	— —	— —	
1856	60,490	500.00	600.00	800.00	2500.00	5750.00	25000.00	
1856 0	14,500	500.00	650.00	900.00	2750.00	— —	— —	
1856S	68,000	500.00	600.00	850.00	2600.00	— —	— —	
1857	16,606	500.00	600.00	850.00	2600.00	— —	— —	
1857 0	5,500	900.00	1400.00	2750.00	5500.00	— —	— —	
1857S	26,000	500.00	600.00	800.00	2500.00	— —	— —	
1858	2,521	4500.00	6500.00	9000.00	20000.00	— —	— —	
1858 0	20,000	500.00	600.00	800.00	2500.00	6500.00	25000.00	
1858S	11,800	500.00	600.00	800.00	2500.00	— —	— —	
1859	16,093	500.00	600.00	850.00	2750.00	6500.00	— —	
1859 0	2,300	2000.00	3500.00	5000.00	12500.00	— —	— —	
1859S	7,000	1000.00	1500.00	2500.00	4500.00	— —	— —	
1860	15,105	500.00	600.00	800.00	2500.00	5750.00	25000.00	— —
1860 0	11,100	500.00	650.00	900.00	2750.00	6000.00	25000.00	
1860 S	5,000	900.00	1500.00	2250.00	4000.00	— —	— —	
1861	113,233	500.00	600.00	800.00	2500.00	5250.00	25000.00	— —
1861S	15,500	500.00	650.00	900.00	2750.00	— —	— —	
1862	10,995	550.00	700.00	950.00	3000.00	— —	— —	— —
1862S	12,500	550.00	700.00	950.00	3000.00	— —	— —	
1863	1,248	3000.00	4500.00	6500.00	17500.00	— —	— —	— —
1863S	10,000	700.00	1000.00	1750.00	4250.00	— —	— —	
1864	3,500	1100.00	1750.00	3000.00	6500.00	— —	— —	— —
1864S	2,500	2250.00	4000.00	7500.00	15000.00	— —	— —	

$10.00 GOLD
EAGLES

DATE	MINTAGE	F-15	VF-30	EF-45	AU-50	UNC-60	UNC-65	PROOF-65
1865	4,005	900.00	1500.00	2250.00	4000.00	— —	— —	— —
1865S		750.00	1250.00	1750.00	4000.00	— —	— —	
1865S over	16,700							
invert 186 .		750.00	1250.00	1750.00	4000.00	— —	— —	
1866S	8,500	1500.00	2500.00	4000.00	7500.00	— —	— —	

IN 1866 THE MOTTO WAS ADDED TO THE REVERSE ABOVE THE EAGLE.

1866	3,780	650.00	1000.00	1500.00	3250.00	— —	— —	55000.00
1866S	11,500	550.00	800.00	1250.00	2500.00	— —	— —	
1867	3,140	600.00	900.00	1500.00	3250.00	— —	— —	45000.00
1867S	9,000	550.00	800.00	1750.00	4000.00	— —	— —	
1868	10,655	550.00	800.00	1250.00	2500.00	— —	— —	45000.00
1868S	13,500	500.00	700.00	1100.00	2250.00	— —	— —	
1869	1,855	1500.00	2500.00	4000.00	7500.00	— —	— —	45000.00
1869S	6,430	600.00	900.00	1400.00	2750.00	— —	— —	
1870	4,025	750.00	1250.00	1750.00	4250.00	— —	— —	45000.00
1870CC . . .	5,908	1250.00	3000.00	5000.00	— —	— —	— —	
1870S	8,000	550.00	800.00	1250.00	2500.00	— —	— —	
1871	1,820	1000.00	1750.00	3000.00	6500.00	— —	— —	45000.00
1871CC . . .	8,085	800.00	1250.00	2000.00	3500.00	— —	— —	
1871S	16,500	550.00	750.00	1250.00	2750.00	— —	— —	
1872	1,650	1250.00	2000.00	3500.00	7500.00	— —	— —	45000.00
1872CC . . .	4,600	700.00	1250.00	2000.00	3500.00	— —	— —	
1872S	17,300	550.00	750.00	1200.00	2500.00	— —	— —	
1873	825	2000.00	3500.00	5500.00	10000.00	— —	— —	65000.00
1873CC . . .	4,543	1200.00	1750.00	3250.00	7000.00	— —	— —	
1873S	12,000	550.00	750.00	1200.00	2500.00	— —	— —	
1874	53,160	500.00	650.00	800.00	2000.00	2750.00	5500.00	47500.00
1874CC . . .	16,767	600.00	800.00	1200.00	2500.00	— —	— —	
1874S	10,000	600.00	800.00	1250.00	2750.00	— —	— —	
1875	120	EXTREMELY RARE		— —	— —	— —	— —	— —
1875CC . . .	7,715	900.00	1250.00	2000.00	3750.00	— —	— —	
1876	732	2250.00	3500.00	6500.00	— —	— —	— —	45000.00
1876CC . . .	4,696	1300.00	2000.00	3000.00	7250.00	— —	— —	
1876S	5,000	650.00	1200.00	2000.00	3750.00	— —	— —	
1877	817	1750.00	2750.00	4000.00	— —	— —	— —	70000.00
1877CC . . .	3,332	1200.00	1750.00	2750.00	6500.00	— —	— —	
1877S	17,000	550.00	800.00	1200.00	2500.00	— —	6600.00	
1878	73,800	500.00	600.00	750.00	1250.00	1850.00	4250.00	45000.00
1878CC . . .	3,244	1500.00	2500.00	3500.00	7750.00	— —	— —	
1878S	26,100	500.00	600.00	800.00	1750.00	— —	— —	
1879	384,770	500.00	600.00	750.00	1250.00	1650.00	4250.00	40000.00
1879CC . . .	1,762	4000.00	6000.00	10000.00	— —	— —	— —	
1879 0	1,500	1500.00	2500.00	4000.00	8500.00	— —	— —	
1879S	224,000	500.00	600.00	750.00	1250.00	— —	4250.00	

$10.00 GOLD
EAGLES

DATE	MINTAGE	F-15	VF-30	EF-45	AU-50	UNC-60	UNC-65	PROOF-65
1880	1,644,876	450.00	500.00	600.00	900.00	1100.00	3750.00	40000.00
1880CC ...	11,190	500.00	600.00	750.00	1200.00	1500.00	5500.00	
1880 O	9,200	550.00	700.00	850.00	1500.00	1850.00	6600.00	
1880S	506,250	450.00	500.00	600.00	900.00	1100.00	3750.00	
1881	3,877,260	450.00	500.00	600.00	900.00	1100.00	3750.00	40000.00
1881CC ...	24,015	450.00	550.00	700.00	1000.00	1200.00	5000.00	
1881 O	8,350	450.00	550.00	750.00	1100.00	1300.00	5500.00	
1881S	970,000	450.00	500.00	600.00	900.00	1100.00	3750.00	
1882	2,324,480	450.00	500.00	600.00	800.00	1000.00	3750.00	40000.00
1882CC ...	6,764	550.00	650.00	800.00	1100.00	1300.00	5000.00	
1882 O	10,820	500.00	600.00	750.00	1000.00	1200.00	4400.00	
1882S	132,000	450.00	500.00	600.00	800.00	1000.00	3750.00	
1883	208,740	450.00	500.00	600.00	800.00	1000.00	3750.00	40000.00
1883CC ...	12,000	500.00	600.00	750.00	1000.00	1200.00	5000.00	
1883 O	800	2000.00	3000.00	5000.00	7500.00	— —	— —	
1883S	38,000	500.00	600.00	750.00	950.00	1150.00	3850.00	
1884	76,905	500.00	600.00	700.00	900.00	1100.00	3750.00	85000.00
1884CC ...	9,925	550.00	650.00	800.00	1100.00	1400.00	5000.00	
1884S	124,250	450.00	500.00	600.00	750.00	900.00	3750.00	
1885	253,527	450.00	500.00	600.00	750.00	900.00	3750.00	35000.00
1885S	228,000	450.00	500.00	600.00	750.00	900.00	3750.00	
1886	236,160	450.00	500.00	600.00	750.00	900.00	3750.00	35000.00
1886S	826,000	450.00	500.00	600.00	750.00	900.00	3750.00	
1887	53,680	450.00	500.00	600.00	750.00	900.00	3750.00	35000.00
1887S	817,000	450.00	500.00	600.00	750.00	900.00	3750.00	
1888	132,996	450.00	500.00	600.00	750.00	900.00	3750.00	35000.00
1888 O	21,335	450.00	500.00	600.00	750.00	900.00	3750.00	
1888S	648,700	450.00	500.00	600.00	750.00	900.00	3750.00	
1889	4,485	550.00	650.00	850.00	1100.00	1400.00	5000.00	35000.00
1889S	425,400	450.00	500.00	600.00	750.00	900.00	3750.00	
1890	58,043	450.00	500.00	600.00	750.00	900.00	3750.00	35000.00
1890CC ...	17,500	550.00	650.00	850.00	1100.00	1400.00	5000.00	
1891	91,868	450.00	500.00	600.00	750.00	900.00	3750.00	35000.00
1891CC ...	103,732	450.00	500.00	600.00	750.00	900.00	3750.00	
1892	797,552	450.00	500.00	600.00	750.00	900.00	3750.00	35000.00
1892CC ...	40,000	550.00	650.00	850.00	1100.00	1400.00	5000.00	
1892 O	28,688	450.00	500.00	600.00	750.00	900.00	3750.00	
1892S	115,500	450.00	500.00	600.00	750.00	900.00	3750.00	
1893	1,840,895	450.00	500.00	600.00	750.00	900.00	3750.00	35000.00
1893CC ...	14,000	550.00	650.00	850.00	1100.00	1400.00	5000.00	
1893 O	17,000	550.00	650.00	850.00	1100.00	1400.00	5000.00	
1893S	141,350	450.00	500.00	600.00	750.00	900.00	3750.00	
1894	2,470,778	450.00	500.00	600.00	750.00	900.00	3750.00	35000.00
1894 O	107,500	450.00	500.00	600.00	750.00	900.00	3750.00	
1894S	25,000	450.00	500.00	600.00	750.00	900.00	3750.00	
1895	567,826	450.00	500.00	600.00	750.00	900.00	3750.00	35000.00
1895 O	98,000	450.00	500.00	600.00	750.00	900.00	3750.00	
1895S	49,000	450.00	500.00	600.00	750.00	900.00	3750.00	
1896	76,348	450.00	500.00	600.00	750.00	900.00	3750.00	35000.00
1896S	123,750	450.00	500.00	600.00	750.00	900.00	3750.00	
1897	1,000,159	450.00	500.00	600.00	750.00	900.00	3750.00	35000.00
1897 O	42,500	450.00	500.00	600.00	750.00	900.00	3750.00	
1897S	234,750	450.00	500.00	600.00	750.00	900.00	3750.00	
1898	812,197	450.00	500.00	600.00	750.00	900.00	3750.00	35000.00
1898S	473,600	450.00	500.00	600.00	750.00	900.00	3750.00	
1899	1,262,305	450.00	500.00	600.00	750.00	900.00	3750.00	35000.00
1899 O	37,047	450.00	500.00	600.00	750.00	900.00	3750.00	

$10.00 GOLD
EAGLES

DATE	MINTAGE	F-15	VF-30	EF-45	AU-50	UNC-60	UNC-65	PROOF-65
1899S	841,000	450.00	500.00	600.00	750.00	900.00	3750.00	
1900	293,960	450.00	500.00	600.00	750.00	900.00	3750.00	35000.00
1900S	81,000	450.00	500.00	600.00	750.00	900.00	3750.00	
1901	1,718,825	450.00	500.00	600.00	750.00	900.00	3750.00	35000.00
1901 O	72,041	450.00	500.00	600.00	750.00	900.00	3750.00	
1901S	2,812,750	450.00	500.00	600.00	750.00	900.00	3750.00	
1902	82,513	450.00	500.00	600.00	750.00	900.00	3750.00	35000.00
1902S	469,500	450.00	500.00	600.00	750.00	900.00	3750.00	
1903	125,926	450.00	500.00	600.00	750.00	900.00	3750.00	35000.00
1903 O	112,771	450.00	500.00	600.00	750.00	900.00	3750.00	
1903S	538,000	450.00	500.00	600.00	750.00	900.00	3750.00	
1904	162,038	450.00	500.00	600.00	750.00	900.00	3750.00	35000.00
1904 O	108,950	450.00	500.00	600.00	750.00	900.00	3750.00	
1905	201,078	450.00	500.00	600.00	750.00	900.00	3750.00	35000.00
1905S	369,250	450.00	500.00	600.00	750.00	900.00	3750.00	
1906	165,497	450.00	500.00	600.00	750.00	900.00	3750.00	35000.00
1906D	981,000	450.00	500.00	600.00	750.00	900.00	3750.00	
1906 O	86,895	450.00	500.00	600.00	750.00	900.00	3750.00	
1906S	457,000	450.00	500.00	600.00	750.00	900.00	3750.00	
1907	1,203,973	450.00	500.00	600.00	750.00	900.00	3750.00	35000.00
1907D	1,030,000	450.00	500.00	600.00	750.00	900.00	3750.00	
1907S	210,500	450.00	500.00	600.00	750.00	900.00	3750.00	

Indian Head
1907-1933
Designer, Augustus Saint-Gaudens

F-Obverse: "LIBERTY" on headband is complete. Feathers at headband are worn into each other.
Reverse: Some of the eagle's feathers show.

VF-Obverse: Most of the feather details in the bonnet show.
Reverse: Most of the eagle's feathers show.

EF-Obverse: All details show with slight wear on high points of feathers and hair.
Reverse: All details show with slight wear on head and wing edge at neckline.

NO MOTTO ON REVERSE

$10.00 GOLD
EAGLES

DATE	MINTAGE	F-15	VF-30	EF-45	AU-50	UNC-60	UNC-65	PROOF-65
1907 Wire Edge Periods in •E•PLURIBUS•UNUM•	500	3750.00	4500.00	6000.00	7500.00	14500.00	37500.00	40000.00
1907 Round Edge Periods in •E•PLURIBUS•UNUM•	42	Proof only						85000.00
1907 w/o Periods ...	239,406	500.00	600.00	700.00	1050.00	1500.00	9000.00	
1908	33,500	650.00	750.00	875.00	1225.00	4450.00	25000.00	
1908D	210,000	500.00	625.00	800.00	1200.00	2500.00	12500.00	

MOTTO "IN GOD WE TRUST" ADDED TO THE REVERSE

DATE	MINTAGE	F-15	VF-30	EF-45	AU-50	UNC-60	UNC-65	PROOF-65
1908	341,486	500.00	600.00	700.00	1050.00	1300.00	7500.00	35000.00
1908D	836,500	500.00	600.00	700.00	1050.00	2250.00	13500.00	
1908S	59,850	750.00	950.00	1225.00	1750.00	7500.00	27500.00	
1909	184,863	500.00	600.00	700.00	950.00	1500.00	8750.00	35000.00
1909D	121,540	500.00	600.00	700.00	950.00	2500.00	11500.00	
1909S	292,350	500.00	600.00	700.00	950.00	3650.00	17000.00	
1910	318,704	500.00	600.00	700.00	950.00	1200.00	7500.00	35000.00
1910D	2,356,640	500.00	600.00	700.00	950.00	1250.00	7150.00	
1910S	811,000	500.00	600.00	700.00	950.00	3500.00	12500.00	
1911	505,595	500.00	600.00	700.00	950.00	1150.00	6500.00	35000.00
1911D	30,100	1000.00	1250.00	1575.00	2600.00	12500.00	40000.00	
1911S	51,000	700.00	850.00	1100.00	1750.00	6250.00	25000.00	
1912	405,083	500.00	600.00	700.00	950.00	1200.00	7500.00	35000.00
1912S	300,000	500.00	600.00	700.00	950.00	4750.00	22000.00	
1913	442,071	500.00	600.00	700.00	950.00	1200.00	6750.00	35000.00
1913S	66,000	1000.00	1250.00	1575.00	1750.00	30000.00	125000.00	
1914	151,050	500.00	600.00	700.00	950.00	1375.00	8250.00	37500.00
1914D	343,500	500.00	600.00	700.00	950.00	1500.00	10000.00	
1914S	208,000	500.00	600.00	700.00	950.00	3750.00	17500.00	
1915	351,075	500.00	600.00	700.00	950.00	1125.00	6500.00	35000.00
1915S	59,000	700.00	850.00	1000.00	1400.00	7500.00	33500.00	
1916S	138,500	550.00	650.00	750.00	1000.00	3500.00	16500.00	
1920S	126,500	12500.00	15000.00	26500.00	37500.00	82500.00	125000.00	
1926	1,014,000	500.00	600.00	700.00	875.00	1000.00	6250.00	
1930S	96,000	6000.00	7500.00	9500.00	12500.00	21500.00	40000.00	
1932	4,463,000	500.00	600.00	700.00	875.00	1000.00	5500.00	
1933	312,500	37500.00	50000.00	65000.00	82500.00	— —	— —	

$20.00 GOLD
DOUBLE EAGLES
1849-1933

Authorized on March 3, 1849. Several pieces of the Double Eagle coins were produced in 1849 but only one example is known to survive today and is exhibited in the U.S. Mint collection at the Smithsonian Institution. All Double Eagles were made of 90% gold, 10% copper.

Liberty Head
1849-1907
Designer, James B. Longacre

F-Obverse: "LIBERTY" legible but very weak. Some details can be seen in curls at the neck.
Reverse: Some feathers show.

VF-Obverse: "LIBERTY" sharp. Most details show. Definite wear on hair around ear.
Reverse: All of the wing feathers show but some are weak.

EF-Obverse: All details show. Wear only on high points of hair.
Reverse: The wing feathers are sharp. Some wear evident on head and shield.

DATE	MINTAGE	F-15	VF-30	EF-45	AU-50	UNC-60	UNC-65
1850	1,170,261	800.00	900.00	1000.00	1500.00	4250.00	25000.00
1850 O	141,000	1000.00	1200.00	1500.00	2250.00	4750.00	30000.00
1851	2,087,155	800.00	900.00	1000.00	1500.00	3500.00	19500.00
1851 O	315,000	900.00	1150.00	1500.00	2250.00	4000.00	25000.00
1852	2,053,026	825.00	900.00	1000.00	1350.00	3500.00	19500.00
1852 O	190,000	900.00	1150.00	1500.00	2250.00	4000.00	25000.00
1853	1,261,326	825.00	900.00	1000.00	1350.00	3500.00	19500.00
1853 O	71,000	1000.00	1200.00	1500.00	2250.00	4750.00	30000.00
1854	757,899	825.00	900.00	1000.00	1350.00	3500.00	19500.00
1854 O	3,250	— —	— —	35000.00	— —	— —	— —
1854S	141,468	800.00	900.00	1000.00	1500.00	5000.00	36000.00
1855	364,666	825.00	900.00	1000.00	1350.00	3500.00	19500.00
1855 O	8,000	1200.00	2000.00	3500.00	5000.00	6750.00	— —
1855S	879,675	825.00	900.00	1000.00	1350.00	3900.00	19500.00
1856	329,878	825.00	900.00	1000.00	1350.00	4000.00	19500.00
1856 O	2,250	20000.00	27500.00	35000.00	— —	— —	— —
1856S	1,189,750	825.00	900.00	1000.00	1350.00	4000.00	19500.00

$20.00 GOLD
DOUBLE EAGLES

DATE	MINTAGE	F-15	VF-30	EF-45	AU-50	UNC-60	UNC-65	PROOF-65
1857	439,375	825.00	900.00	1000.00	1350.00	3500.00	19500.00	
1857 0	30,000	950.00	1550.00	2250.00	3000.00	4750.00	30000.00	
1857S	970,500	825.00	900.00	1000.00	1350.00	3500.00	19500.00	
1858	211,714	825.00	900.00	1000.00	1350.00	3500.00	19500.00	
1858 0·	35,250	950.00	1400.00	2000.00	3000.00	5500.00	— —	
1858S	846,710	825.00	900.00	1000.00	1350.00	3750.00	19500.00	
1859	43,597	800.00	900.00	1000.00	1500.00	3850.00	22000.00	
1859 0	9,100	1200.00	2500.00	3500.00	5000.00	8500.00	— —	
1859S	636,445	825.00	900.00	1000.00	1350.00	3850.00	19500.00	
1860	577,670	825.00	900.00	1000.00	1350.00	3500.00	19500.00	— —
1860 0	6,600	2000.00	3250.00	4500.00	7500.00	— —	— —	
1860S	544,950	825.00	900.00	1000.00	1350.00	3800.00	19500.00	
1861	2,976,453	825.00	900.00	1000.00	1350.00	3500.00	19500.00	— —
1861 0	17,741	1250.00	2500.00	3500.00	5000.00	7500.00	— —	
1861S	768,000	825.00	900.00	1000.00	1350.00	3500.00	19500.00	

In 1861 a new reverse designed by Anthony C. Paquet, was used. The new design caused a great deal of die breakage around the rim, so it was discontinued. Several coins were struck at the Philadelphdia Mint and several thousands at the San Francisco Mint, all dated 1861.

DATE	MINTAGE	F-15	VF-30	EF-45	AU-50	UNC-60	UNC-65	PROOF-65
1861 A.C. PAQUET . .		EXTREMELY RARE						
1861S A.C. PAQUET . .		4000.00	6000.00	7500.00	12500.00	— —	— —	
1862	92,133	800.00	900.00	1000.00	1500.00	3850.00	27500.00	— —
1862S	854,173	825.00	900.00	1000.00	1350.00	3500.00	19500.00	
1863	142,790	825.00	900.00	1000.00	1350.00	4000.00	22000.00	— —
1863S	966,570	825.00	900.00	1000.00	1350.00	3500.00	19500.00	
1864	204,285	825.00	900.00	1000.00	1350.00	4000.00	22000.00	— —
1864S	793,660	825.00	900.00	1000.00	1350.00	3500.00	19500.00	
1865	351,200	825.00	900.00	1000.00	1350.00	3500.00	19500.00	— —
1865S	1,042,500	825.00	900.00	1000.00	1350.00	4500.00	19500.00	
1866S	120,000	875.00	1200.00	1650.00	2400.00	5000.00	27500.00	

IN 1866 THE MOTTO "IN GOD WE TRUST" WAS ADDED TO THE REVERSE ABOVE THE EAGLE.

DATE	MINTAGE	F-15	VF-30	EF-45	AU-50	UNC-60	UNC-65	PROOF-65
1866	698,775	825.00	900.00	1000.00	1350.00	2650.00	16500.00	— —
1866S	722,250	825.00	900.00	1000.00	1350.00	1750.00	13750.00	
1867	251,065	825.00	900.00	1000.00	1350.00	1600.00	10000.00	— —
1867S	920,750	825.00	900.00	1000.00	1350.00	1900.00	11000.00	
1868	98,600	825.00	900.00	1000.00	1350.00	1950.00	12000.00	— —
1868S	837,500	825.00	900.00	1000.00	1350.00	2000.00	11000.00	
1869	175,155	825.00	900.00	1000.00	1350.00	1750.00	13250.00	— —
1869S	686,750	825.00	900.00	1000.00	1350.00	1750.00	12000.00	
1870	155,185	825.00	900.00	1000.00	1350.00	1750.00	13250.00	— —
1870CC . . .	3,789	15000.00	22500.00	30000.00	37500.00	— —	— —	
1870S	982,000	725.00	800.00	900.00	1250.00	1850.00	10500.00	
1871	80,150	700.00	800.00	900.00	1250.00	1700.00	13750.00	— —
1871CC . . .	17,387	1250.00	2000.00	3250.00	4600.00	5500.00	— —	
1871S	928,000	825.00	900.00	1000.00	1350.00	1500.00	10000.00	
1872	251,880	825.00	900.00	1000.00	1350.00	1500.00	11500.00	— —
1872CC . . .	26,900	950.00	1500.00	1850.00	2750.00	3000.00	— —	
1872S	780,000	825.00	900.00	1000.00	1350.00	1500.00	8750.00	
1873	1,709,825	825.00	900.00	1000.00	1350.00	1500.00	7750.00	— —

$20.00 GOLD
DOUBLE EAGLES

DATE	MINTAGE	F-15	VF-30	EF-45	AU-50	UNC-60	UNC-65	PROOF-65
1873CC ...	22,410	950.00	1600.00	2000.00	3000.00	3500.00	– –	
1873S	1,040,600	825.00	900.00	1000.00	1350.00	1500.00	7750.00	
1874	366,800	825.00	900.00	1000.00	1350.00	1500.00	7750.00	– –
1874CC ...	115,085	850.00	1000.00	1250.00	1750.00	2100.00	13750.00	
1874S	1,214,000	825.00	900.00	1000.00	1350.00	1500.00	7750.00	
1875	295,740	825.00	900.00	1000.00	1350.00	1500.00	7750.00	– –
1875CC ...	111,151	800.00	950.00	1200.00	1750.00	2000.00	9350.00	
1875S	1,230,000	825.00	900.00	1000.00	1350.00	1500.00	7750.00	
1876	583,905	800.00	900.00	1050.00	1350.00	1500.00	7750.00	– –
1876CC ...	138,441	850.00	1000.00	1250.00	1750.00	2000.00	8750.00	
1876S	1,597,000	800.00	900.00	1000.00	1350.00	1500.00	7750.00	
1877	397,670	800.00	900.00	1000.00	1350.00	1450.00	7750.00	65000.00
1877CC ...	42,565	850.00	1000.00	1250.00	1750.00	2000.00	5500.00	
1877S	1,735,000	800.00	900.00	1000.00	1350.00	1450.00	1900.00	
1878	543,645	800.00	900.00	1000.00	1350.00	1450.00	1900.00	65000.00
1878CC ...	13,180	1000.00	1200.00	1500.00	2250.00	2750.00	8250.00	
1878S	1,739,000	800.00	900.00	1000.00	1350.00	1450.00	1900.00	
1879	207,630	800.00	900.00	1000.00	1350.00	1450.00	1900.00	65000.00
1879CC ...	10,708	1250.00	1650.00	2250.00	3000.00	3500.00	9350.00	
1879O	2,325	3500.00	4250.00	6000.00	8000.00	10000.00	– –	
1879S	1,223,800	800.00	900.00	1000.00	1350.00	1450.00	1900.00	60000.00
1880	51,456	825.00	900.00	1000.00	1350.00	1500.00	2500.00	
1880S	836,000	800.00	900.00	1000.00	1350.00	1450.00	1900.00	
1881	2,260	2750.00	4000.00	7000.00	9500.00	11500.00	– –	– –
1881S	727,000	800.00	900.00	1000.00	1350.00	1450.00	1900.00	
1882	630	3000.00	7500.00	12500.00	17500.00	22500.00	– –	– –
1882CC ...	39,140	950.00	1200.00	1500.00	2250.00	2650.00	3850.00	
1882S	1,125,000	800.00	900.00	1000.00	1350.00	1450.00	1900.00	
1883	92	Proof only						– –
1883CC ...	59,962	800.00	1000.00	1250.00	2000.00	2250.00	3850.00	
1883S	1,189,000	800.00	900.00	1000.00	1350.00	1450.00	1900.00	
1884	71	Proof only						– –
1884CC ...	81,139	800.00	1000.00	1250.00	1750.00	2000.00	3000.00	
1884S	916,000	800.00	900.00	1000.00	1350.00	1450.00	1900.00	
1885	828	3250.00	6000.00	9500.00	15000.00	17000.00	– –	– –
1885CC ...	9,450	1000.00	1500.00	2000.00	3000.00	3500.00	8250.00	
1885S	683,500	800.00	900.00	1000.00	1350.00	1450.00	1900.00	
1886	1,106	3500.00	6000.00	8000.00	10500.00	12500.00	– –	– –
1887	121	Proof only						– –
1887S	283,000	800.00	900.00	1000.00	1350.00	1500.00	2500.00	
1888	226,266	800.00	900.00	1000.00	1350.00	1450.00	1900.00	60000.00
1888S	859,600	800.00	900.00	1000.00	1350.00	1450.00	1900.00	
1889	44,111	800.00	900.00	1000.00	1350.00	1500.00	2500.00	60000.00
1889CC ...	30,945	850.00	1000.00	1250.00	1750.00	2000.00	3850.00	
1889S	774,700	800.00	900.00	1000.00	1350.00	1550.00	2250.00	
1890	75,995	800.00	900.00	1000.00	1350.00	1450.00	2500.00	60000.00
1890CC ...	91,209	850.00	1000.00	1250.00	1750.00	2000.00	3850.00	
1890S	802,750	800.00	900.00	1000.00	1350.00	1450.00	1900.00	
1891	1,442	2000.00	3000.00	4250.00	6500.00	8000.00	25000.00	60000.00
1891CC ...	5,000	1500.00	2250.00	3000.00	4500.00	5500.00	13750.00	
1891S	1,288,125	800.00	900.00	1000.00	1350.00	1450.00	1900.00	
1892	4,523	1400.00	2500.00	3250.00	5000.00	6000.00	13750.00	60000.00
1892CC ...	27,265	1200.00	2000.00	2500.00	3500.00	4250.00	11000.00	
1892S	930,150	800.00	900.00	1000.00	1350.00	1500.00	3850.00	
1893	344,339	800.00	900.00	1000.00	1350.00	1450.00	1900.00	45000.00
1893CC ...	18,402	850.00	1000.00	1250.00	1750.00	2100.00	3250.00	

$20 GOLD
DOUBLE EAGLES

DATE	MINTAGE	F-15	VF-30	EF-45	AU-50	UNC-60	UNC-65	PROOF-65
1893S	996,175	800.00	900.00	1000.00	1350.00	1450.00	1900.00	
1894	1,368,990	800.00	900.00	1000.00	1350.00	1450.00	1900.00	45000.00
1894S	1,048,550	800.00	900.00	1000.00	1350.00	1450.00	1900.00	
1895	1,114,656	800.00	900.00	1000.00	1350.00	1450.00	1900.00	45000.00
1895S	1,143,500	800.00	900.00	1000.00	1350.00	1450.00	1900.00	
1896	792,663	800.00	900.00	1000.00	1350.00	1450.00	1900.00	45000.00
1896S	1,403,925	800.00	900.00	1000.00	1350.00	1450.00	1900.00	
1897	1,383,261	800.00	900.00	1000.00	1350.00	1450.00	1900.00	45000.00
1897S	1,470,250	800.00	900.00	1000.00	1350.00	1450.00	1900.00	
1898	170,470	800.00	900.00	1000.00	1350.00	1450.00	1900.00	45000.00
1898S	2,575,175	800.00	900.00	1000.00	1350.00	1450.00	1900.00	
1899	1,669,384	800.00	900.00	1000.00	1350.00	1450.00	1900.00	45000.00
1899S	2,010,300	800.00	900.00	1000.00	1350.00	1450.00	1900.00	
1900	1,874,584	800.00	900.00	1000.00	1350.00	1450.00	1900.00	45000.00
1900S	2,459,500	800.00	900.00	1000.00	1350.00	1450.00	1900.00	
1901	111,526	800.00	900.00	1000.00	1350.00	1450.00	1900.00	45000.00
1901S	1,596,000	800.00	900.00	1000.00	1350.00	1450.00	1900.00	
1902	31,254	800.00	900.00	1000.00	1350.00	1450.00	2500.00	45000.00
1902S	1,753,625	800.00	900.00	1000.00	1350.00	1450.00	1900.00	45000.00
1903	287,428	800.00	900.00	1000.00	1350.00	1450.00	1900.00	45000.00
1903S	954,000	800.00	900.00	1000.00	1350.00	1450.00	1900.00	
1904	6,256,797	800.00	900.00	1000.00	1350.00	1450.00	1900.00	45000.00
1904S	5,134,175	800.00	900.00	1000.00	1350.00	1450.00	1900.00	
1905	59,011	800.00	900.00	1000.00	1350.00	1450.00	2500.00	45000.00
1905S	1,813,000	800.00	900.00	1000.00	1350.00	1450.00	1900.00	
1906	69,690	800.00	900.00	1000.00	1350.00	1450.00	2500.00	45000.00
1906D	620,250	800.00	900.00	1000.00	1350.00	1450.00	1900.00	
1906S	2,065,750	800.00	900.00	1000.00	1350.00	1450.00	1900.00	
1907	1,451,864	800.00	900.00	1000.00	1350.00	1450.00	1900.00	45000.00
1907D	842,250	800.00	900.00	1000.00	1350.00	1450.00	1900.00	
1907S	2,165,800	800.00	900.00	1000.00	1350.00	1450.00	1900.00	

Saint Gaudens
1907-1932
Designer, Augustus Saint-Gaudens

F-Obverse: Some details show. Liberty's right breast worn smooth. Considerable wear shows on Liberty's right knee and leg.
Reverse: Some feather details show. Breast feathers worn almost smooth.

VF-Obverse: Most details show. Liberty's gown at breasts and legs shows strong.
Reverse: Most feathers show. The high edge of eagle's left wing has considerable wear. Evidence of some breast feathers is visible.

EF-Obverse: All details show. Slight wear shows only of the tip of Liberty's right knee and breast.
Reverse: All feathers including the breast are clear. Slight wear shows on edge of eagle's left wing.

$20.00 GOLD
DOUBLE EAGLES

WITHOUT MOTTO ON REVERSE

DATE	MINTAGE	F-15	VF-30	EF-45	AU-50	UNC-60	UNC-65	PROOF-65
1907 Wire Edge Date MCMVII ..	11,250	— —	— —	7000.00	10500.00	21000.00	41500.00	
1907 Flat Edge Date MCMVII ..		— —	— —	7000.00	10500.00	21000.00	41500.00	
1907 Date Arabic Numerals .	361,667	775.00	825.00	900.00	1100.00	1500.00	3750.00	
1908	4,271,551	750.00	800.00	875.00	1000.00	1350.00	2500.00	55000.00
1908D	663,750	750.00	800.00	875.00	1000.00	1450.00	4000.00	

IN 1908 THE MOTTO "IN GOD WE TRUST" WAS ADDED TO THE REVERSE BELOW THE EAGLE.

DATE	MINTAGE	F-15	VF-30	EF-45	AU-50	UNC-60	UNC-65	PROOF-65
1908	156,359	750.00	800.00	875.00	1000.00	1350.00	6500.00	
1908D	349,500	750.00	800.00	875.00	1000.00	1400.00	5750.00	
1908S	22,000	1000.00	1250.00	1600.00	2600.00	7000.00	18000.00	
1909		800.00	850.00	1000.00	1400.00	1900.00	9000.00	55000.00
1909 over 8	161,282	800.00	850.00	1000.00	1400.00	2850.00	9750.00	
1909D	52,500	900.00	950.00	1150.00	2000.00	4500.00	14750.00	
1909S	2,774,925	750.00	800.00	875.00	1000.00	1275.00	3150.00	
1910	482,167	750.00	800.00	875.00	1000.00	1250.00	3000.00	55000.00
1910D	429,000	750.00	800.00	875.00	1000.00	1275.00	3200.00	
1910S	2,128,250	750.00	800.00	875.00	1000.00	1225.00	3500.00	
1911	197,350	750.00	800.00	875.00	1000.00	1350.00	4500.00	55000.00
1911D	846,500	750.00	800.00	875.00	1000.00	1200.00	3000.00	
1911S	775,750	750.00	800.00	875.00	1000.00	1200.00	3500.00	
1912	149,824	750.00	800.00	875.00	1050.00	1600.00	6500.00	55000.00
1913	168,838	750.00	800.00	875.00	1000.00	1275.00	4000.00	
1913D	393,500	750.00	800.00	875.00	1000.00	1250.00	3500.00	
1913S	34,000	950.00	1000.00	1250.00	1550.00	2600.00	6250.00	
1914	95,320	750.00	800.00	875.00	1000.00	1650.00	6500.00	55000.00
1914D	453,000	750.00	800.00	875.00	1000.00	1250.00	3000.00	
1914S	1,498,000	750.00	800.00	875.00	1000.00	1250.00	3000.00	
1915	152,050	750.00	800.00	875.00	1000.00	1300.00	3650.00	57500.00
1915S	567,500	750.00	800.00	875.00	1000.00	1200.00	3000.00	
1916S	796,000	750.00	800.00	875.00	1000.00	1200.00	4650.00	
1920	228,250	750.00	800.00	875.00	1000.00	1300.00	4350.00	
1920S	558,000	11000.00	13000.00	17500.00	22500.00	35,000.00	— —	
1921	528,500	19500.00	22500.00	31500.00	38500.00	45000.00	— —	

$20.00 GOLD
DOUBLE EAGLES

DATE	MINTAGE	F-15	VF-30	EF-45	AU-50	UNC-60	UNC-65	PROOF-65
1922	1,375,500	750.00	800.00	875.00	1000.00	1400.00	2000.00	
1922S	2,658,000	850.00	950.00	1050.00	1200.00	2250.00	7000.00	
1923	566,000	750.00	800.00	875.00	1050.00	1400.00	1900.00	
1923D	1,702,250	750.00	800.00	875.00	1050.00	1300.00	2100.00	
1924	4,323,500	750.00	800.00	875.00	1050.00	1175.00	1500.00	
1924D	3,049,500	1050.00	1400.00	2250.00	3000.00	3850.00	10500.00	
1924S	2,927,500	950.00	1150.00	1400.00	1800.00	2750.00	9000.00	
1925	2,831,750	750.00	800.00	875.00	1050.00	1175.00	1500.00	
1925D	2,938,500	1000.00	1250.00	1550.00	2150.00	4250.00	12750.00	
1925S	3,776,500	950.00	1100.00	1400.00	2150.00	3500.00	12000.00	
1926	816,750	750.00	800.00	875.00	1050.00	1175.00	1500.00	
1926D	481,000	1350.00	1550.00	1850.00	2350.00	5000.00	14750.00	
1926S	2,041,500	900.00	1000.00	1200.00	1550.00	3000.00	8500.00	
1927	2,946,750	750.00	800.00	850.00	1050.00	1100.00	1500.00	
1927D	18,000	EXCEEDINGLY RARE — NO LATE INFORMATION						
1927S	3,107,000	4750.00	6000.00	7000.00	10500.00	19000.00	— —	
1928	8,816,000	750.00	800.00	875.00	1050.00	1200.00	1500.00	
1929	1,779,750	4500.00	5250.00	6350.00	8750.00	18000.00	— —	
1930S	74,000	9500.00	13000.00	18000.00	25000.00	35000.00	— —	
1931	2,938,250	11000.00	13000.00	15000.00	18500.00	30000.00	— —	
1931D	106,500	13000.00	15000.00	18000.00	25000.00	32500.00	— —	
1932	1,101,750	15000.00	18000.00	21000.00	26000.00	42500.00	— —	
1933		NONE ISSUED FOR CIRCULATION						

Coin Check List
Half Cents

DATE	QUANTITY MINTED	AG	G	VG	F	VF	EF	AU	UNC	PROOF
1793	35,334									
1794	81,600									
1795	134,600									
1796	6,480									
1797	119,215									
1800	211,530									
1802	14,366									
1803	97,900									
1804	1,055,312									
1805	814,464									
1806	356,000									
1807	476,000									
1808	400,000									
1809	1,154,572									
1810	215,000									
1811	63,140									
1825	63,000									
1826	234,000									
1828	606,000									
1829	487,000									
1831	2,200									
1832	154,000									
1833	120,000									
1834	141,000									
1835	398,000									
1836										
1840										
1840										
1841										
1841										
1842										
1842										
1843										
1843										
1844										
1844										
1845										
1845										
1846										
1846										
1847										
1847										
1848										
1848										
1849	39,864									
1850	39,812									
1851	147,672									
1852										
1853	129,694									
1854	55,358									
1855	56,500									
1856	40,430									
1857	35,180									

Coin Check List
Large Cents

DATE	QUANTITY MINTED	AG	G	VG	F	VF	EF	AU	UNC	PROOF
1793 Chain Ameri	36,103									
1793 Chain America ..										
1793 Wreath type	63,353									
1793 Liberty cap	11,056									
1794	918,521									
1795	538,500									
1796	109,825									
1796	363,375									
1797	897,500									
1798	1,841,700									
1799	2,822,175									
1800	2,822,175									
1801	1,362,837									
1802	3,435,100									
1803	3,131,691									
1804	96,500									
1805	941,116									
1806	348,000									
1807	829,221									
1808	1,109,000									
1809	222,867									
1810	1,458,500									
1811	218,025									
1812	1,075,500									
1813	418,000									
1814	357,830									
1816	2,820,982									
1817	3,948,400									
1818	3,167,000									
1819	2,671,000									
1820	4,407,550									
1821	389,000									
1822	2,072,339									
1823	855,730									
1824	1,262,000									
1825	1,461,100									
1826	1,517,425									
1827	2,357,732									
1828	2,260,624									
1829	1,414,500									
1830	1,711,500									
1831	3,359,260									
1832	2,362,000									
1833	2,739,000									
1834	1,855,100									
1835	3,878,400									
1836	2,111,000									
1837	5,558,300									

Coin Check List
Large Cents

DATE	QUANTITY MINTED	AG	G	VG	F	VF	EF	AU	UNC	PROOF
1838	6,370,200									
1839	3,128,661									
1840	2,462,700									
1841	1,597,367									
1842	2,383,390									
1843	2,428,320									
1844	2,398,752									
1845	3,894,804									
1846	4,120,800									
1847	6,183,669									
1848	6,415,799									
1849	4,178,500									
1850	4,426,844									
1851	9,889,707									
1852	5,063,094									
1853	6,641,131									
1854	4,236,156									
1855	1,574,829									
1856	2,690,463									
1857	333,456									

Coin Check List
Small Cents

DATE	QUANTITY MINTED	AG	G	VG	F	VF	EF	AU	UNC	PROOF
1856	1,000									
1857	17,450,000									
1858	24,600,000									
1859	36,400,000									
1860	20,566,000									
1861	10,100,000									
1862	28,075,000									
1863	49,840,000									
1864	13,740,000									
1864 / 1864L	39,233,714									
1865	35,429,286									
1866	9,826,500									
1867	9,821,000									
1868	10,266,500									
1869	6,420,000									
1870	5,275,000									
1871	3,929,500									
1872	4,042,000									
1873	11,676,500									
1874	14,187,500									
1875	13,528,000									
1876	7,944,000									
1877	852,500									
1878	5,799,850									
1879	16,231,200									
1880	38,964,955									
1881	39,211,575									
1882	38,581,100									
1883	45,598,109									
1884	23,261,742									
1885	11,765,384									
1886	17,654,290									
1887	45,226,483									
1888	37,494,414									
1889	48,869,361									
1890	57,182,854									
1891	47,072,350									
1892	37,649,832									
1893	46,642,195									
1894	16,752,132									
1895	38,343,636									
1896	39,057,293									
1897	50,466,330									
1898	49,823,079									
1899	53,600,031									
1900	66,833,764									
1901	79,611,143									
1902	87,376,722									
1903	85,094,493									
1904	61,328,015									
1905	80,719,163									
1906	96,022,255									
1907	108,138,618									
1908	32,327,987									

Coin Check List
Small Cents

DATE	QUANTITY MINTED	AG	G	VG	F	VF	EF	AU	UNC	PROOF
1908S	1,115,000									
1909	14,370,645									
1909S	309,000									
1909 V.D.B. ...	27,995,000									
1909 VDB-S ...	484,000									
1909	72,702,618									
1909S	1,825,000									
1910	146,801,218									
1910S	6,045,000									
1911	101,177,787									
1911D	12,672,000									
1911S	4,026,000									
1912	68,153,060									
1912D	10,411,000									
1912S	4,431,000									
1913	76,532,352									
1913D	15,804,000									
1913S	6,101,000									
1914	75,238,432									
1914D	1,193,000									
1914S	4,137,000									
1915	29,092,120									
1915D	22,050,000									
1915S	4,833,000									
1916	131,833,677									
1916D	35,956,000									
1916S	22,510,000									
1917	196,429,785									
1917D	55,120,000									
1917S	32,620,000									
1918	288,104,634									
1918D	47,830,000									
1918S	34,680,000									
1919	392,021,000									
1919D	57,154,000									
1919S	139,760,000									
1920	310,165,000									
1920D	49,280,000									
1920S	46,220,000									
1921	39,157,000									
1921S	15,274,000									
1922 ...... 1922D	7,160,000									
1923	74,723,000									
1923S	8,700,000									
1924	75,178,000									
1924D	2,520,000									
1924S	11,696,000									
1925	139,949,000									
1925D	22,580,000									
1925S	26,380,000									
1926	157,088,000									
1926D	28,020,000									

Coin Check List
Small Cents

DATE	QUANTITY MINTED	AG	G	VG	F	VF	EF	AU	UNC	PROOF
1926S	4,550,000									
1927	144,440,000									
1927D	27,170,000									
1927S	14,276,000									
1928	134,116,000									
1928D	31,170,000									
1928S	17,266,000									
1929	185,262,000									
1929D	41,730,000									
1929S	50,148,000									
1930	157,415,000									
1930D	40,100,000									
1930S	24,286,000									
1931	19,396,000									
1931D	4,480,000									
1931S	866,000									
1932	9,062,000									
1932D	10,500,000									
1933	14,360,000									
1933D	6,200,000									
1934	219,080,000									
1934D	28,446,000									
1935	245,388,000									
1935D	47,000,000									
1935S	38,702,000									
1936	309,637,569									
1936D	40,620,000									
1936S	29,130,000									
1937	309,179,320									
1937D	50,430,000									
1937S	34,500,000									
1938	156,696,734									
1938D	20,010,000									
1938S	15,180,000									
1939	316,479,520									
1939D	15,160,000									
1939S	52,070,000									
1940	586,825,872									
1940D	81,390,000									
1940S	112,940,000									
1941	887,039,100									
1941D	128,700,000									
1941S	92,360,000									
1942	657,828,600									
1942D	206,698,000									
1942S	85,590,000									
1943	684,628,670									
1943D	217,660,000									
1943S	191,550,000									
1944	1,435,400,000									
1944D	430,578,000									
1944S	282,760,000									
1945	1,040,515,000									
1945D	226,268,000									
1945S	181,770,000									

Coin Check List
Small Cents

DATE	QUANTITY MINTED	AG	G	VG	F	VF	EF	AU	UNC	PROOF
1946	991,655,000									
1946D	315,690,000									
1946S	198,100,000									
1947	190,555,000									
1947D	194,750,000									
1947S	99,000,000									
1948	317,570,000									
1948D	172,637,500									
1948S	81,735,000									
1949	217,490,000									
1949D	154,370,500									
1949S	64,290,000									
1950	272,686,386									
1950D	334,950,000									
1950S	118,505,000									
1951	294,633,500									
1951D	625,355,000									
1951S	136,010,000									
1952	186,856,980									
1952D	746,130,000									
1952S	137,800,004									
1953	256,883,800									
1953D	700,515,000									
1953S	181,835,000									
1954	71,873,350									
1954D	251,552,500									
1954S	96,190,000									
1955										
1955 ...... Double Die	330,958,200									
1955D	563,257,500									
1955S	44,610,000									
1956	421,414,384									
1956D	1,098,201,100									
1957	283,787,952									
1957D	1,051,342,000									
1958	253,400,652									
1958D	800,953,300									
1959	610,864,291									
1959D	1,279,760,000									
1960 large date										
1960 small date	588,096,602									
1960D large date										
1960D small date	1,580,884,000									
1961	756,373,244									
1961D	1,753,266,700									
1962	609,263,019									
1962D	1,793,148,400									
1963	757,185,645									
1963D	1,774,020,400									
1964	2,652,525,762									

Coin Check List
Small Cents

DATE	QUANTITY MINTED	AG	G	VG	F	VF	EF	AU	UNC	PROOF
1964D	3,799,071,500									
1865	1,497,224,900									
1966	2,188,147,783									
1967	3,048,667,100									
1968	1,707,880,970									
1968D	2,886,269,600									
1968S	261,311,510									
1969	1,136,910,000									
1969D	4,002,832,200									
1969S	547,309,631									
1970	1,898,315,000									
1970D	2,891,438,900									
1970S	693,192,814									
1971	1,919,490,000									
1971D	2,911,045,600									
1971S	528,354,192									
1972										
1972 ...... Double impression.	2,933,255,000									
1972D	2,665,071,400									
1972S	380,200,104									
1973	3,728,245,000									
1973D	3,549,576,588									
1973S	319,937,634									
1974	4,232,140,523									
1974D	4,235,098,000									
1974S	412,039,228									
1975	5,451,476,142									
1975D	4,505,275,300									
1975S* ...	2,845,450									
1976	4,674,292,426									
1976D	4,221,592,455									
1976S* ...	4,149,730									
1977	4,469,930,000									
1977D	4,194,062,300									
1977S* ...	3,251,152									
1978	5,266,905,000									
1978D	4,280,233,400									
1978S* ...	3,127,781									
1979	5,266,790,000									
1979D	4,139,357,254									
1979S	751,725,000									
1980	6,230,115,000									
1980D	5,140,098,660									
1980S	1,184,590,000									
1981										
1981D										
1981S										

*Proof only

Coin Check List
Two Cents

DATE	QUANTITY MINTED	AG	G	VG	F	VF	EF	AU	UNC	PROOF
1864	19,847,500									
1865	13,640,000									
1866	3,177,000									
1867	2,938,750									
1868	2,803,750									
1869	1,546,500									
1870	861,250									
1871	721,250									
1872	65,000									
1873	1,100									

Coin Check List
Three Cents Silver

DATE	QUANTITY MINTED	AG	G	VG	F	VF	EF	AU	UNC	PROOF
1851	5,447,400									
1851 O	720,000									
1852	18,663,500									
1853	11,400,000									
1854	671,000									
1855	139,000									
1856	1,458,000									
1857	1,042,000									
1858	1,604,000									
1859	365,000									
1860	286,000									
1861	499,000									
1862	363,500									
1863	21,460									
1864	12,470									
1865	8,500									
1866	22,725									
1867	4,625									
1868	4,100									
1869	5,100									
1870	4,000									
1871	4,360									
1872	1,950									
1873	600									

Coin Check List
Nickel Three Cent Pieces

DATE	QUANTITY MINTED	AG	G	VG	F	VF	EF	AU	UNC	PROOF
1865	11,382,000									
1866	4,801,000									
1867	3,915,000									
1868	3,252,000									
1869	1,604,000									
1870	1,335,000									
1871	604,000									
1872	862,000									
1873	1,173,000									
1874	790,000									
1875	228,000									
1876	162,000									
1877	510									
1878	2,350									
1879	41,200									
1880	24,955									
1881	1,080,575									
1882	25,300									
1883	10,609									
1884	5,642									
1885	4,790									
1886	4,290									
1887	7,961									
1888	41,083									
1889	21,561									

Coin Check List
Five Cent Nickel

DATE	QUANTITY MINTED	AG	G	VG	F	VF	EF	AU	UNC	PROOF
1866 Rays .	14,742,500									
1867 Rays .	30,909,500									
1867										
1868	28,817,000									
1869	16,395,000									
1870	4,806,000									
1871	561,000									
1872	6,036,000									
1873	4,550,000									
1874	3,538,000									
1875	2,097,000									
1876	2,530,000									
1877	500									
1878	2,350									
1879	29,100									
1880	19,955									
1881	72,375									
1882	11,476,000									
1883	1,456,919									
1883 Without Cents	5,479,519									
1883	16,032,983									
1884	11,273,942									
1885	1,476,490									
1886	3,330,290									
1887	15,263,652									
1888	10,720,483									
1889	15,881,361									
1890	16,259,272									
1891	16,834,350									
1892	11,699,642									
1893	13,370,195									
1894	5,413,132									
1895	9,979,884									
1896	8,842,920									
1897	20,428,735									
1898	12,532,087									
1899	26,029,031									
1900	27,255,995									
1901	26,480,213									
1902	31,480,579									
1903	28,006,725									
1904	21,404,984									
1905	29,827,276									
1906	38,613,725									
1907	39,214,800									
1908	22,686,177									
1909	11,590,526									
1910	30,169,353									
1911	39,559,372									
1912	26,236,714									
1912D	8,474,000									
1912S	238,000									
1913	30,993,520									

Coin Check List
Five Cent Nickels

DATE	QUANTITY MINTED	AG	G	VG	F	VF	EF	AU	UNC	PROOF
1913D	5,337,000									
1913S	2,105,000									
1913	29,853,700									
1913D	4,156,000									
1913S	1,209,000									
1914	20,665,738									
1914D	3,912,000									
1914S	3,470,000									
1915	20,987,270									
1915D	7,569,500									
1915S	1,505,000									
1916	63,498,066									
1916D	13,333,000									
1916S	11,860,000									
1917	51,424,029									
1917D	9,910,800									
1917S	4,193,000									
1918	32,086,314									
1918D	8,362,000									
1918S	4,882,000									
1919	60,868,000									
1919D	8,006,000									
1919S	7,521,000									
1920	63,093,000									
1920D	9,418,000									
1920S	9,689,000									
1921	10,663,000									
1921S	1,557,000									
1923	35,715,000									
1923S	6,142,000									
1924	21,620,000									
1924D	5,258,000									
1924S	1,437,000									
1925	35,565,000									
1925D	4,450,000									
1925S	6,256,000									
1926	44,693,000									
1926D	5,638,000									
1926S	970,000									
1927	37,981,000									
1927D	5,730,000									
1927S	3,430,000									
1928	23,411,000									
1928D	6,436,000									
1928S	6,936,000									
1929	36,446,000									
1929D	8,370,000									
1929S	7,754,000									
1930	22,849,000									
1930S	5,435,000									
1931S	1,200,000									
1934	20,213,000									
1934D	7,480,000									
1935	58,264,000									
1935D	12,092,000									

Coin Check List
Five Cent Nickels

DATE	QUANTITY MINTED	AG	G	VG	F	VF	EF	AU	UNC	PROOF
1935S	10,300,000									
1936	119,001,420									
1936D	24,418,000									
1936S	14,930,000									
1937	79,485,769									
1937D										
1937D	17,826,000									
3 Legged ..										
1937S	5,635,000									
1938D	7,020,000									
1938	19,515,365									
1938D	5,376,000									
1938S	4,105,000									
1939	120,627,535									
1939D	3,514,000									
1939S	6,630,000									
1940	176,499,158									
1940D	43,540,000									
1940S	39,690,000									
1941	203,283,720									
1941D	53,432,000									
1941S	43,445,000									
1942	49,818,600									
1942D	13,938,000									
1942P	57,900,600									
1942S	32,900,000									
1943P	271,165,000									
1943D	15,294,000									
1943S	104,060,000									
1944P	119,150,000									
1944D	32,309,000									
1944S	21,640,000									
1945P	119,408,100									
1945D	37,158,000									
1945S	58,939,000									
1946	161,116,000									
1946D	45,292,200									
1946S	13,560,000									
1947	95,000,000									
1947D	37,882,000									
1947S	24,720,000									
1948	89,348,000									
1948D	44,734,000									
1948S	11,300,000									
1949	60,652,000									
1949D	35,238,000									
1949S	9,716,000									
1950	9,847,386									
1950D	2,630,030									
1951	28,689,500									
1951D	20,460,000									
1951S	7,776,000									
1952	64,069,980									
1952D	30,638,000									
1952S	20,572,000									

Coin Check List
Five Cent Nickels

DATE	QUANTITY MINTED	AG	G	VG	F	VF	EF	AU	UNC	PROOF
1953	46,772,800									
1953D	59,878,600									
1953S	19,210,900									
1954	47,917,350									
1954D	117,183,060									
1954S	29,384,000									
1955	8,266,200									
1955D	74,464,100									
1956	35,885,384									
1956D	67,222,940									
1957	39,655,952									
1957D	136,828,900									
1958	17,963,652									
1958D	168,249,120									
1959	28,397,291									
1959D	160,738,240									
1960	57,107,602									
1960D	192,582,180									
1961	76,668,244									
1961D	229,342,760									
1962	100,602,019									
1962D	280,195,720									
1963	178,851,645									
1963D	276,829,460									
1964	1,028,622,762									
1964D	1,787,297,160									
1965	136,131,380									
1966	156,208,283									
1967	107,325,800									
1968D	91,227,880									
1968S	103,437,510									
1969D	202,807,500									
1969S	123,089,631									
1970D	515,485,380									
1970S	241,464,814									
1971	106,884,000									
1971D	316,144,800									
1971S* . . .	3,220,733									
1972	202,036,000									
1972D	351,694,600									
1972S* . . .	3,260,996									
1973	384,396,000									
1973D	261,405,400									
1973S* . . .	2,760,339									
1974	601,752,000									
1974D	277,373,000									
1974S* . . .	2,612,568									
1975	181,772,000									
1975D	401,875,300									
1975S* . . .	2,845,450									
1976	367,124,000									
1976D	563,964,147									
1976S* . . .	4,123,056									
1977	585,376,000									
1977D	297,313,422									

Coin Check List
Five Cent Nickels

DATE	QUANTITY MINTED	AG	G	VG	F	VF	EF	AU	UNC	PROOF
1977S* ...	3,251,152									
1978	391,308,000									
1978D	313,092,780									
1978S* ...	3,127,781									
1979	463,188,000									
1979D	325,867,672									
1979S* ...	3,677,175									
1980P	593,004,000									
1980D	502,323,448									
1980S* ...	2,144,231									
1981P										
1981D										
1981S										

*Proof only

Coin Check List
Half Dimes

DATE	QUANTITY MINTED	AG	G	VG	F	VF	EF	AU	UNC	PROOF
1794	86,416									
1795										
1796	10,230									
1797	44,527									
1800	24,000									
1801	33,910									
1802	13,010									
1803	37,850									
1805	15,600									
1829	1,230,000									
1830	1,240,000									
1831	1,242,700									
1832	965,000									
1833	1,370,000									
1834	1,480,000									
1835	2,760,000									
1836	1,900,000									
1837	871,000									
1837	1,405,000									
1838 0 No Stars	70,000									
1838	2,255,000									
1839	1,069,150									
1839 0	981,550									
1840 No Drapery	1,344,085									
1840 With Drapery										
1840 0 No Drapery	935,000									
1840 0 With Drapery										
1841	1,150,000									
1841 0	815,000									
1842	815,000									
1842 0	350,000									
1843	1,165,000									
1844	430,000									
1844 0	220,000									
1845	1,564,000									
1846	27,000									
1847	1,274,000									
1848	668,000									
1848 0	600,000									
1849	1,309,000									
1849 0	140,000									
1850	955,000									
1850 0	690,000									
1851	781,000									
1851 0	860,000									
1852	1,000,500									
1852 0	260,000									
1853 No Arrows	135,000									

Coin Check List
Half Dimes

DATE	QUANTITY MINTED	AG	G	VG	F	VF	EF	AU	UNC	PROOF
1853 0 No Arrows ...	160,000									
1853	13,210,020									
1853 0	2,200,000									
1854	5,740,000									
1854 0	1,560,000									
1855	1,750,000									
1855 0	600,000									
1856										
1856 0										
1857										
1857 0										
1858	3,500,000									
1858 0	1,660,000									
1859	340,000									
1859 0	560,000									
1860	799,000									
1860 0	1,060,000									
1861	3,360,000									
1862	1,492,550									
1863	18,460									
1863S	100,000									
1864	48,470									
1864S	90,000									
1865	13,500									
1865S	120,000									
1866	10,725									
1866S	120,000									
1867	8,625									
1867S	120,000									
1868	89,200									
1868S	280,000									
1869	208,600									
1869S	230,000									
1870	536,000									
1871	1,873,960									
1871S	161,000									
1872	2,947,950									
1872S	537,000									
1873	712,600									
1873S	324,000									

Coin Check List
Dimes

DATE	QUANTITY MINTED	AG	G	VG	F	VF	EF	AU	UNC	PROOF
1796	22,135									
1797	25,261									
1798	27,550									
1800	21,760									
1801	34,640									
1802	10,975									
1803	33,040									
1804	8,265									
1805	120,780									
1807	165,000									
1809	51,065									
1811	65,180									
1814	421,500									
1820	942,587									
1821	1,186,512									
1822	100,000									
1823	440,000									
1824	100,000									
1825	410,000									
1827	1,215,000									
1828	125,000									
1829	770,000									
1830	510,000									
1831	771,350									
1832	522,500									
1833	485,000									
1834	635,000									
1835	1,410,000									
1836	1,190,000									
1837	1,042,000									
1838 0	402,434									
1838	1,992,500									
1839	1,053,115									
1839 0	1,243,272									
1840 No Drapery	1,358,580									
1840 0	1,175,000									
1840 With Drapery	Mintage in 1840 above									
1841	1,622,500									
1841 0	2,007,500									
1842	1,887,500									
1842 0	2,020,000									
1843	1,370,000									
1843 0	150,000									
1844	72,500									
1845	1,755,000									
1845 0	230,000									
1846	31,300									
1847	245,000									
1848	451,500									
1849	839,000									
1849 0	300,000									
1850	1,931,500									
1850 0	510,000									

Coin Check List
Dimes

DATE	QUANTITY MINTED	AG	G	VG	F	VF	EF	AU	UNC	PROOF
1851	1,026,500									
1851 0	400,000									
1852	1,535,500									
1852 0	430,000									
1853 No Arrows ...	95,000									
1853 With Arrows ...	12,078,010									
1853 0	1,100,000									
1854	4,470,000									
1854 0	1,770,000									
1855	2,075,000									
1856	5,780,000									
1856 0	1,180,000									
1856S	70,000									
1857	5,580,000									
1857 0	1,540,000									
1858	1,540,000									
1858 0	290,000									
1858S	60,000									
1859	430,000									
1859 0	480,000									
1859S	60,000									
1860S	140,000									
1860	607,000									
1860 0	40,000									
1861	1,884,000									
1861S	172,500									
1862	847,550									
1862S	180,750									
1863	14,460									
1863S	157,500									
1864	11,470									
1864S	230,000									
1865	10,500									
1865S	175,000									
1866	8,725									
1866S	135,000									
1867	6,625									
1867S	140,000									
1868	464,600									
1868S	260,000									
1869	256,600									
1869S	450,000									
1870	471,500									
1870S	50,000									
1871	907,710									
1871CC ...	20,100									
1871S	320,000									
1872	2,396,450									
1872CC ...	35,480									
1872S	190,000									
1873CC ...	12,400									
1873	1,568,600									
1873	2,378,500									

Coin Check List
Dimes

DATE	QUANTITY MINTED	AG	G	VG	F	VF	EF	AU	UNC	PROOF
1873CC ...	18,791									
1873S	455,000									
1874	2,940,000									
1874CC ...	10,817									
1874S	240,000									
1875	10,350,700									
1875CC ...	4,645,000									
1875S	9,070,000									
1876	11,461,150									
1876CC ...	8,270,000									
1876S	10,420,000									
1877	7,310,510									
1877CC ...	7,700,000									
1877S	2,340,000									
1878	1,678,800									
1878CC ...	200,000									
1879	15,100									
1880	37,355									
1881	24,975									
1882	3,911,100									
1883	7,675,712									
1884	3,366,380									
1884S	564,969									
1885	2,533,427									
1885S	43,690									
1886	6,377,570									
1886S	206,524									
1887	11,283,939									
1887S	4,454,450									
1888	5,496,487									
1888S	1,720,000									
1889	7,380,711									
1889S	972,678									
1890	9,911,541									
1890S	1,423,076									
1891	15,310,600									
1891 O	4,540,000									
1891S	3,196,116									
1892	12,121,245									
1892 O	3,841,700									
1892S	990,710									
1893	3,340,792									
1893 O	1,760,000									
1893S	2,491,401									
1894	1,330,972									
1894 O	720,000									
1894S	24									
1895	690,880									
1895 O	440,000									
1895S	1,120,000									
1896	2,000,762									
1896 O	610,000									
1896S	575,056									
1897	10,869,264									
1897 O	666,000									

Coin Check List
Dimes

DATE	QUANTITY MINTED	AG	G	VG	F	VF	EF	AU	UNC	PROOF
1897S	1,342,844									
1898	16,320,735									
1898 0	2,130,000									
1898S	1,702,507									
1899	19,580,846									
1899 0	2,650,000									
1899S	1,867,493									
1900	17,600,912									
1900 0	2,010,000									
1900S	5,168,270									
1901	18,860,478									
1901 0	5,620,000									
1901S	593,022									
1902	21,380,777									
1902 0	4,500,000									
1902S	2,070,000									
1903	19,500,755									
1903 0	8,180,000									
1903S	613,300									
1904	14,601,027									
1904S	800,000									
1905	14,552,350									
1905 0	3,400,000									
1905S	6,855,199									
1906	19,958,406									
1906D	4,060,000									
1906 0	2,610,000									
1906S	3,136,640									
1907	22,220,575									
1907D	4,080,000									
1907 0	5,058,000									
1907S	3,178,470									
1908	10,600,545									
1908D	7,490,000									
1908 0	1,789,000									
1908S	3,220,000									
1909	10,240,650									
1909D	954,000									
1909 0	2,287,000									
1909S	1,000,000									
1910	11,520,551									
1910D	3,490,000									
1910S	1,240,000									
1911	18,870,543									
1911D	11,209,000									
1911S	3,520,000									
1912	19,350,700									
1912D	11,760,000									
1912S	3,420,000									
1913	19,760,622									
1913S	510,000									
1914	17,360,655									
1914D	11,908,000									
1914S	2,100,000									
1915	5,620,450									

Coin Check List
Dimes

DATE	QUANTITY MINTED	AG	G	VG	F	VF	EF	AU	UNC	PROOF
1915S	960,000									
1916	18,490,000									
1916S	5,820,000									
1916	22,180,080									
1916D	264,000									
1916S	10,450,000									
1917	55,230,000									
1917D	9,402,000									
1917S	27,330,000									
1918	26,680,000									
1918D	22,674,800									
1918S	19,300,000									
1919	35,740,000									
1919D	9,939,000									
1919S	8,850,000									
1920	59,030,000									
1920D	19,171,000									
1920S	13,820,000									
1921	1,230,000									
1921D	1,080,000									
1923	50,130,000									
1923S	6,440,000									
1924	24,010,000									
1924D	6,810,000									
1924S	7,120,000									
1925	25,610,000									
1925D	5,117,000									
1925S	5,850,000									
1926	32,160,000									
1926D	6,828,000									
1926S	1,520,000									
1927	28,080,000									
1927D	4,812,000									
1927S	4,770,000									
1928	19,480,000									
1928D	4,161,000									
1928S	7,400,000									
1929	25,970,000									
1929D	5,034,000									
1929S	4,730,000									
1930	6,770,000									
1930S	1,843,000									
1931	3,150,000									
1931D	1,260,000									
1931S	1,800,000									
1934	24,080,000									
1934D	6,772,000									
1935	58,830,000									
1935D	10,477,000									
1935S	15,840,000									
1936	87,504,130									
1936D	16,132,000									
1936S	9,210,000									
1937	56,865,756									
1937D	14,146,000									

Coin Check List
Dimes

DATE	QUANTITY MINTED	AG	G	VG	F	VF	EF	AU	UNC	PROOF
1937S	9,740,000									
1938	22,198,728									
1938D	5,537,000									
1938S	8,090,000									
1939	67,749,321									
1939D	24,394,000									
1939S	10,540,000									
1940	65,361,827									
1940D	21,198,000									
1940S	21,560,000									
1941	175,106,557									
1941D	45,634,000									
1941S	43,090,000									
1942	205,432,329									
1942D over 1	60,740,000									
1942S	49,300,000									
1943	191,710,000									
1943D	71,949,000									
1943S	60,400,000									
1944	231,410,000									
1944D	62,224,000									
1944S	49,490,000									
1945	159,130,000									
1945D	40,245,000									
1945	41,920,000									
1946	225,250,000									
1946D	61,043,500									
1946S	27,900,000									
1947	121,520,000									
1947D	46,835,000									
1947S	34,840,000									
1948	74,950,000									
1948D	52,841,000									
1948S	35,520,000									
1949	30,940,000									
1949D	26,034,000									
1949S	13,510,000									
1950	50,181,500									
1950D	46,803,000									
1950S	20,440,000									
1951	130,937,602									
1951D	56,529,000									
1951S	31,630,000									
1952	99,122,073									
1952D	122,100,000									
1952S	44,419,500									
1953	53,618,920									
1953D	136,433,000									
1953S	39,180,000									
1954	114,243,503									
1954D	106,397,000									
1954S	22,860,000									
1955	12,828,381									
1955D	13,959,000									

Coin Check List
Dimes

DATE	QUANTITY MINTED	AG	G	VG	F	VF	EF	AU	UNC	PROOF
1955S	18,510,000									
1956	109,309,384									
1956D	108,015,100									
1957	161,407,952									
1957D	113,354,330									
1958	32,785,652									
1958D	136,564,600									
1959	86,929,291									
1959D	164,919,790									
1960	72,081,602									
1960D	200,160,400									
1961	96,758,244									
1961D	209,146,550									
1962	75,668,019									
1962D	334,948,380									
1963	126,725,645									
1963D	421,476,530									
1964	933,310,762									
1964D	1,357,517,180									
1965	1,652,140,570									
1966	1,382,734,540									
1967	2,244,007,320									
1968	424,470,400									
1968D	480,748,280									
1968S*	3,041,506									
1969	145,790,000									
1969D	563,323,870									
1969S* ...	2,934,631									
1970	345,570,000									
1970D	754,942,100									
1970S* ...	2,632,810									
1971	162,690,000									
1971D	377,914,240									
1971S* ...	3,220,733									
1972	431,540,000									
1972D	330,290,000									
1972S* ...	3,260,996									
1973	315,670,000									
1973D	455,032,426									
1973S* ...	2,760,339									
1974	470,248,000									
1974D	571,083,000									
1974S* ...	2,612,568									
1975	585,673,900									
1975D	313,705,300									
1975S* ...	2,845,450									
1976	568,760,000									
1976D	695,222,774									
1976S* ...	4,149,730									
1977	796,930,000									
1977D	376,607,228									
1977S* ...	3,251,152									
1978	663,980,000									
1978D	282,847,540									
1978S* ...	3,127,781									

Coin Check List
Dimes

DATE	QUANTITY MINTED	AG	G	VG	F	VF	EF	AU	UNC	PROOF
1979	315,440,000									
1979D	390,921,184									
1979S* ...	3,677,175									
1980P	735,170,000									
1980D	719,354,321									
1980S* ...	2,144,231									
1981P										
1981D										
1981S										

*Proof only

Coin Check List
Twenty Cents

DATE	QUANTITY MINTED	AG	G	VG	F	VF	EF	AU	UNC	PROOF
1875	39,700									
1875CC . . .	133,290									
1875S	1,155,000									
1876	15,900									
1876CC . . .	10,000									
1877	510									
1878	600									

Coin Check List
Quarter Dollars

DATE	QUANTITY MINTED	AG	G	VG	F	VF	EF	AU	UNC	PROOF
1796	6,146									
1804	6,738									
1805	121,394									
1806	206,124									
1807	220,643									
1815	89,235									
1818	361,174									
1819	144,000									
1820	127,444									
1821	216,851									
1822	64,080									
1823	17,800									
1824	24,000									
1825	148,000									
1827	4,000									
1828	102,000									
1831	398,000									
1832	320,000									
1833	156,000									
1834	286,000									
1835	1,952,000									
1836	472,000									
1837	252,400									
1838	366,000									
1838	466,000									
1839	491,146									
1840	188,127									
1840 0	425,200									
1841	120,000									
1841 0	452,000									
1842	88,000									
1842 0	769,000									
1843	645,600									
1843 0	968,000									
1844	421,200									
1844 0	740,000									
1845	922,000									
1846	510,000									
1847	734,000									
1847 0	368,000									
1848	146,000									
1849	340,000									
1849 0	16,000									
1850	190,800									
1850 0	396,000									
1851	160,000									
1851 0	88,000									
1852	177,060									
1852 0	96,000									
1853	44,200									
1853 Rays .	15,210,020									
1853 0										
Rays	1,332,000									
1854	12,380,000									
1854 0	1,484,000									

Coin Check List
Quarter Dollars

DATE	QUANTITY MINTED	AG	G	VG	F	VF	EF	AU	UNC	PROOF
1855	2,857,000									
1855 O	176,000									
1855S	396,400									
1856	7,264,000									
1856 O	968,000									
1856S	286,000									
1857	9,644,000									
1857 O	1,180,000									
1857S	82,000									
1858	7,368,000									
1858 O	520,000									
1858S	121,000									
1859	1,344,000									
1859 O	260,000									
1859S	80,000									
1860	805,400									
1860 O	388,000									
1860S	56,000									
1861	4,854,600									
1861S	96,000									
1862	932,550									
1862S	67,000									
1863	192,000									
1864	94,070									
1864S	20,000									
1865	59,300									
1865S	41,000									
1866	17,525									
1866S	28,000									
1867	20,625									
1867S	48,000									
1868	30,000									
1868S	96,000									
1869	16,600									
1869S	76,000									
1870	87,400									
1870CC . . .	8,340									
1871	119,160									
1871CC . . .	10,890									
1871S	30,900									
1872	182,950									
1872CC . . .	22,850									
1872S	83,000									
1873	212,600									
1873CC . . .	4,000									
1873 Arrows . . .	1,271,700									
1873CC Arrows . . .	12,462									
1873S Arrows . . .	156,000									
1874 Arrows . . .	471,900									
1874S Arrows . . .	392,000									

Coin Check List
Quarter Dollars

DATE	QUANTITY MINTED	AG	G	VG	F	VF	EF	AU	UNC	PROOF
1875	4,293,500									
1875CC ...	140,000									
1875S	680,000									
1876	17,817,150									
1876CC ...	4,944,000									
1876S	8,596,000									
1877	10,911,710									
1877CC ...	4,192,000									
1877S	8,996,000									
1878	2,260,800									
1878CC ...	996,000									
1878S	140,000									
1879	14,700									
1880	14,955									
1881	12,975									
1882	16,300									
1883	15,439									
1884	8,875									
1885	14,530									
1886	5,886									
1887	10,710									
1888	10,833									
1888S	1,216,000									
1889	12,711									
1890	80,590									
1891	3,920,600									
1891 0	68,000									
1891S	2,216,000									
1892	8,237,245									
1892 0	2,640,000									
1892S	964,079									
1893	5,444,815									
1893 0	3,396,000									
1893S	1,454,535									
1894	3,432,972									
1894 0	2,852,000									
1894S	2,648,821									
1895	4,440,880									
1895 0	2,816,000									
1895S	1,764,681									
1896	3,874,762									
1896 0	1,484,000									
1896S	188,039									
1897	8,140,731									
1897 0	1,414,800									
1897S	542,229									
1898	11,100,735									
1898 0	1,868,000									
1898S	1,020,592									
1899	12,624,846									
1899 0	2,644,000									
1899S	708,000									
1900	10,016,912									
1900 0	3,146,000									
1900S	1,858,585									

Coin Check List
Quarter Dollars

DATE	QUANTITY MINTED	AG	G	VG	F	VF	EF	AU	UNC	PROOF
1901	8,892,813									
1901 0	1,612,000									
1901S	72,664									
1902	12,197,744									
1902 0	4,748,000									
1902 S	1,524,612									
1903	9,670,064									
1903 0	3,500,000									
1903S	1,036,000									
1904	9,588,813									
1904 0	2,456,000									
1905	4,968,250									
1905 0	1,230,000									
1905S	1,884,000									
1906	3,656,435									
1906D	3,280,000									
1906 0	2,056,000									
1907	7,192,575									
1907D	2,484,000									
1907 0	4,560,000									
1907S	1,360,000									
1908	4,232,545									
1908D	5,788,000									
1908 0	6,244,000									
1908S	784,000									
1909	9,268,650									
1909D	5,114,000									
1909 0	712,000									
1909S	1,348,000									
1910	2,244,551									
1910D	1,500,000									
1911	3,720,543									
1911D	933,600									
1911S	988,000									
1912	4,400,700									
1912S	708,000									
1913	484,613									
1913D	1,450,800									
1913S	40,000									
1914	6,244,610									
1914D	3,046,000									
1914S	264,000									
1915	3,480,450									
1915D	3,694,000									
1915S	704,000									
1916	1,788,000									
1916D	6,540,800									
1916	52,000									
1917	8,792,000									
1917D	1,509,200									
1917S	1,952,000									
1917	13,880,000									
1917D	6,224,400									
1917S	5,552,000									
1918	14,240,000									

Coin Check List
Quarter Dollars

DATE	QUANTITY MINTED	AG	G	VG	F	VF	EF	AU	UNC	PROOF
1918D	7,380,000									
1918S	11,072,000									
1919	11,324,000									
1919D	1,944,000									
1919S	1,836,000									
1920	27,860,000									
1920D	3,586,400									
1920S	6,380,000									
1921	1,916,000									
1923	9,716,000									
1923S	1,360,000									
1924	10,920,000									
1924D	3,112,000									
1924S	2,860,000									
1925	12,280,000									
1926	11,316,000									
1926D	1,716,000									
1926S	2,700,000									
1927	11,912,000									
1927D	976,400									
1927S	396,000									
1928	6,336,000									
1928D	1,627,600									
1928S	2,644,000									
1929	11,140,000									
1929D	1,358,000									
1929S	1,764,000									
1930	5,632,000									
1930S	1,556,000									
1932	5,404,000									
1932D	436,800									
1932S	408,000									
1934	31,912,052									
1934D	3,527,200									
1935	32,484,000									
1935D	5,780,000									
1935S	5,660,000									
1936	41,303,837									
1936D	5,374,000									
1936S	3,828,000									
1937	19,701,542									
1937D	7,189,600									
1937S	1,652,000									
1938	9,480,045									
1938S	2,832,000									
1939	33,548,795									
1939D	7,092,000									
1939S	2,628,000									
1940	35,715,246									
1940D	2,797,600									
1940S	8,244,000									
1941	79,047,287									
1941D	16,714,800									
1941S	16,080,000									
1942	102,117,123									

Coin Check List
Quarter Dollars

DATE	QUANTITY MINTED	AG	G	VG	F	VF	EF	AU	UNC	PROOF
1942D	17,487,200									
1942S	19,384,000									
1943	99,700,000									
1943D	16,095,600									
1943S	21,700,000									
1944	104,956,000									
1944D	14,600,000									
1944S	12,560,000									
1945	74,372,000									
1945D	12,341,600									
1945S	17,004,001									
1946	53,436,000									
1946D	9,072,800									
1946S	4,204,000									
1947	22,556,000									
1947D	15,338,400									
1947S	5,532,000									
1948	35,196,000									
1948D	16,766,800									
1948S	15,960,000									
1949	9,312,000									
1949D	10,068,400									
1950	24,971,512									
1950D	21,075,600									
1950S	10,284,004									
1951	43,505,602									
1951D	35,354,800									
1951S	9,048,000									
1952	38,862,073									
1952D	49,795,200									
1952S	13,707,800									
1953	18,664,920									
1953D	56,112,400									
1953S	14,016,000									
1954	54,645,503									
1954D	46,305,500									
1954S	11,834,722									
1955	18,558,381									
1955D	3,182,400									
1956	44,813,384									
1956D	32,334,500									
1957	47,779,952									
1957D	77,924,160									
1958	7,235,652									
1958D	78,124,900									
1959	25,533,291									
1959D	62,054,232									
1960	30,855,602									
1960D	63,000,324									
1961	40,064,244									
1961D	83,656,928									
1962	39,374,019									
1962D	127,554,756									
1963	77,391,645									
1963D	135,288,184									

Coin Check List
Quarter Dollars

DATE	QUANTITY MINTED	AG	G	VG	F	VF	EF	AU	UNC	PROOF
1964	564,341,347									
1964D	704,135,528									
1965	1,819,717,540									
1966	821,101,500									
1967	1,524,031,848									
1968	220,731,500									
1968D	101,534,000									
1968S* . . .	3,041,506									
1969	176,212,000									
1969D	114,372,000									
1969S* . . .	2,934,631									
1970	136,420,000									
1970D	417,341,364									
1970S* . . .	2,632,810									
1971	109,284,000									
1971D	258,634,428									
1971S* . . .	3,220,733									
1972	215,048,000									
1972D	311,067,732									
1972S* . . .	3,260,996									
1973	346,924,000									
1973D	232,977,400									
1973S* . . .	2,760,399									
1974	801,456,000									
1974D	353,160,300									
1974S* . . .	2,612,568									
1976	809,784,016									
1976D	860,118,839									
1976S* . . .	7,059,099									
1977	468,566,000									
1977D	256,524,978									
1977S* . . .	3,251,152									
1978	521,452,000									
1978D	287,373,152									
1978S* . . .	3,127,781									
1979	515,708,000									
1979D	489,789,780									
1979S* . . .	3,677,175									
1980P	635,832,000									
1980D	518,327,487									
1980S* . . .	2,144,231									
1981P										
1981D										
1981S										

*Proof only

Coin Check List
Half Dollars

DATE	QUANTITY MINTED	AG	G	VG	F	VF	EF	AU	UNC	PROOF
1794	23,464									
1795	299,680									
1796	3,918									
1797										
1801	30,289									
1802	29,820									
1803	188,234									
1805	211,722									
1806	839,576									
1807	301,076									
1807	750,500									
1808	1,368,600									
1809	1,405,810									
1810	1,276,276									
1811	1,203,644									
1812	1,628,059									
1813	1,241,903									
1814	1,039,075									
1815	47,150									
1817	1,215,567									
1818	1,960,322									
1819	2,208,000									
1820	751,122									
1821	1,305,797									
1822	1,559,573									
1823	1,694,200									
1824	3,504,954									
1825	2,943,166									
1826	4,004,180									
1827	5,493,400									
1828	3,075,200									
1829	3,712,156									
1830	4,764,800									
1831	5,873,660									
1832	4,797,000									
1833	5,206,000									
1834	6,412,004									
1835	5,352,006									
1836	6,545,200									
1836	1,200									
1837	3,629,820									
1838	3,546,000									
1838 0	20									
1839	1,362,160									
1839 0	162,976									
1839	1,972,400									
1840	1,435,008									
1840 0	855,100									
1841	310,000									
1841 0	401,000									
1842	2,012,764									
1842 0	957,000									
1843	3,844,000									
1843 0	2,268,000									
1844	1,766,000									

Coin Check List
Half Dollars

DATE	QUANTITY MINTED	AG	G	VG	F	VF	EF	AU	UNC	PROOF
1844 0	2,005,000									
1845	580,000									
1845 0	2,094,000									
1846	2,210,000									
1846 0	2,304,000									
1847	1,156,000									
1847 0	2,584,000									
1848	580,000									
1848 0	3,180,000									
1849	1,252,000									
1849 0	2,310,000									
1850	227,000									
1850 0	2,456,000									
1851	200,750									
1851 0	402,000									
1852	77,130									
1852 0	144,000									
1853	3,532,000									
1853 0	1,328,000									
1854	2,982,000									
1854 0	5,240,000									
1855	759,500									
1855 0	3,688,000									
1855S	129,950									
1856	938,000									
1856 0	2,658,000									
1856S	211,000									
1857	1,988,000									
1857 0	818,000									
1857S	158,000									
1858	4,226,000									
1858 0	7,294,000									
1858S	476,000									
1859	748,000									
1859 0	2,834,000									
1859S	566,000									
1860	303,700									
1860 0	1,290,000									
1860S	472,000									
1861	2,888,400									
1861 0	2,532,633									
1861S	939,500									
1862	253,550									
1862S	1,352,000									
1863	503,660									
1863S	916,000									
1864	379,570									
1864S	658,000									
1865	511,900									
1865S	675,000									
1866S	1,054,000									
1866	745,625									
1866S	1,054,000									
1867	449,925									
1867S	1,196,000									

227

Coin Check List
Half Dollars

DATE	QUANTITY MINTED	AG	G	VG	F	VF	EF	AU	UNC	PROOF
1868	418,200									
1868S	1,160,000									
1869	795,900									
1869S	656,000									
1870	634,900									
1870CC . . .	54,617									
1870S	1,004,000									
1871	1,204,560									
1871CC . . .	139,950									
1871S	2,178,000									
1872	881,550									
1872CC . . .	272,000									
1872S	580,000									
1873	801,800									
1873CC . . .	122,500									
1873 Arrows	1,815,700									
1873CC Arrows . . .	214,560									
1873S Arrows . . .	228,000									
1874	2,360,300									
1874CC . . .	59,000									
1874S	394,000									
1875	6,027,500									
1875CC . . .	1,008,000									
1875S	3,200,000									
1876	8,419,150									
1876CC . . .	1,956,000									
1876S	4,528,000									
1877	8,304,510									
1877CC . . .	1,420,000									
1877S	5,356,000									
1878	1,378,400									
1878CC . . .	62,000									
1878S	12,000									
1879	5,900									
1880	9,755									
1881	10,975									
1882	5,500									
1883	9,039									
1884	5,275									
1885	6,130									
1886	5,886									
1887	5,710									
1888	12,833									
1889	12,711									
1890	12,590									
1891	200,600									
1892	935,245									
1892 0	390,000									
1892S	1,029,028									
1893	1,826.792									
1893 0	1,389,000									
1893S	740,000									
1894	1,148,972									

Coin Check List
Half Dollars

DATE	QUANTITY MINTED	AG	G	VG	F	VF	EF	AU	UNC	PROOF
1894 0	2,138,000									
1894S	4,048,690									
1895	1,835,218									
1895 0	1,766,000									
1895S	1,108,086									
1896	950,762									
1896 0	924,000									
1896S	1,140,948									
1897	2,480,731									
1897 0	632,000									
1897S	933,900									
1898	2,956,735									
1898 0	874,000									
1898S	2,358,550									
1899	5,538,846									
1899 0	1,724,000									
1899S	1,686,411									
1900	4,762,912									
1900 0	2,744,000									
1900S	2,560,322									
1901	4,268,813									
1901 0	1,124,000									
1901S	847,044									
1902	4,922,777									
1902 0	2,526,000									
1902S	1,460,670									
1903	2,278,755									
1903 0	2,100,000									
1903S	1,920,772									
1904	2,992,670									
1904 0	1,117,600									
1904S	553,038									
1905	662,727									
1905 0	505,000									
1905S	2,494,000									
1906	2,638,675									
1906D	4,028,000									
1906 0	2,446,000									
1906S	1,740,154									
1907	2,598,575									
1907D	3,856,000									
1907 0	3,946,600									
1907S	1,250,000									
1908	1,354,545									
1908D	3,280,000									
1908 0	5,360,000									
1908S	1,644,828									
1909	2,368,650									
1909 0	925,400									
1909S	1,764,000									
1910	418,551									
1910S	1,948,000									
1911	1,406,543									
1911D	695,080									
1911S	1,272,000									

Coin Check List
Half Dollars

DATE	QUANTITY MINTED	AG	G	VG	F	VF	EF	AU	UNC	PROOF
1912	1,550,700									
1912D	2,300,800									
1912S	1,370,000									
1913	188,627									
1913D	534,000									
1913S	604,000									
1914	124,610									
1914S	992,000									
1915	138,450									
1915D	1,170,400									
1915S	1,604,000									
1916	608,000									
1916D on Obverse . .	1,014,400									
1916S on Obverse . .	508,000									
1917	12,292,000									
1917D on Obverse . .	765,400									
1917D	1,940,000									
1917S on Obverse . .	952,000									
1917S	5,554,000									
1918	6,634,000									
1918D	3,853,040									
1918S	10,282,000									
1919	962,000									
1919D	1,165,000									
1919S	1,552,000									
1920	6,372,000									
1920D	1,551,000									
1920S	4,624,000									
1921	246,000									
1921D	208,000									
1921S	548,000									
1923S	2,178,000									
1927S	2,392,000									
1928S	1,940,000									
1929D	1,001,200									
1929S	1,902,000									
1933S	1,786,000									
1934	6,964,000									
1934D	2,361,400									
1934S	3,652,000									
1935	9,162,000									
1935D	3,003,800									
1935S	3,854,000									
1936	12,617,901									
1936D	4,252,400									
1936S	3,884,000									
1937	9,527,728									
1937D	1,676,000									
1937S	2,090,000									
1938	4,118,152									
1938D	491,600									

Coin Check List
Half Dollars

DATE	QUANTITY MINTED	AG	G	VG	F	VF	EF	AU	UNC	PROOF
1939	6,820,808									
1939D	4,267,800									
1939S	2,552,000									
1940	9,167,279									
1940S	4,550,000									
1941	24,207,412									
1941D	11,248,400									
1941S	8,098,000									
1942	47,839,120									
1942D	10,973,800									
1942S	12,708,000									
1943	53,190,000									
1943D	11,346,000									
1943S	13,450,000									
1944	28,206,000									
1944D	9,769,000									
1944S	8,904,000									
1945	31,502,000									
1945D	9,966,800									
1945S	10,156,000									
1946	12,118,000									
1946D	2,151,100									
1946S	3,724,000									
1947	4,094,000									
1947D	3,900,600									
1948	3,006,814									
1948D	4,028,600									
1949	5,614,000									
1949D	4,120,600									
1949S	3,744,000									
1950	7,793,509									
1950D	8,031,600									
1951	16,859,602									
1951D	9,475,200									
1951S	13,696,000									
1952	21,274,073									
1952D	25,395,600									
1952S	5,526,000									
1953	2,796,920									
1953D	20,900,400									
1953S	4,148,000									
1954	13,421,503									
1954D	25,445,580									
1954S	4,993,400									
1955	2,876,381									
1956	4,701,384									
1957	6,361,952									
1957D	19,966,850									
1958	4,917,652									
1958D	23,962,412									
1959	7,349,291									
1959D	13,053,750									
1960	7,716,602									
1960D	18,215,812									
1961	8,290,000									

Coin Check List
Half Dollars

DATE	QUANTITY MINTED	AG	G	VG	F	VF	EF	AU	UNC	PROOF
1961D	20,276,442									
1962	12,932,019									
1962D	35,473,281									
1963	25,239,645									
1963D	67,069,292									
1964	277,254,766									
1964D	156,205,446									
1965	65,879,366									
1966	108,984,932									
1967	295,046,978									
1968D	246,951,930									
1968S* ...	3,041,506									
1969D	129,881,800									
1969S* ...	2,934,631									
1970D	2,150,000									
1970S* ...	2,632,810									
1971	155,164,000									
1971D	302,097,424									
1971S* ...	3,220,733									
1972	153,180,000									
1972D	141,890,000									
1972S* ...	3,260,996									
1973	64,964,000									
1973D	83,171,400									
1973S* ...	2,760,339									
1974	201,596,000									
1974D	79,066,300									
1974S* ...	2,612,568									
1976	234,308,000									
1976D	287,565,248									
1976S* ...	7,059,099									
1976S Silver Clad mintage figures not released										
1977	43,598,000									
1977D	31,449,106									
1977S* ...	3,251,152									
1978	14,350,000									
1978D	13,765,799									
1978S* ...	3,127,781									
1979	68,312,000									
1979D	15,815,422									
1979S* ...	3,677,175									
1980P	44,134,000									
1980D	33,456,449									
1980S* ...	2,144,231									
1981P										
1981D										
1981S										

*Proof only

Coin Check List
Silver Dollars

DATE	QUANTITY MINTED	AG	G	VG	F	VF	EF	AU	UNC	PROOF
1794	1,758									
1795	160,295									
1795	42,738									
1796	72,920									
1797	7,776									
1798 Small Eagle										
1798 Large Eagle	327,536									
1799	423,515									
1800	220,920									
1801	54,454									
1802	41,650									
1803	85,634									
1840	61,005									
1841	173,000									
1842	184,618									
1843	165,100									
1844	20,000									
1845	24,500									
1846	110,600									
1846 0	59,000									
1847	140,750									
1848	15,000									
1849	62,600									
1850	7,500									
1850 0	40,000									
1851	1,300									
1852	1,100									
1853	46,110									
1854	33,140									
1855	26,000									
1856	63,500									
1857	94,000									
1858	80									
1859	256,500									
1859 0	360,000									
1859S	20,000									
1860	218,930									
1860 0	515,000									
1861	78,500									
1862	12,090									
1863	27,660									
1864	31,170									
1865	47,000									
1866	49,625									
1867	47,525									
1868	162,700									
1869	424,300									
1870	416,000									
1870CC . . .	12,462									
1870S	Unknown									
1871	1,074,760									
1871CC . . .	1,376									
1872	1,106,450									

Coin Check List
Silver Dollars

DATE	QUANTITY MINTED	AG	G	VG	F	VF	EF	AU	UNC	PROOF
1872CC ...	3,150									
1872S	9,000									
1873	293,600									
1873CC ...	2,300									
1873S	700									
1878	10,509,550									
1878CC ...	2,212,000									
1878S	9,774,000									
1879	14,807,100									
1879CC ...	756,000									
1879 0	2,887,000									
1879S	9,110,000									
1880	12,601,355									
1880CC ...	591,000									
1880 0	5,305,000									
1880S	8,900,000									
1881	9,163,975									
1881CC ...	296,000									
1881 0	5,708,000									
1881S	12,760,000									
1882	11,101,100									
1882CC ...	1,133,000									
1882 0	6,090,000									
1882S	9,250,000									
1883	12,291,039									
1883CC ...	1,204,000									
1883 0	8,725,000									
1883S	6,250,000									
1884	14,070,875									
1884CC ...	1,136,000									
1884 0	9,730,000									
1884S	3,200,000									
1885	17,787,767									
1885CC ...	228,000									
1885 0	9,185,000									
1885S	1,497,000									
1886	19,963,886									
1886 0	10,710,000									
1886S	750,000									
1887	20,290,710									
1887 0	11,550,000									
1887S	1,771,000									
1888	19,183,833									
1888 0	12,150,000									
1888S	657,000									
1889	21,726,811									
1889CC ...	350,000									
1889 0	11,875,000									
1889S	700,000									
1890	16,802,590									
1890CC ...	2,309,041									
1890 0	10,701,000									
1890S	8,230,373									
1891	8,694,206									

Coin Check List
Silver Dollars

DATE	QUANTITY MINTED	AG	G	VG	F	VF	EF	AU	UNC	PROOF
1891CC ...	1,618,000									
1891 O	7,954,529									
1891S	5,296,000									
1892	1,037,245									
1892CC ...	1,352,000									
1892 O	2,744,000									
1892S	1,200,000									
1893	378,792									
1893 O	677,000									
1893S	300,000									
1893	100,000									
1894	110,972									
1894 O	1,723,000									
1894S	1,260,000									
1895	12,880									
1895 O	450,000									
1895S	400,000									
1896	9,976,762									
1896 O	4,900,000									
1896S	5,000,000									
1897	2,822,731									
1897 O	4,004,000									
1897S	5,825,000									
1898	5,884,735									
1898 O	4,440,000									
1898S	4,102,000									
1899	330,846									
1899 O	12,290,000									
1899S	2,562,000									
1900	8,830,912									
1900 O	12,590,000									
1900S	3,540,000									
1901	6,962,813									
1901 O	13,320,000									
1901S	2,284,000									
1902	7,994,777									
1902 O	8,636,000									
1902S	1,530,000									
1903	4,652,755									
1903 O	4,450,000									
1903S	1,241,000									
1904	2,788,650									
1904 O	3,720,000									
1904S	2,304,000									
1921	44,690,000									
1921D	20,345,000									
1921S	21,695,000									
1921	1,006,473									
1922	51,737,000									
1922D	15,063,000		—	—						
1922S	17,475,000						—	—		
1923	30,800,000									
1923D	6,811,000									
1923S	19,020,000									
1924	11,811,000									

Coin Check List
Silver Dollars

DATE	QUANTITY MINTED	AG	G	VG	F	VF	EF	AU	UNC	PROOF
1924S	1,728,000									
1925	10,198,000									
1925S	1,610,000									
1926	1,939,000									
1926D	2,348,700									
1926S	6,980,000									
1927	848,000									
1927D	1,268,900									
1927S	866,000									
1928	360,649									
1928S	1,632,000									
1934	954,057									
1934D	1,569,500									
1934S	1,011,000									
1935	1,576,000									
1935S	1,964,000									

Coin Check List
Clad Dollars

DATE	QUANTITY MINTED	AG	G	VG	F	VF	EF	AU	UNC	PROOF
1971 CN ..	47,799,000									
1971D CN .	68,587,424									
1971S Silver										
Clad	6,868,5330									
1972 CN ..	75,890,000									
1972D CN .	92,548,511									
1972S Silver										
Clad	2,193,056									
1973 CN ..	2,000,056									
1973D CN .	2,000,000									
1973S CN .	2,760,399									
1973 Silver										
Clad	1,883,140									
1974 CN ..	27,366,000									
1974D CN .	45,517,000									
1974S CN*	2,612,568									
1974S Silver										
Clad	1,900,000									
Bicentennial Dollars										
1976 Type I										
CN	4,019,000									
1976 Type II										
CN	113,318,000									
1976D										
Type I CN .	21,048,710									
1976D										
Type II										
CN	82,179,564									
1976S*										
Type I CN .	2,845,450									
1976S*										
Type II										
CN	4,149,730									
Clad Dollars										
1976S Silver	(approx.									
Clad	3,300,000)									
1977	12,596,000									
1977D	32,983,006									
1977S* . . .	3,251,152									
1978	25,702,000									
1978D	23,012,890									
1978S* . . .	3,127,781									
1979	360,222,000									
1979D	288,015,744									
1979S	109,576,000									
1980P	27,610,000									
1980D	41,628,708									
1980S	20,422,000									
1981P										
1981D										
1981S										

Coin Check List
Trade Dollars

DATE	QUANTITY MINTED	AG	G	VG	F	VF	EF	AU	UNC	PROOF
1873	397,500									
1873CC . . .	124,500									
1873S	703,000									
1874	987,800									
1874CC . . .	1,373,200									
1874S	2,549,000									
1875	218,900									
1875CC . . .	1,573,700									
1875S	4,487,000									
1876	456,150									
1876CC . . .	509,000									
1876S	5,227,000									
1877	3,039,710									
1977CC . . .	534,000									
1877S	9,519,000									
1878	900									
1878CC . . .	97,000									
1878S	4,162,000									
1879	1,541									
1880	1,987									
1881	960									
1882	1,097									
1883	979									
1884	10									
1885	5									

Coin Check List
Commemorative Silver Coins

DATE	QUANTITY MINTED	AG	G	VG	F	VF	EF	AU	UNC	PROOF
1892 Columbian Exposition	950,000									
1893 Columbian Exposition	1,550,000									
1893 Isabella Quarter Dollar	24,214									
1900 Lafayette Dollar	36,026									
1915S Panama Pacific Exposition	27,134									
1918 Illinois Centennial	100,058									
1920 Maine Centennial	50,028									
1921 Missouri Centennial	15,428									
1921 Missouri Centennial 2 x 4 in field	5,000									
1920 Pilgrim Tercentenary	152,112									
1921 Pilgrim Tercentenary	20,053									
1921 Alabama Centennial	59,038									
1921 Ala. Centennial 2 x 2 in obv. field	6,002									
1922 Grant Memorial	67,405									
1922 Grant Memorial, star in obv field	4,256									
1923S Monroe Doctrine Centennial	274,077									

Coin Check List
Commemorative Silver Coins

DATE	QUANTITY MINTED	AG	G	VG	F	VF	EF	AU	UNC	PROOF
1924 Huguenot-Walloon Tercentenary	142,080									
1925 Lexington-Concord Sesquicent	162,013									
1925 Stone Mountain Memorial . .	1,314,709									
1925S California Diamond Jubilee	86,594									
1925S Fort Vancouver Centennial .	14,994									
1926 Sesquicent of American Independ . .	141,120									
1926 Oregon Trail Memorial . .	47,955									
1926S Oregon Trail Memorial .	83,055									
1928 Oregon Trail Memorial . .	6,028									
1933D Oregon Trail Memorial . .	5,008									
1934D Oregon Trail Memorial . .	7,006									
1936 Oregon Trail Memorial . .	10,006									
1936S Oregon Trail Memorial . .	5,006									
1937D Oregon Trail Memorial . .	12,008									
1938 Oregon Trail Memorial . .	6,006									
1938D Oregon Trail Memorial . .	6,005									
1938S Oregon Trail Memorial . .	6,006									

Coin Check List
Commemorative Silver Coins

DATE	QUANTITY MINTED	AG	G	VG	F	VF	EF	AU	UNC	PROOF
1939 Oregon Trail Memorial ..	3,004									
1939D Oregon Trail Memorial ..	3,004									
1939S Oregon Trail Memorial ..	3,005									
1927 Vermont Sesquicent (Bennington)	28,162									
1928 Hawaiian Sesquiu-cenntenial .	10,008									
1934 Maryland Tercenten-ary	25,015									
1934 Texas Centennial .	61,350									
1935 Texas Centennial .	9,994									
1935D Texas Centennial .	10,007									
1935S Texas Centennial .	10,008									
1936 Texas Centennial .	8,911									
1936D Texas Centennial .	9,039									
1936S Texas Centennial .	9,064									
1937 Texas Centennial .	6,571									
1937D Texas Centennial .	6,605									
1937S Texas Centennial .	6,637									
1938 Texas Centennial .	3,780									
1938D Texas Centennial .	3,775									
1938S Texas Centennial .	3,816									
1934 Daniel Boone Bi-centennial .	10,007									
1935 Daniel Boone Bi-centennial .	10,010									

Coin Check List
Commemorative Silver Coins

DATE	QUANTITY MINTED	AG	G	VG	F	VF	EF	AU	UNC	PROOF
1935D Daniel Boone Bi-centennial .	5,005									
1935S Daniel Boone Bi-centennial .	5,005									
1935 Daniel Boone Bicent. 1934 on rev. ...	10,008									
1935D Daniel Boone Bicent. 1934 on rev. ...	2,003									
1935S Daniel Boone . Bicent. 1934 on rev. ...	2,004									
1936 Daniel Boone Bicent. 1934 on rev. ...	12,012									
1936D Daniel Boone Bicent. 1934 on rev. ...	5,005									
1936S Daniel Boone Bicent. 1934 on rev. ...	5,006									
1937 Daniel Boone Bicent. 1934 on rev. ...	9,810									
1937D Daniel Boone Bicent. 1934 on rev. ...	2,506									
1937S Daniel Boone Bicent. 1934 on rev. ...	2,506									
1938 Daniel Boone Bicent. 1934 on rev. ...	2,100									

Coin Check List
Commemorative Silver Coins

DATE	QUANTITY MINTED	AG	G	VG	F	VF	EF	AU	UNC	PROOF
1938D Daniel Boone Bicent. 1934 on rev. ...	2,100									
1938S Daniel Boone Bicent. 1934 on rev. ...	2,100									
1935 Connecticut Tercentenary	25,018									
1935 Arkansas Centennial.	13,012									
1935D Arkansas Centennial.	5,505									
1935S Arkansas Centennial.	5,506									
1936 Arkansas Centennial.	9,660									
1936D Arkansas Centennial.	9,660									
1936S Arkansas Centennial.	9,662									
1937 Arkansas Centennial.	5,505									
1937D Arkansas Centennial.	5,505									
1937S Arkansas Centennial.	5,506									
1938 Arkansas Centennial.	3,156									
1938D Arkansas Centennial.	3,155									
1938S Arkansas Centennial.	3,156									
1939 Arkansas Centennial.	2,104									
1939D Arkansas Centennial.	2,104									

Coin Check List
Commemorative Silver Coins

DATE	QUANTITY MINTED	AG	G	VG	F	VF	EF	AU	UNC	PROOF
1939S Arkansas Centennial .	2,105									
1935 Hudson, N.Y. Sesquicentennial	10,008									
1935S San Diego, Cal. Pacific Exposition ...	70,132									
1936D San Diego, Cal. Pacific Exposition ...	30,092									
1935 Old Spanish Trail, 1535-1935	10,008									
1936 Rhode Island Tercentenary .	20,013									
1936D Rhode Island Tercentenary	15,010									
1936S Rhode Island Tercentenary	15,011									
1936 Cleveland, Great Lakes Exposition ...	50,030									
1936 Wisconsin Centennial	25,015									
1936 Cincinnati Musical Center	5,005									
1936D Cincinnati Musical Center	5,005									
1936S Cincinnati Musical Center	5,006									
1936 Long Island Tercentenary .	81,826									
1936 York County Maine Tercentenary .	25,015									

Coin Check List
Commemorative Silver Coins

DATE	QUANTITY MINTED	AG	G	VG	F	VF	EF	AU	UNC	PROOF
1936 Bridgeport Connecticut Centennial.	25,015									
1936 Lynchburg Virginia Sesquicent	20,013									
1936 Elgin Illinois Centennial.	20,015									
1936 Albany New York Charter ...	17,671									
1936S San Francisco Oakland Bay Bridge	71,424									
1936 Columbia, S.C. Sesquicentennial	9,007									
1936D Columbia, S.C. Sesquicentennial	8,009									
1936D Columbia S.C. Sesquicentennial	8,007									
1936 Arkansas Centennial (Robinson)	25,265									
1936 Delaware Tercentenary	20,993									
1936 Battle of Gettysburg 1863-1938	26,928									
1936 Norfolk, Virginia Bicentennial .	16,936									
1937 Roanoke Island, N.C. 1587-1937 .	29,030									
1937 Battle of Antietam 1862-1937 .	18,028									

Coin Check List
Commemorative Silver Coins

DATE	QUANTITY MINTED	AG	G	VG	F	VF	EF	AU	UNC	PROOF
1938 New Rochelle, N.Y. 1688-1938	15,266									
1946 Iowa Centennial .	100,057									
1946 Booker T. Washington Memorial . .	1,000,546									
1946D Booker T. Washington Memorial . .	200,113									
1946S Booker T. Washington Memorial . .	500,279									
1947 Booker T. Washington Memorial . .	100,017									
1947D Booker T. Washington Memorial . .	100,017									
1947S Booker T. Washington Memorial . .	100,017									
1948 Booker T. Washington Memorial . .	8,005									
1948D Booker T. Washington Memorial . .	8,005									
1948S Booker T. Washington Memorial . .	8,005									
1949 Booker T. Washington Memorial . .	6,004									
1949D Booker T. Washington Memorial . .	6,004									
1949S Booker T. Washington Memorial . .	6,004									

Coin Check List
Commemorative Silver Coins

DATE	QUANTITY MINTED	AG	G	VG	F	VF	EF	AU	UNC	PROOF
1950 Booker T. Washington Memorial . .	6,004									
1950D Booker T. Washington Memorial . .	6,004									
1950S Booker T. Washington Memorial . .	512,091									
1951 Booker T. Washington Memorial . .	510,082									
1951D Booker T. Washington Memorial . .	7,004									
1951S Booker T. Washington Memorial . .	7,004									
1951 Washington Carver	110,018									
1951D Washington Carver	10,004									
1951S Washington Carver	10,004									
1952 Washington Carver	2,006,292									
1952D Washington Carver	8,006									
1952S Washington Carver	8,006									
1953 Washington Carver	8,003									
1953D Washington Carver	8,003									
1953S Washington Carver	108,020									
1954 Washington Carver	12,006									

Coin Check List
Commemorative Silver Coins

DATE	QUANTITY MINTED	AG	G	VG	F	VF	EF	AU	UNC	PROOF
1954D Washington Carver	12,006									
1954S Washington Carver	122,024									

Coin Check List
Proof Sets

DATE	QUANTITY MINTED	AG	G	VG	F	VF	EF	AU	UNC	PROOF
1936	3,837									
1937	5,542									
1938	8,045									
1939	8,795									
1940	11,246									
1941	15,287									
1942 . . . . . . } 1942 Ty. II . }	21,120									
1950	51,386									
1951	57,500									
1952	81,980									
1953	128,800									
1954	233,300									
1955	378,200									
1956	669,384									
1957	1,247,952									
1958	875,652									
1959	1,149,291									
1960 . . . . . . } 1960 Sm. . }	1,691,602									
1961	3,028,244									
1962	3,218,019									
1963	3,075,645									
1964	3,950,762									
1968S	3,041,509									
1969S	2,934,631									
1970 . . . . . . } 1970 Sm. . }	2,632,810									
1971S (Dollar only)	3,220,733									
1972S	3,260,996									
1973S	2,760,339									
1974S	2,612,568									
1975S	2,845,450									
1976S	4,123,056									
1976S 3 piece . . .	3,295,666									
1977S	3,251,152									
1978S	3,127,781									
1979S	3,677,175									
1980S	2,144,231									

Coin Check List
Gold Dollars

DATE	QUANTITY MINTED	AG	G	VG	F	VF	EF	AU	UNC	PROOF
1849	688,567									
1849C	11,634									
1849D	21,588									
1849 0	215,000									
1850	481,953									
1850C	6,966									
1850D	8,382									
1850 0	14,000									
1851	3,317,671									
1851C	41,267									
1851D	9,882									
1851 0	290,000									
1852	2,045,351									
1852C	9,434									
1852D	6,360									
1852 0	140,000									
1853	4,076,051									
1853C	11,515									
1853D	6,583									
1853 0	290,000									
1854	736,709									
1854D	2,935									
1854S	14,632									
1854	902,736									
1855	758,269									
1855C	9,803									
1855D	1,811									
1855 0	55,000									
1856S	24,600									
1856	1,762,936									
1856D	1,460									
1857	774,789									
1857C	13,280									
1857D	3,533									
1857S	10,000									
1858	117,995									
1858D	3,477									
1858S	10,000									
1859	168,244									
1859C	5,235									
1859D	4,952									
1859S	15,000									
1860	36,668									
1860D	1,566									
1860S	13,000									
1861	527,499									
1861D										
1862	1,361,390									
1863	6,250									
1864	5,950									
1865	3,725									
1866	7,130									
1867	5,250									
1868	10,525									
1869	5,925									

Coin Check List
Gold Dollars

DATE	QUANTITY MINTED	AG	G	VG	F	VF	EF	AU	UNC	PROOF
1870	6,335									
1870S	3,000									
1871	3,900									
1872	3,530									
1873	125,125									
1874	198,820									
1875	420									
1876	3,245									
1877	3,920									
1878	3,020									
1879	3,030									
1880	1,636									
1881	7,707									
1882	5,125									
1883	11,007									
1884	6,236									
1885	12,261									
1886	6,016									
1887	8,543									
1888	16,580									
1889	30,729									

Coin Check List
$2.50 Gold Dollars
(Quarter Eagles)

DATE	QUANTITY MINTED	AG	G	VG	F	VF	EF	AU	UNC	PROOF
1796 No Stars	963									
1796 Stars	432									
1797	427									
1798	1,094									
1802 over 01	3,035									
1804 13 Stars Reverse . . .	3,327									
1804 14 Stars Reverse . . .										
1805	1,781									
1806 over 04	1,616									
1806 over 05										
1807	6,812									
1808	2,710									
1821	6,448									
1824 over 21	2,600									
1825	4,434									
1826 over 25	760									
1827	2,800									
1829	3,403									
1830	4,540									
1831	4,520									
1832	4,400									
1833	4,160									
1834	4,000									
1834	112,234									
1835	131,402									
1836	547,986									
1837	45,080									
1838	47,030									
1838C	7,880									
1839	27,021									
1839C	18,140									
1839D	13,674									
1839 0	17,781									
1840	18,859									
1840C	12,822									
1840D	3,532									
1840 0	33,580									
1841										
1841C	10,281									
1841D	4,164									
1842	2,823									
1842C	6,737									
1842D	4,643									
1842 0	19,800									

Coin Check List
$2.50 Gold Dollars
(Quarter Eagles)

DATE	QUANTITY MINTED	AG	G	VG	F	VF	EF	AU	UNC	PROOF
1843	100,546									
1843C	26,064									
1843D	36,209									
1843 0	368,002									
1844	6,784									
1844C	11,622									
1844D	17,332									
1845	91,051									
1845D	19,460									
1845 0	4,000									
1846	21,598									
1846C	4,808									
1846D	19,303									
1846 0	62,000									
1847	29,814									
1847C	23,226									
1847D	15,784									
1847 0	124,000									
1848	7,497									
1848 Cal ..	1,389									
1848C	16,788									
1848D	13,771									
1849	23,294									
1849C	10,220									
1849D	10,945									
1850	252,923									
1850C	9,148									
1850D	12,148									
1850 0	84,000									
1851	1,372,748									
1851C	14,923									
1851D	11,264									
1851 0	148,000									
1852	1,159,681									
1852C	9,772									
1852D	4,078									
1852 0	140,000									
1853	1,404,668									
1853D	3,178									
1854	596,258									
1854C	7,295									
1854D	1,760									
1854 0	153,000									
1854S	246									
1855	235,480									
1855C	3,677									
1855D	1,123									
1856	384,240									
1856C	7,913									
1856D	874									
1856 0	21,100									
1856S	72,120									
1857	214,130									
1857D	2,364									

Coin Check List
$2.50 Gold Dollars
(Quarter Eagles)

DATE	QUANTITY MINTED	AG	G	VG	F	VF	EF	AU	UNC	PROOF
1857 0	34,000									
1857S	69,200									
1858	47,377									
1858C	9,056									
1859	39,444									
1859D	2,244									
1859S	15,200									
1860	22,675									
1860C	7,469									
1860S	35,600									
1861	1,283,878									
1861S	24,000									
1862 ...... 1862 over 1	98,543									
1862S	8,000									
1863	30									
1863S	10,800									
1864	2,874									
1865	1,545									
1865S	23,376									
1866	3,110									
1866S	38,960									
1867	3,250									
1867S	28,000									
1868	3,625									
1868S	34,000									
1869	4,345									
1869S	29,500									
1870	4,555									
1870S	16,000									
1871	5,350									
1871S	22,000									
1872	3,030									
1872S	18,000									
1873	178,025									
1873S	27,000									
1874	3,940									
1875	420									
1875S	11,600									
1876	4,221									
1876S	5,000									
1877	1,652									
1877S	35,400									
1878	286,260									
1878S	178,000									
1879	88,990									
1879S	43,500									
1880	2,996									
1881	691									
1882	4,067									
1883	2,002									
1884	2,023									
1885	887									

Coin Check List
$2.50 Gold Dollars
(Quarter Eagles)

DATE	QUANTITY MINTED	AG	G	VG	F	VF	EF	AU	UNC	PROOF
1886	4,088									
1887	6,282									
1888	16,098									
1889	17,648									
1890	8,813									
1891	11,040									
1892	2,545									
1893	30,106									
1894	4,122									
1895	6,119									
1896	19,202									
1897	29,904									
1898	24,165									
1899	27,350									
1900	67,205									
1901	91,323									
1902	133,733									
1903	201,257									
1904	160,960									
1905	217,944									
1906	176,490									
1907	336,448									
1908	565,057									
1909	441,899									
1910	492,682									
1911	704,191									
1911D	55,680									
1912	616,192									
1913	722,165									
1914	240,117									
1914D	448,000									
1915	606,100									
1925D	578,000									
1926	446,000									
1927	388,000									
1928	416,000									
1929	532,000									

Coin Check List
$3.00 Gold Dollars
(Quarter Eagles)

DATE	QUANTITY MINTED	AG	G	VG	F	VF	EF	AU	UNC	PROOF
1854	138,618									
1854D	1,120									
1854 O	24,000									
1855	50,555									
1855S	6,600									
1856	26,010									
1856S	34,500									
1857	20,891									
1857S	14,000									
1858	2,133									
1859	15,638									
1860	7,155									
1860S	7,000									
1861	6,072									
1862	5,785									
1863	5,039									
1864	2,680									
1865	1,165									
1866	4,030									
1867	2,650									
1868	4,875									
1869	2,525									
1870	3,535									
1870S	2									
1871	1,330									
1872	2,030									
1873	25									
1874	41,820									
1875	20									
1876	45									
1877	1,488									
1878	82,324									
1879	3,030									
1880	1,036									
1881	554									
1882	1,576									
1883	989									
1884	1,106									
1885	910									
1886	1,142									
1887	6,160									
1888	5,291									
1889	2,429									

Coin Check List
$5.00 Gold Dollars
Half Eagles

DATE	QUANTITY MINTED	AG	G	VG	F	VF	EF	AU	UNC	PROOF
1795	8,707									
1796	6,196									
1792 15 Stars ..... 1797 16 Stars	3,609									
1798	*									
1795	*									
1797 7 over 5	*									
1798 13 Stars ..... 1798 14 Stars	*24,867									
1799	7,451									
1800	37,628									
1802 2 over 1	53,176									
1803 3 over 2	33,506									
1804	30,475									
1805	33,183									
1806	64,093									
1807	32,488									
1807	51,605									
1808 ...... 1808 over 7	55,578									
1809 over 8	33,875									
1810	100,287									
1811	99,581									
1812	58,087									
1813	95,428									
1814 over 3	15,454									
1815	635									
1818	48,588									
1819	51,723									
1820	263,806									
1821	34,641									
1822	17,796									
1823	14,485									
1824	17,340									
1825 over 1 1825 over 4	29,060									
1826	18,069									
1827	24,913									
1828 ...... 1828 over 7	28,029									
1829	57,442									
1830	126,351									
1831	140,504									
1832 12 Stars ..... 1832 13 Stars	157,487									

Coin Check List
$5.00 Gold Dollars
Half Eagles

DATE	QUANTITY MINTED	AG	G	VG	F	VF	EF	AU	UNC	PROOF
1833	193,630									
1834 ...... 1834 Serf 4	50,141									
1834 ...... 1834 Serf 4	657,460									
1835	371,534									
1836	553,174									
1837	207,121									
1838	286,588									
1838C	17,179									
1838D	20,583									
1839	118,143									
1839C	17,205									
1839D	18,939									
1840	137,382									
1840C	18,992									
1840D	22,896									
1840 0	40,120									
1841	15,833									
1841C	21,467									
1841D	29,392									
1841 0	50									
1842	27,578									
1842C	27,432									
1842D	59,608									
1842 0	16,400									
1843	611.205									
1843C	44,277									
1843D	98,452									
1843 0 Sm. Letters ...	19,075									
1843 0 Lg. Letters ...	82,000									
1844	340,330									
1844C	23,631									
1844D	88,982									
1844 0	364,600									
1845	417,099									
1845D	90,629									
1845 0	41,000									
1846	395,942									
1846C	12,995									
1846D	80,294									
1846 0	58,000									
1847	915,981									
1847C	84,151									
1847D	64,405									
1847 0	12,000									
1848	260,775									
1848C	64,472									
1848D	47,465									
1849	133,070									
1849C	64,472									

Coin Check List
$5.00 Gold Dollars
Half Eagles

DATE	QUANTITY MINTED	AG	G	VG	F	VF	EF	AU	UNC	PROOF
1849D	39,036									
1850	64,491									
1850C	63,591									
1850D	43,984									
1851	377,505									
1851C	49,176									
1851D	62,710									
1851 0	41,000									
1852	573,901									
1852C	72,574									
1852D	91,584									
1853	305,770									
1853C	65,571									
1853D	89,678									
1854	160,675									
1854C	39,283									
1854D	56,413									
1854 0	46,000									
1854S	268									
1855	117,098									
1855C	39,788									
1855D	22,432									
1855 0	11,100									
1855S	61,000									
1856	197,990									
1856C	28,457									
1856D	19,786									
1856 0	10,000									
1856S	105,100									
1857	98,188									
1857C	31,360									
1857D	17,046									
1857 0	13,000									
1857S	87,000									
1858	15,136									
1858C	38,856									
1858D	15,362									
1858S	18,600									
1859	16,814									
1859C	31,847									
1859D	10,366									
1859S	13,220									
1860	19,825									
1860C	14,813									
1860D	14,635									
1860S	21,200									
1861	688,150									
1861C	6,879									
1861D	1,597	—								
1861S	18,000						—	—		
1862	4,465									—
1862S	9,500									
1863	2,472									

Coin Check List
$5.00 Gold Dollars
Half Eagles

DATE	QUANTITY MINTED	AG	G	VG	F	VF	EF	AU	UNC	PROOF
1863S	17,000									
1864	4,200									
1864S	3,888									
1865	1,295									
1865S	27,612									
1866S	9,000									
1866	6,730									
1866S	34,920									
1867	6,920									
1867S	29,000									
1868	5,725									
1868S	52,000									
1869	1,785									
1869S	31,000									
1870	4,035									
1870CC ...	7,675									
1870S	17,000									
1871	3,230									
1871CC ...	20,770									
1871S	25,000									
1872	1,690									
1872CC ...	16,980									
1872S	36,400									
1873	112,505									
1873CC ...	7,416									
1873S	31,000									
1874	3,508									
1874CC ...	21,198									
1874S	16,000									
1875	220									
1875CC ...	11,828									
1875S	9,000									
1876	1,477									
1876CC ...	6,887									
1876S	4,000									
1877	1,152									
1877CC ...	8,680									
1877S	26,700									
1878	131,740									
1878CC ...	9,054									
1878S	144,700									
1879	301,950									
1879CC ...	17,281									
1879S	426,200									
1880	3,166,436									
1880CC ...	51,017									
1880S	1,348,900									
1881	5,708,802									
1881CC ...	13,886									
1881S	969,000									
1882	2,514,568									
1882CC ...	82,817									
1882S	969,000									

Coin Check List
$5.00 Gold Dollars
Half Eagles

DATE	QUANTITY MINTED	AG	G	VG	F	VF	EF	AU	UNC	PROOF
1883	233,461									
1883CC ...	12,958									
1883S	83,200									
1884	191,078									
1884CC ...	16,402									
1884S	177,000									
1885	601,506									
1885S	1,211,500									
1886	388,432									
1886S	3,268,000									
1887	87									
1887S	1,912,000									
1888	18,296									
1888S	293,900									
1889	7,565									
1890	4,328									
1890CC ...	53,800									
1891	61,413									
1891CC ...	208,000									
1892	753,572									
1892CC ...	82,968									
1892 0	10,000									
1892S	298,400									
1893	1,528,197									
1893CC ...	60,000									
1893 0	110,000									
1893S	224,000									
1894	957,955									
1894 0	16,600									
1894S	55,900									
1895	1,345,936									
1895S	112,000									
1896	59,063									
1896S	155,400									
1897	867,883									
1897S	354,000									
1898	633,495									
1898S	1,397,400									
1899	1,710,729									
1899S	1,545,000									
1900	1,405,730									
1900S	329,000									
1901	616,040									
1901S	3,648,000									
1902	172,562									
1902S	939,000									
1903	227,024									
1903S	1,855,000									
1904	392,136									
1904S	97,000									
1905	302,308									
1905S	880,700									
1906	348,820									

Coin Check List
$5.00 Gold Dollars
Half Eagles

DATE	QUANTITY MINTED	AG	G	VG	F	VF	EF	AU	UNC	PROOF
1906D	320,000									
1906S	598,000									
1907	626,192									
1907D	888,000									
1908	421,874									
1908	578,012									
1908D	148,000									
1908S	82,000									
1909	627,138									
1909D	3,423,560									
1909 0	34,200									
1909S	297,200									
1910	604,250									
1910D	193,600									
1910S	770,200									
1911	915,139									
1911D	72,500									
1911S	1,416,000									
1912	790,144									
1912S	392,000									
1913	916,000									
1913S	408,000									
1914	247,125									
1914D	247,000									
1914S	263,000									
1915	588,075									
1915S	164,000									
1916S	240,000									
1929	662,000									

Coin Check List
$10.00 Gold
Eagles

DATE	QUANTITY MINTED	AG	G	VG	F	VF	EF	AU	UNC	PROOF
1795	5,583									
1796	4,146									
1797	3,615									
1797	10,940									
1798 4 star right	900									
1798 6 star right	842									
1799	37,449									
1800	5,999									
1801	44,344									
1803	15,017									
1804	3,757									
1838	7,200									
1839 Lg. Letters . . .	25,801									
1839 Sm. Letters . . .	12,447									
1840	47,338									
1841	63,131									
1841 0	2,500									
1842	81,507									
1842 0	27,400									
1843	75,462									
1843 0	175,162									
1844	6,361									
1844 0	118,700									
1845	26,153									
1845 0	47,500									
1846	20,095									
1846 0	81,780									
1847	862,258									
1847 0	571,500									
1848	145,484									
1848 0	35,850									
1849	653,618									
1849 0	23,900									
1850	291,451									
1850 0	57,500									
1851	176,328									
1851 0	263,000									
1852	263,106									
1852 0	18,000									
1853 . . . . . / 1853 over 2	201,253									
1853 0	51,000									
1854	54,250									
1854 0	52,500									
1854S . . .	123,826									
1855	121,701									
1855 0	18,000									
1855S	9,000									
1856	60,490									
1856 0	14,500									

Coin Check List
$10.00 Gold
Eagles

DATE	QUANTITY MINTED	AG	G	VG	F	VF	EF	AU	UNC	PROOF
1856S	68,000									
1857	16,606									
1857 0	5,500									
1857S	26,000									
1858	2,521									
1858 0	20,000									
1858S	11,800									
1859	16,093									
1859 0	2,300									
1859S	7,000									
1860	15,105									
1860 0	11,100									
1860S	5,000									
1861	113,233									
1861S	15,500									
1862	10,995									
1862S	12,500									
1863	1,248									
1863S	10,000									
1864	3,500									
1864S	2,500									
1865	4,005									
1865S .... 1865S over invert 186 .	16,700									
1866S	8,500									
1866	3,780									
1866S	11,500									
1867	3,140									
1867S	9,000									
1868	10,655									
1868S	13,500									
1869	1,855									
1869S	6,430									
1870	4,025									
1870CC ...	5,908									
1870S	8,000									
1871	1,820									
1871CC ...	8,085									
1871S	16,500									
1872	1,650									
1872CC ...	4,600									
1872S	17,300									
1873	825									
1873CC ...	4,543									
1873S	12,000									
1874	53,160									
1874CC ...	16,767									
1874S	10,000									
1875	120									
1875CC ...	7,715									
1876	732									
1876CC ...	4,696									

Coin Check List
$10.00 Gold
Eagles

DATE	QUANTITY MINTED	AG	G	VG	F	VF	EF	AU	UNC	PROOF
1876S	5,000									
1877	817									
1877CC ...	3,332									
1877S	17,000									
1878	73,800									
1878CC ...	3,244									
1878S	26,100									
1879	384,770									
1879CC ...	1,762									
1879 0	1,500									
1879S	224,000									
1880	1,644,876									
1880CC ...	11,190									
1880 0	9,200									
1880S	506,250									
1881	3,877,260									
1881CC ...	24,015									
1881 0	8,350									
1881S	970,000									
1882	2,324,480									
1882CC ...	6,764									
1882 0	10,820									
1882S	132,000									
1883	208,740									
1883CC ...	12,000									
1883 0	800									
1883S	38,000									
1884	76,905									
1884CC ...	9,925									
1884S	124,250									
1885	253,527									
1885S	228,000									
1886	236,160									
1886S	826,000									
1887	53,680									
1887S	817,000									
1888	132,996									
1888 0	21,335									
1888S	648,700									
1889	4,485									
1889S	425,400									
1890	58,043									
1890CC ...	17,500									
1891	91,868									
1891CC ...	103,732									
1892	797,552									
1892CC ...	40,000									
1892 0	28,688									
1892S	115,500									
1893	1,840,895									
1893CC ...	14,000									
1893 0	17,000									
1893S	141,350									

Coin Check List
$10.00 Gold
Eagles

DATE	QUANTITY MINTED	AG	G	VG	F	VF	EF	AU	UNC	PROOF
1894	2,470,778									
1894 0	107,500									
1894S	25,000									
1895	567,826									
1895 0	98,000									
1895S	49,000									
1896	76,348									
1896S	123,750									
1897	1,000,159									
1897 0	42,500									
1897S	234,750									
1898	812,197									
1898S	473,600									
1899	1,262,305									
1899 0	37,047									
1899S	841,000									
1900	293, 960									
1900S	81,000									
1901	1,718,825									
1901 0	72,041									
1901S	2,812,750									
1902	82,513									
1902S	469,500									
1903	125,926									
1903 0	112,771									
1903S	538,000									
1904	162,038									
1904 0	108,950									
1905	201,078									
1905S	369,250									
1906	165,497									
1906D	981,000									
1906 0	86,895									
1906S	457,000									
1907	1,203,973									
1907D	1,030,000									
1907S	210,500									
1907 Wire edge periods IN•E• PLURI- BUS• UNUM• . .	500									
1907 Round edge periods IN•E• PLURI- BUS• UNUM• . .	42									
1907 w/o Periods . . .	239,406									
1908	33,500									
1908D	210,000									

Coin Check List
$10.00 Gold
Eagles

DATE	QUANTITY MINTED	AG	G	VG	F	VF	EF	AU	UNC	PROOF
1908	341,486									
1908D	836,500									
1908S	59,850									
1909	184,863									
1909D	121,540									
1909S	292,350									
1910	318,704									
1910D	2,356,640									
1910S	811,000									
1911	505,595									
1911D	30,100									
1911S	51,000									
1912	405,083									
1912S	300,000									
1913	442,071									
1913S	66,000									
1914	151,050									
1914D	343,500									
1914S	208,000									
1915	351,075									
1915S	59,000									
1916S	138,500									
1920S	126,500									
1926	1,014,000									
1930S	96,000									
1932	4,463,000									
1933	312,500									

Coin Check List
$20.00 Gold
Double Eagles

DATE	QUANTITY MINTED	AG	G	VG	F	VF	EF	AU	UNC	PROOF
1850	1,170,261									
1850 O	141,000									
1851	2,087,155									
1851 O	315,000									
1852	2,053,026									
1852 O	190,000									
1853	1,261,326									
1853 O	71,000									
1854	757,899									
1854 O	3,250									
1854S	141,468									
1855	364,666									
1855 O	8,000									
1855S	879,675									
1856	329,878									
1856 O	2,250									
1856S	1,189,750									
1857	439,375									
1857 O	30,000									
1857S	970,500									
1858	211,714									
1858 O	35,250									
1858S	846,710									
1859	43,597									
1859 O	9,100									
1859S	636,445									
1860	577,670									
1860 O	6,600									
1860S	544,950									
1861	2,976,453									
1861 O	17,741									
1861S	768,000									
1862	92,133									
1862S	854,173									
1863	142,790									
1863S	966,570									
1864	204,285									
1864S	793,660									
1865	351,200									
1865S	1,042,500									
1866S	120,000									
1866	698,775									
1866S	722,250									
1867	251,065									
1867S	920,750									
1868	98,600									
1868S	837,500									
1869	175,155									
1869S	686,750									
1870	155,185									
1870CC . . .	3,789									
1870S	982,000									
1871	80,150									

Coin Check List
$20.00 Gold
Double Eagles

DATE	QUANTITY MINTED	AG	G	VG	F	VF	EF	AU	UNC	PROOF
1871CC ...	17,387									
1871S	928,000									
1872	251,880									
1872CC ...	26,900									
1872S	780,000									
1873	1,709,825									
1873CC ...	22,410									
1873S	1,040,600									
1874	366,800									
1874CC ...	155,085									
1874S	1,214,000									
1875	295,740									
1875CC ...	111,151									
1875S	1,230,000									
1876	583,905									
1876CC ...	138,441									
1876S	1,597,000									
1877	397,670									
1877CC ...	42,565									
1877S	1,735,000									
1878	543,645									
1878CC ...	13,180									
1878S	1,739,000									
1879	207,630									
1879CC ...	10,708									
1879 0	2,325									
1879S	1,223,800									
1880	51,456									
1880S	836,000									
1881	2,260									
1881S	727,000									
1882	630									
1882CC ...	39,140									
1882S	1,125,000									
1883	92									
1883CC ...	59,962									
1883S	1,189,000									
1884	71									
1884CC ...	81,139									
1884S	916,000									
1885	828									
1885CC ...	9,450									
1885S	683,500									
1886	1,106									
1887	1211									
1888	283,000									
1888S	226,266									
1889	859,600									
1889CC ...	44,111									
1889S	30,945									
1890	774,700									
1890CC ...	75,995									
1890S	91,209									

Coin Check List
$20.00 Gold
Double Eagles

DATE	QUANTITY MINTED	AG	G	VG	F	VF	EF	AU	UNC	PROOF
1891	802,750									
1891CC ...	1,442									
1891S	5,000									
1892	1,288,125									
1892CC ...	4,523									
1892S	27,265									
1893	930,150									
1893CC ...	18,402									
1893C	996,175									
1894	1,368,990									
1894S	1,048,550									
1895	1,114,656									
1895S	1,143,500									
1896	792,663									
1896S	1,403,925									
1897	1,383,261									
1897S	1,470,250									
1898	170,470									
1898S	2,575,175									
1899	1,669,384									
1899S	2,010,300									
1900	1,875,584									
1900S	2,459,500									
1901	111,526									
1901S	1,596,000									
1902	31,254									
1902S	1,753,625									
1903	287,428									
1903S	954,000									
1904	6,256,797									
1904S	5,134,175									
1905	59,011									
1905S	1,813,000									
1906	69,690									
1906D	620,250									
1906S	2,065,750									
1907	1,451,864									
1907D	842,250									
1907S	2,165,800									
1907 Wire Edge Date MCMVII 1907 Flat Edge Date MCMVII ..	11,250									
1907 Date Arabic Numerals .	361,667									
1908	4,271,551									
1908D	663,750									
1908	156,359									
1908D	349,500									
1908S	22,000									

Coin Check List
$20.00 Gold
Double Eagles

DATE	QUANTITY MINTED	AG	G	VG	F	VF	EF	AU	UNC	PROOF
1909 ...... 1909 over 8	161,282									
1909D	52,500									
1909S	2,774,925									
1910	482,167									
1910D	429,000									
1910S	2,128,250									
1911	197,350									
1911D	846,500									
1911S	775,750									
1912	149,824									
1913	168,838									
1913D	393,500									
1913S	34,000									
1914	95,320									
1914D	453,000									
1914S	1,498,000									
1915	152,050									
1915S	567,500									
1916S	796,000									
1920	228,250									
1920S	558,000									
1921	528,500									
1922	1,375,500									
1922S	2,658,000									
1923	566,000									
1923D	1,702,250									
1924	4,323,500									
1924D	3,049,500									
1924S	2,927,500									
1925	2,831,750									
1925D	2,938,500									
1925S	3,776,500									
1926	816,750									
1926D	481,000									
1926S	2,041,500									
1927	2,946,750									
1927D	180,000									
1927S	3,107,000									
1928	8,816,000									
1929	1,779,750									
1930S	74,000									
1931	2,938,250									
1931D	106,500									
1932	1,101,750									
1933	None									

INDEX

Welcome to the world of coin collecting and investing. A fascinating hobby awaits you. Bowers & Ruddy Rare Coin Galleries, the world's largest rare coin firm, will be pleased to put you on its mailing list to insure that you will receive publications listing hundreds of coins for sale, special offers, and articles of interest. You will be able to keep updated on the latest trends in the coin market.

Fill out the convenient coupon below or, to leave your catalog intact, write directly to Bowers & Ruddy Galleries, Inc., Dept. HCU, 6922 Hollywood Blvd., Suite 600, Los Angeles, California 90028.

Respond today — soon you will be a part of the Bowers & Ruddy Galleries world-wide family of coin collectors and investors.

TO: Bowers & Ruddy Rare Coin Galleries
   Dept. HCU, 6922 Hollywood Blvd., Suite 600
   Los Angeles, CA 90028

Please put me on your current mailing list — no obligation of course.

NAME: _____

STREET: _____

CITY/STATE/ZIP: _____

Start a coin collection today with these Harris folder albums — ask for them at your dealers!

The Harris coin folders are 8½ x 11", with openings for coins punched in heavy card stock. Covers are rich blue finely-textured stock, printed in white and decorated with brilliant metallic silver embossed coin designs (copper for pennies). Presidential Series provides a dated space for each mint variation of each year, and the quantity minted of each coin. Blank spaces are provided for future issues. Each folder is 2 pages. Price $2.50 per folder.

2150	Lincoln Memorial Cents, 1959 to Present	$2.50
2155	Jefferson Nickels, 1951 to Present	$2.50
2160	Roosevelt Dimes, 1965 to Present	$2.50
2165	Washington Quarters, 1965 to Present	$2.50
2170	Kennedy Half-Dollars, 1964 to Present	$2.50
2175	Eisenhower/Anthony Dollars, 1971 to Present	$2.50

COLLECT ONE COIN FOR EACH YEAR

These 8½ x 11" blue folders have openings punched for one coin per year, disregarding mint mark variations. Each space is dated, with blank spaces for future years. Cents begin with first Lincoln penny issued in 1909, nickels with first Buffalo nickel, and dimes with the first "Mercury" dime. Rich metallic coin design, $2.50 per folder.

2185	Cents, 1909 to Present	$2.50
2190	Nickels, 1913 to Present	$2.50
2195	Dimes, 1916 to Present	$2.50

BLANK CREATE-A-COLLECTION FOLDERS

With these folders, you may assemble any collection you wish. The 8½ x 11" blue folders with metallic coin design have openings for many coins, but no dates printed. Price $2.50 per folder.

2220	Cents	$2.50	2235 Quarters	$2.50
2225	Nickels	2.50	2240 Half-Dollars	2.50
2230	Dimes	2.50	2245 Dollars	2.50

Fine Magnifiers for Numismatists Available By Mail From Harris

FINE QUALITY READING GLASSES — Choice of 3 Sizes

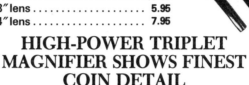

Clear lenses of the highest quality mounted in wide chromium plated brass rims . . . solid black ebonite handles.

Y773 Reading Glass 2" lens $3.95
Y774 Reading Glass 3" lens 5.95
Y775 Reading Glass 4" lens 7.95

HIGH-POWER TRIPLET MAGNIFIER SHOWS FINEST COIN DETAIL

The finest pocket magnifier on the market today. Its lens consists of three highest quality optical lenses expertly ground and bonded to form one triplex lens. An excellent glass where crystal clarity is needed for critical inspection. . . glass is mounted in heavy nickel plated brass with an attractive silver matte finish. Genuine cowhide leather case.

Y777 Ten-Power Triplet Magnifier $34.95

STAND MAGNIFIER LEAVES HANDS FREE

These adjustable ball-jointed magnifiers leave both hands free to examine coins. A really superb magnifier for the most discriminating collector. Generous 2" diameter lens, 3x magnification. Rugged all-metal construction to last a lifetime. Lens swivels to any angle and locks in place with thumb screw.

Y772 Stand Magnifier $17.95

ELECTRO-OPTIX LIGHTED STAND MAGNIFIER

Highest quality magnifier/illuminator. Distortion-free 3" lens, two-position switch for brilliant momentary or fixed light. Perfect for examining stamps, coins, maps, fine print, etc. Attractive charcoal-and-bone-colored impact-resistant plastic housing. Operates on 2 "C" cells, not incl. A superior instrument!

Y807 Electro-Optix Illuminated Magnifier $19.95

EXTRA 5X LENS

BIG 4-INCH MAGNIFIER
With High-Power Extra
Lens Built Right In
Lights Up Viewing Area

The wide field lens of this magnifier lets you view an area the size of a paperback book page all at once, and a built-in light shines a powerful beam on the viewing area. The big 3-power lens is 4" in diameter. A unique bifocal feature gives you an extra 5-power lens set right into the big lens, so you can get ultra-close magnification at a glance. Satin black plastic case is 10" long with thumb-operated light switch. Uses 2 "C" batteries, includes.

Y798 Bifocal Magnifier $19.95

5X LIGHTED POCKET MAGNIFIER WITH CASE

Light-up pocket magnifier has 5-power lens 7/8" in diameter. Shines a bright beam of light on your work; eliminates shadows and dark areas that make magnifiers hard to use. Push button switch at top for easy one hand use. Rugged 2 x2" rigid plastic frame; soft plastic case. Uses 2 "AAA" batteries, included.

Y797 5X Scanner Magnifier....$5.95

MAGNA-LITE SHINES LIGHT DIRECTLY ON YOUR COINS

Handy magnifying flashlight has powerful 3.5x optical quality lens — ideal for examining coins, stamps, maps, documents, anything with fine detail. Light, compact, fits pocket or purse. Use 2 AAA penlight batteries.

Y805 Magna-Lite Flashlight Magnifier $4.95

FOLDING POCKET MAGNIFIERS

Lenses of good magnifying power which fold back into their own handles for pocket carrying.

Y752 Folding Magnifier, excellent quality 1 ¼ "lens . $5.95
Y753 Folding Magnifier, good quality 1 ¾ "lens 1.95

| MAIL TO: H.E. HARRIS & CO., INC., BOX O, BOSTON, MA 02117 |

Please send these magnifiers: _____

TOTAL $ _____   Add $1.75 for postage and handling up to $10, $3.00 if $10.01 or more in U.S. In Canada, add $2.25 up to $10, $4.25 over.

NAME _____

ADDRESS _____

CITY _____ STATE _____ ZIP _____

NOTES

NOTES

NOTES

NOTES

NOTES

NOTES